D0526047

P.C.P. SERIES IN ACCOUNTING AND FINANCE

Consulting Editor: Michael J. Sherer

The aim of this series is to publish lively and readable textbooks for university, polytechnic and professional students, and important, up-to-date reference books for researchers, managers and practising accountants. All the authors have been commissioned because of their specialist knowledge of their subjects and their established reputations as lecturers and researchers. All the major topics in accounting and finance will be included and the series will give special emphasis to recent developments in the field and to issues of continuing debate and controversy.

CASES IN PUBLIC SECTOR ACCOUNTING

CASES IN PUBLIC SECTOR ACCOUNTING

Brian A Rutherford
PhD, F.C.C.A.
Professor of Accounting
The University of Kent at Canterbury

Michael Sherer
MA (Econ.), F.C.A.
Royal London Professor of Finance
University of Essex

and

Robert Wearing
MSc, F.C.A.
Senior Lecturer in Accounting
University of Essex

P·C·P
Paul Chapman
Publishing Ltd

Paul Chapman Publishing Ltd
144 Liverpool Road
London
N1 1LA

British Library Cataloguing in Publication Data
Rutherford, Brian
  Cases in public sector accounting.
  I. Title II. Sherer, Michael III. Wearing, Robert
  657.83500941

ISBN 1 85396 072 1

Typeset by Best-set Typesetter Ltd., Hong Kong
Printed by St Edmundsbury Press Ltd.,
Bury St. Edmunds, and
bound by W.H. Ware Ltd., Clevedon

A B C D E F G 8 7 6 5 4 3 2

Contents

Acknowledgements

We would like to thank all the public sector organizations below for their permission to reproduce in this book material originally published by them and for the helpful comments made on the text. Without their co-operation this book could not have been written. The background commentaries and the analyses of the case study material are, of course, the responsibility of the authors and do not necessarily reflect the views or opinions of the public sector organizations themselves.

British Railways Board
Chartered Institute of Public Finance and Accountancy
Cheshire County Council
Colchester County High School for Girls
Essex County Council
Greater Manchester Transport Authority
HMSO (reproduced with the permission of the Controller of Her Majesty's Stationery Office)
London Borough of Tower Hamlets
North East Essex Health Authority
Public Finance Foundation
Severn Trent Water Company
University of Essex
West Suffolk District Hospital

We would also like to thank Marianne Lagrange and Cathy Blishen of Paul Chapman Publishing for their unstinting support and encouragement of this book, and for their belief in us even when we missed successive deadlines for completing the manuscript.

BAR
MJS
RTW
September 1991

Introduction:
Learning From Case Studies

AIMS OF THE BOOK

The origins of this book lie in our experience of teaching public sector accounting courses to undergraduates at the Universities of Kent and Essex. Whilst several textbooks dealing with public sector accounting are available (see for example Rutherford (1983), Henley *et al.* (1989), Jones and Pendlebury (1988), their primary concern is with concepts, general principles and an overview of accounting practice. This book is intended to complement these textbooks by offering lecturers and their students the opportunity to undertake an in-depth analysis of financial and management accounting reports of actual public sector organizations in the UK. In this way, the concepts and general principles of accounting and reporting in the public sector described in the textbooks can be compared and contrasted with the actual accounting reports prepared by particular public sector organizations, for example a government trading body, a local authority, a district hospital or a regional transport authority.

The book contains fourteen case studies of accounting and reporting in the public sector and is designed to be used in a ten- to twelve-week course on public sector accounting. The number of case studies will allow one case study to be analysed in the classroom each week and for some or all of the remaining cases to be set as written assignments. The choice of which cases to use for each purpose may be a matter for the course lecturer alone or an agreed decision of the lecturer and the students. We would suggest, however, that the way the cases are used for learning in the classroom is somewhat different from the way they are used for written assignments, and this is discussed in the two sections below.

CLASSROOM DISCUSSION

The way the case studies are used for classroom discussions will of course depend upon how the course has been structured, including whether or not the classes have been preceded by lectures, and whether the course is designed around organizations or concepts and principles. Where classes are used to support lectures a case study relating to the material introduced in the lecture may be selected for class discussion one or two weeks later. It is important that all members of the class are encouraged to read the selected case study in advance of the class and to prepare notes in answer to the questions listed at the end of the case. Without such preparation there is a danger that the discussion will be dominated by just one or two students, or that the silence of the class will be filled by a mini-lecture from the class teacher.

Where a course comprises just seminars or classes the case studies can be used as the focus for discussion of both concepts and principles, and accounting and reporting practice. Thorough preparation in advance of the seminars is also important here, although the additional discussion time available will provide an opportunity for the class to have a more flexible format than the fifty-minute class. The first part of the seminar might be used to identify the general theoretical and applied issues arising from the case study while in the second part students can be directed to the specific questions asked.

Although the structure of *Cases in Public Sector Accounting* is consistent with a course designed around the different types of organization to be found in the public sector, for example central government, local government and health authorities, it can also be used to support a conceptually based course. For example, the principles and methods of financial accounting in the public sector are illustrated by Cases 1, 2, 4, 7, 8, 11, 12 and 13, issues of management control and financial management by Cases 3, 4, 5, 6 and 10, and the concept of accountability to multiple stakeholders by Cases 3, 7, 8, 9, 11, 12, 13 and 14.

WRITTEN ASSIGNMENTS

Written assignments based on the case studies in the book may be set either to give some practice for examinations or other types of formal assessment, or as part of the formal assessment itself. Written assignments are intended to be more rigorous and more structured than the class discussions which may precede them. One of the main aims of a written case analysis report is to identify the relevant material and evidence in the accounting statements and annual reports which illustrate and support the students' analyses of the problems and the recommended solutions to those problems. It is often the ability to distinguish between relevant and irrelevant data, and the clarity with which arguments are presented and substantiated which marks out the good quality case report. In addition, a concise and well-focused report will tend earn higher marks than a report which is unstructured and identifies the main issues only on the last page. For a detailed, and very helpful guide to the preparation of written case study assignments see Easton (1992).

AUTHORS' NOTES ON END-OF-CHAPTER QUESTIONS

At the end of each case study we have listed several questions for discussion and/or written assignments. Although we would not wish to encourage the view that there are unique answers to these questions we recognize that lecturers (and their students!) often find some brief guidance notes helpful in preparing a full answer. Accordingly, we have prepared a short companion volume to this text, *Cases in Public Sector Accounting – Guidance Notes for lecturers*, which lecturers who have adopted the book for their course can purchase from Paul Chapman Publishing Limited.

REFERENCES

Easton, G. (1992) *Learning from Case Studies*, 2nd edition, Prentice-Hall International, London.

Henley, D., Holtham, C., Likierman, A. and Perrin J. (1989) *Public Sector Accounting and Financial Control*, 3rd edition, Van Nostrand Reinhold, London.

Jones, R. and Pendlebury, M. (1988) *Public Sector Accounting*, 2nd edition, Pitman, London.

Rutherford, B. A. (1983) *Financial Reporting in the Public Sector*, Butterworths, London.

CENTRAL GOVERNMENT

Case 1
Appropriation Accounts

OBJECTIVES

1. To examine the appropriation accounting system and the terminology associated with that system.
2. To investigate the nature of cash accounting and its relationship to accruals accounting.
3. To consider how appropriation accounts should be interpreted.

MATERIALS

1. Appropriation Accounts 1988–89: Class XII: Department of Education and Science: Summary (Appropriation Accounts 1988–89: Volume 7: Classes XII and XIII: Education and Science and Arts and Libraries, HC 1989–90 15-VII, HMSO, pp. 6–7) (Exhibit 1.1).
2. Appropriation Accounts 1988–89: Class XII: Department of Education and Science: Vote 1: Schools, Further Education and Other Educational Services (Appropriation Accounts 1988–89: Volume 7: Classes XII and XIII: Education and Science and Arts and Libraries, HC 1989–90 15-VII, HMSO, pp. 8–12) (Exhibit 1.2).

INTRODUCTION

Appropriation accounts are detailed financial statements covering expenditure by central government departments. They are designed to record the sums voted by Parliament to be spent on specified activities ('the supply grant' shown in the column headed 'grant') and the amount actually spent. Sums granted but not spent are 'surrendered' by departments at the end of the year. The statement also contains brief explanations of major variations between expenditure and grant.

ANALYSIS

Since appropriation accounts provide detailed information and are prepared on an annual basis, audited and published, they are the nearest equivalent to the annual report and accounts of companies. However, there are a number of very significant differences between company and central government financial statements.

Perhaps the most obvious difference is in coverage. Whereas companies and groups of companies produce statements dealing with the whole of their operations in a particular year, each appropriation account covers a block of expenditure (called a 'vote') on related services within a government department met from the main central government fund (the Consolidated Fund). The vote is the basic unit of control within the framework of parliamentary scrutiny of the expenditure process: Parliament approves expenditure plans on a vote-by-vote basis (see Case 4) and thereafter the government may not divert monies from one vote to another. Expenditure is broken down within each vote into categories, sections and subheads but the government can transfer sums ('vire') within the vote without seeking the approval of Parliament.

Thus appropriation accounting is highly disaggregated: each separate financial statement covers a group of activities smaller than a department. Where a function is carried out by more than one department, or by more than one branch of the public sector, expenditure will appear in several different places. Thus, because state schools are administered by local authorities, the bulk of central government spending on schools appears as financial support for local government (in the relevant vote) so that although the DES is responsible for central government's management of schools, central government funding of them appears elsewhere. Further, approximately a quarter of central government expenditure is not covered by the system at all. This includes payments which are predetermined and thus do not need parliamentary approval (such as amounts provided for the repayment of government debt and payments to the EC), expenditure on activities which, for constitutional reasons, Parliament wishes to keep independent of the government of the day (such as the salaries of the judiciary) and expenditure met from other funds (for example payments from the National Insurance Fund).

Although some incidental receipts are reflected in appropriation accounts as reductions in expenditure ('appropriations in aid') or as memorandum amounts (the sums being paid directly to the Consolidated Fund) the bulk of the revenue raised to fund central government operations – tax receipts and borrowing – is not included in the appropriation accounting system at all since the system is designed to focus on expenditure.

Of course the government does account for the receipts and expenditures omitted from appropriation accounts: financial statements are published covering all transactions on the Consolidated Fund (at a highly aggregated level); the transactions of other funds (see Case 2); and tax receipts and borrowing. In addition, aggregate information on government revenue and expenditure is published in a variety of locations, for example in the national income statistics. However, it is largely left to the user to piece all the information together and the central point, namely that in the detailed audited financial statements attention on the expenditure side is focused at a highly disaggregated level, remains true.

Another major difference between appropriation and company accounting is that the former is conducted on a cash basis: expenditures are recognized in the statements as payments are made and not as real resources are consumed, and revenues are recognized as cash is received rather than as claims on real resources arise. This basis of accounting is used, in part at least, to reflect the focus of attention in the parliamentary scrutiny of government spending, which is on controlling the executive's powers to raise cash from taxation and to disburse that cash.

The use of cash accounting makes it impossible in principle to determine from the financial statements what real level of activity (as indicated by the consumption of resources) has taken place in a year: for example, if the NHS uses more drugs in year 2 than in year 1 by running down stocks already paid for at the beginning of year 2 this will not appear in the appropriation accounts for that year; equally, if cash is disbursed to increase the level of stocks this will appear as expenditure even though the consumption of drugs (and thus, presumably, the volume of service delivered to the public) has not increased.

In many areas, however, the difference in practice between the numbers produced by cash and accruals accounting will be small. The bulk of government spending is on pay, where the timing difference between payment and the consumption of the resource acquired is insignificant. The level of stockholding will not in general fluctuate widely so that the relationship between payments and consumption will be stable. One device sometimes used in the private sector to influence the level of cash outflows in the short term is to delay (or accelerate) payment to creditors: this device is rather more difficult to employ in appropriation accounting because there is a rule that expenditure that has 'matured for payment' must be charged in the appropriation account for that year, that is, sums must be paid as they fall due. There remains, of course, some discretion at the margin about how much trade credit to take, how speedily to process claims and so on. Note that because the system involves reporting payments against budgeted appropriations there may be an incentive to accelerate payments in order to use up a surplus.

Cash spent on major fixed assets is usually shown separately and so can be excluded from any measurement of current activity. Depreciation is not, of course, included in appropriation accounts but, where the assets are very long-lived (as with buildings) the level of depreciation would usually be small.

Appropriation accounts record payments made from the Consolidated Fund and thus the inclusion of an amount in an appropriation account does not necessarily mean that cash has been paid for the purchase of resources or even paid to a third party outside the public sector. Some institutions in the public sector are financed by 'grants in aid' from votes: cash is paid over to them (and charged in the appropriation accounts) but they can use the money in a different period. Other institutions (which would not be regarded as within the public sector) may receive grants which they will spend in a subsequent period.

Thus cash accounting will not reflect the consumption of real resources, even as a reasonable approximation, where operations involve relatively large amounts of short-lived fixed assets (such as defence); where stockholding is changing significantly from period to period; or where operations are actually financed on a loan, grant or 'grant in aid' basis.

QUESTIONS

1. Explain, giving examples from the case material, what is meant by each of the following:

(a) supply grant;
(b) appropriation in aid;
(c) grant in aid;
(d) virement;
(e) surplus to be surrendered;
(f) receipts not authorized to be used as appropriations in aid.

2. Explain, giving examples from the case material, how each of the following is treated:

(a) capital expenditure;
(b) purchase of a stock of consumables by a government department;
(c) purchase of a stock of consumables by a body funded from grants in aid;
(d) unspent balances of grants in aid;
(e) a loan from a government department.

3. How useful would you find the relevant appropriation accounts in determining whether the volume of resources consumed by each of the following had gone up or down?

(a) bursaries and grants for the training of teachers in shortage subjects;
(b) the Royal College of Art;
(c) music and ballet schools;
(d) the state education system.

4. How useful would you find appropriation accounts in determining whether, for any particular activity, the volume of services delivered had changed and service delivery was efficient and effective?

FURTHER READING

Jones, R. and Pendlebury, M. (1988) *Public Sector Accounting*, 2nd edition, Pitman, London, chapter 8.

Rutherford, B. A. (1983) *Financial Reporting in the Public Sector*, Butterworths, London, chapters 3, 6 and 9.

HM Treasury (1988) *Central Government: Financial Accounting and Reporting Framework*, HM Treasury, London.

Exhibit 1.1 Appropriation Accounts 1988–89: Class XII: Department of Education and Science: Summary (Reproduced with the permission of the Controller of Her Majesty's Stationery Office.)

CLASS XII: DEPARTMENT OF EDUCATION AND SCIENCE

No. of Vote	Service	Estimated Gross Expenditure	Authorized Appro- priations in Aid	Supply Grant
		£000	£000	£000
1	Schools. Further Education and Other Educational Services	491,325	9,868	481,457
2	Student Awards. etc.	794,028	6	794,022
3	Universities. etc.	1,851,353	1,689	1,849,664
4	Department of Education and Science administration	68,804	1,069	67,735
5	Agricultural and Food Research Council	61,158	–	61,158
6	Medical Research Council	149,677	–	149,677
7	Natural Environment Research Council	91,864	–	91,864
8	Science and Engineering Research Council	369,334	–	369,334
9	Economic and Social Research Council	27,657	–	27,657
10	Other Science Research. etc.	9,114	–	9,114
11	'Teachers' Superannuation (England and Wales)	1,490,000	1,259,532	230,468
	Total	5,404,314	1,272,164	4,132,150

Gross Expenditure	Appropriations in Aid applied	Net Expenditure	Gross Expenditure compared with Estimate: Saving or (Excess)	Deficiency of Appropriations in Aid	Amount to be surrendered	Extra Receipts payable to Consolidated Fund
£000	£000	£000	£000	£000	£000	£000
429,325	9,868	419,457	62,000	–	62,000	1,091
789,825	4	789,821	4,203	2	4,201	11
1,851,058	1,606	1,849,452	295	83	212	504
68,258	856	67,402	546	213	333	539
61,158	–	61,158	–	–	–	23
149,677	–	149,677	–	–	–	223
91,864	–	91,864	–	–	–	2
367,595	–	367,595	1,739	–	1,739	851
27,007	–	27,007	650	–	650	111
9,082	–	9,082	32	–	32	1
1,468,079	1,259,532	208,547	21,921	–	21,921	12,160
5,312,928	1,271,866	4,041,062	91,386	298		15,516

Total amount to be surrendered   91,088

Actual total amount to be surrendered   £91,087,019,13

Exhibit 1.2 Appropriation Accounts 1988–89: Class XII: Department of Education and Science: Vote 1: Schools, Further Education and other Educational Services (Reproduced with the permission of the Controller of Her Majesty's Stationery Office.)

SCHOOLS, FURTHER EDUCATION AND OTHER EDUCATIONAL SERVICES

Summary of outturn, and the *Account* of the sum expended, in the year ended 31 March 1989, compared with the sum granted, for expenditure by the Department of Education and Science on schools, further education, teacher training, adult education, miscellaneous educational services and research, including grants in aid and international subscriptions and payments to charities.

SUMMARY OF OUTTURN

Section	Estimated			Actual		
	Gross Expenditure	Appro-priations in Aid	Net Expenditure	Gross Expenditure	Appro-priations in Aid	Net Expenditure
	£000	£000	£000	£000	£000	£000
Schools						
A	76,484	3,977	72,507	75,089	3,428	71,661
B	3,764	–	3,764	3,743	–	3,743
C	18,700	–	18,700	14,343	–	14,343
	98,948	3,977	94,971	93,175	3,428	89,747
Higher and further education						
D	108,730	5,372	103,358	104,849	6,412	98,437
E	17,538	–	17,538	17,379	–	17,379
	126,268	5,372	120,896	122,228	6,412	115,816
Miscellaneous educational services, research and administration						
F	4,444	–	4,444	4,403	–	4,403
G	5,694	–	5,694	5,388	–	5,388
H	42,971	519	42,452	43,496	609	42,887
	53,109	519	52,590	53,287	609	52,678
Other (non-public) expenditure						
I	213,000	–	213,000	160,635	–	160,635
Total	491,325	9,868	481,457	429,325	10,449	418,876*

* This figure is £581,000 less than the net total of expenditure on the Appropriation Account, being the difference between the Appropriations in Aid realized (£10,449,000) and those authorized to be applied (£9,868,000).

ACCOUNT

Service	Grant	Expenditure	Expenditure compared with Grant	
			Less than granted	More than granted
	£000	£000	£000	£000
Section A				
SCHOOLS: Primary and Secondary				
A1 Grants to special schools: capital	847	250	597	–
A2 Aided and special agreement schools: building grants and loans[1]	75,637	74,839	798	–
Section B				
SCHOOLS: Supporting services and fees at non-maintained schools				
B1 Grants to direct grant schools	20	16	4	–
B2 Grants to music and ballet schools[1]	3,744	3,727	17	–
Section C				
SCHOOLS: City Technology Colleges				
C1 City Technology Colleges	18,700	14,343	4,357	–
Section D				
HIGHER AND FURTHER EDUCATION: Voluntary and direct grant				
D1 Grants for further education: grant-aided colleges	83,389	80,521	2,868	–
D2 Grants and loans for further education: capital	3,202	2,725	477	–
D3 Royal College of Art (grant in aid)	6,156	6,148	8	–
D4 Royal College of Art: grant for capital expenditure	2,992	2,036	956	–
D5 Cranfield Institute of Technology (grant in aid)	8,701	9,176	–	475
D6 Cranfield Institute of Technology: grant for capital expenditure	581	621	–	40
D7 Cranfield Information Technology Institute: grant	300	273	27	–
D8 Courses for teachers: grants	323	271	52	–
D9 Teacher training: bursaries and grants for training of teachers in shortage subjects	3,086	3,078	8	–
Section E				
HIGHER AND FURTHER EDUCATION: Adult education				
E1 Adult education	17,538	17,379	159	–

Explanation of the causes of variation between expenditure and grant.
A1 Slippage of projects and delayed starts on new projects.
C1 Difficulties in obtaining suitable sites leading to subsequent delays in starting projects.
D4 Due to slippage on rationalization scheme.

[1] See notes.

Service	Grant	Expenditure	Expenditure compared with Grant	
			Less than granted	More than granted
	£000	£000	£000	£000

Section F
MISCELLANEOUS EDUCATIONAL SERVICES, RESEARCH AND ADMINISTRATION: Youth service

F1 Current expenditure: grants	3,981	3,940	41	–
F2 Capital expenditure: grants	463	463	–	–

Section G
MISCELLANEOUS EDUCATIONAL SERVICES, RESEARCH AND ADMINISTRATION: International services

G1 The European schools	2,905	2,764	141	–
G2 Teachers on interchange grants	938	894	44	–
G3 Organizations concerned with the interchange of teachers and students: grants	1,526	1,416	110	–
G4 Joint United States–United Kingdom Educational Commission (Fulbright Commission): grants	300	289	11	–
G5 Miscellaneous services	25	25	–	–

Section H
MISCELLANEOUS EDUCATIONAL SERVICES, RESEARCH AND ADMINISTRATION: Educational research and other miscellaneous services

H1 Educational Services and Research[1]	19,908	19,846	62	–
H2 Further Education Unit (grant in aid)	3,358	3,525	–	167
H3 Curriculum development	4,673	5,338	–	665
H4 School examination and assessment	3,970	3,681	289	–
H5 Subscriptions to the Organization for Economic Co-operation and Development	161	137	24	–
H6 Polytechnics and colleges	9,000	9,069	–	69
H7 Payment from the European Social Fund	1	–	1	–
H8 Donations to charities	1,900	1,900	–	–

Section I
OTHER (NON-PUBLIC) EXPENDITURE: Education Grants

I1 Education Support Grants	80,000	68,863	11,137	–
I2 In-service teacher training grants	130,000	89,194	40,806	–
I3 Grants to inner London councils	3,000	2,578	422	–

Explanation of the causes of variation between expenditure and grant *contd.*

H3 Due mainly to bulk payment covering pension transfer values payable by DES to the Principal Civil Service Pension Scheme following the admission to PCSPS of staff of the former School Curriculum Development Committee and Secondary Examinations Council.

I1 Delay in the timing of local education authority claims.

I2 Delay in the timing of local education authority claims.

Service	Grant	Expenditure	Expenditure compared with Grant	
			Less than granted	More than granted
	£000	£000	£000	£000	£000

GROSS TOTAL					
Original	473,412				
Supplementary	16,366				
Supplementary	1,547				
	———	491,325	429,325	63,416	1,416

	Estimated	Applied		
Deduct	£000	£000		
Z Appropriations in Aid				
Original	9,757			
Supplementary	111			
	———	9,868	9,868	

NET TOTAL				
Original	463,655			
Supplementary	16,366			
Supplementary	1,436			Surplus
	———	481,457	419,457	62,000

Actual surplus to be surrendered   £61,999,991.39

Receipts

	Estimated	Realized
Receipts payable to Consolidated Fund		
	£000	£000
(i) Receipts of classes authorized to be used as Appropriations in Aid	9,868	10,449
(ii) Receipts of other classes	7	510
Gross Total	9,875	10,959
Appropriated in aid		9,868
Net Total		1,091

Actual sum payable separately to Consolidated Fund   £1,091,457.87

[1] See notes.

Details of Receipts

	Estimated	Realized
	£000	£000

(i) Receipts of classes authorized to be used as Appropriations in Aid

Subhead AZ

	Estimated	Realized
Repayments of grants overpaid in previous years	177	159
Repayment of loans under subhead A2(2)	3,800	3,269
	3,977	3,428

Subhead DZ

	Estimated	Realized
Payments by the governments of the Isle of Man and the Channel Islands for students attending higher education institutions in the United Kingdom	4,699	6,412
Reimbursements from the European Agricultural Guidance and Guarantee Fund of 25 per cent of the costs of certain vocational training and retraining courses in agriculture and horticulture	1	—
Royal College of Art receipts. Proceeds from the sale of property owned by the RCA to be reinvested in the rationalization of the College's accommodation	672	—
	5,372	6,412

Subhead HZ

	Estimated	Realized
Contributions from other sources towards the cost of research projects sponsored by the DES	519	609
Total	9,868	10,449

(ii) Receipts of other classes

	Estimated	Realized
Miscellaneous	1	369
Sale of land and property	6	141
Total	7	510

Notes

	£000
New loans exceeding £100,000	
Expenditure under Subhead A2 included one new loan	212

Subhead B2 includes a capital grant of £150,000 towards the Royal Ballet School's Appeal Fund.

£501,000 of the sum provided from Subhead H1 was transferred to a deposit account with the Paymaster General's Office from which payments will be made to the Department of Customs and Excise if an appeal by the Open University against VAT liability in respect of the Education Counselling and Credit Transfer Information System (ECCTIS) contract should prove unsuccessful.

J. Caines
Accounting Officer   5 September 1989

I certify that I have examined the above account in accordance with the Exchequer and Audit Departments Acts 1866 and 1921 and the National Audit Office auditing standards.

In my opinion the sums expended have been applied for the purposes authorized by Parliament and the account properly presents the expenditure and receipts of Class XII Vote 1 for the year ended 31 March 1989.

John Bourn
Comptroller and Auditor General

Case 2
Fund Accounting

OBJECTIVES

1. To examine the objectives and methods of fund accounting.
2. To consider the extent to which fund accounting achieves its objectives.

MATERIALS

The account of the Home Grown Sugar Beet (Research and Education) Fund, 1988–89 (extracts) (HC 1989–90 131, HMSO) (Exhibit 2.1).

INTRODUCTION

Fund accounting is the name given to the system in which separate accounting entities ('funds') are established to maintain accountability for identified pools of monetary and other resources. Such funds do not necessarily coincide with the operating structure of the organizations which administer them. For an accounting entity to qualify as a fund its records must identify which net assets are associated with the fund balance (so that merely creating a provision or reserve is not sufficient) and there must be a framework of administrative or legal rules against which the accountability of the fund can be tested.

Although the substantive activities with which it is concerned may be rather esoteric, the Home Grown Sugar Beet (Research and Education) Fund (henceforth 'the Fund') provides a classic example of fund accounting. The operations of the Fund are described in the foreword to the account, included in Exhibit 2.1.

ANALYSIS

Funds are established to demonstrate accountability for specific pools of resources, often where the pool of resources does not coincide with organizational boundaries, so that the financial statements of the organization will not provide sufficient information about the use of the resources concerned. As the foreword to the account explains, the Fund covers resources raised from the beet industry to fund relevant research and education. The operation is administered by the ministers with responsibility for the industry, and by maintaining a separate fund they are able to demonstrate that the money raised has been applied for the proper purpose or, where it has yet to be applied, remains available for use.

Although in previous years it was operated on a cash basis, the Fund now uses accruals accounting and so the pool of resources for which the Fund accounts includes fixed assets (see the balance sheet). The audit report on the Fund is included in the exhibit and clearly forms an important part of the process of accountability.

Fund accounting provides a powerful tool for demonstrating accountability for specific pools of resources, but it does concentrate attention on fiduciary accountability and on the application of funding rather than on the underlying operations. Thus the account does little to show how the activities funded from the statutory contributions fit into the programmes of the industry itself, the ministries administering the Fund, or the establishments receiving grants from the Fund. The effect of fund accounting can be to divert attention from the overall activities of organizations to the disaggregated pools of resources they administer.

As an example of this problem consider the following case. A body uses a fund it administers to finance an activity which it previously supported from its own resources whilst running down the fund's support for activities supported in previous years. The net effect is a reduction in operations in a given area but this would not be apparent from the accounts of the fund and might not be clear in the accounts of the body itself, especially if it stated in those accounts that operations were now supported by the fund.

QUESTIONS

1. Explain the purpose of fund accounting using the Home Grown Sugar Beet (Research and Education) Fund as a source of examples.
2. Is expenditure on research and education in the sugar beet industry going up or down?
3. Explain how an organization might use fund accounting to obscure rather than clarify aspects of its underlying operations.

FURTHER READING

Jones, R. and Pendlebury, M. (1988) *Public Sector Accounting*, 2nd edition, Pitman, London, pp. 174–82.
Rutherford, B. A. (1983) *Financial Reporting in the Public Sector*, Butterworths, London, chapter 4.

Exhibit 2.1   The Account of the Home Grown Sugar Beet (Research and Education) Fund, 1988–89 (extracts) (Reproduced by permission of the Controller of Her Majesty's Stationery Office.)

Foreword

Background information

Since 1936, successive Acts of Parliament have provided for research on home-grown sugar beet on the basis of 100 per cent industry funding. Under the current legislation (section 68 of the 1984 Food Act), the Minister of Agriculture, Fisheries and Food and the Secretary of State for Wales have overall responsibility for the Home Grown Sugar Beet (Research and Education) Fund, but are advised by the Sugar Beet Research and Education Committee. This Committee is a non-statutory body appointed by the Minister and the Secretary of State which comprises representatives of British Sugar plc, the National Farmers' Union, the Agricultural and Food Research Council, MAFF and independent members. The Secretariat is provided by MAFF on a cost-recoupment basis.

The Fund commissions research, both strategic and applied, with a number of organizations but most of the work (about 60 per cent) is placed with Broom's Barn Experimental Station (near Bury St Edmunds). Broom's Barn is part of the AFRC's Institute of Arable Crops Research and, as such, belongs to the Lawes Agricultural Trust. Broom's Barn was, however, purchased with monies provided by the SBREF and the Fund meets all recurring costs. Purchase was on the basis that only work on sugar beet should be carried out and the Fund has a reversionary interest in the land and buildings if sold.

The annual orders made under the Act provide for contributions from British Sugar plc and from the growers of home-grown beet to meet the cost of carrying out the programme. The levy income is paid into the Home Grown Sugar Beet (Research and Education) Fund – which is under the control of the Minister. This account of the Fund shows the income and expenditure attributable to the year ended 31 March 1989.

Review of activities and priorities

The programme covered by the period of this account included research into plant nutrition, physiology, agronomy, variety trials, crop husbandry, pest and disease control (including rhizomania and beet yellows virus) and machinery development as well as advice and education to growers through publications, films and demonstrations. Although a statutory programme is for one year at a time, much of the work will take several years to complete. The Committee has therefore formulated a policy in which the following principal areas have been identified as requiring new or further attention: genotype, seedling establishment, physiology and agronomy, pest and diseases, weed control and harvesting losses.

Financial position of the Fund

Contributions to the Fund were levied in accordance with Article 3 of the Order made on 26 February 1988 (SI 1988 No. 336), i.e. from growers at the rate of 10.0p per adjusted tonne of home-grown beet sold for delivery to British Sugar plc and from the company at the rate of 10.0p per adjusted tonne of home-grown beet delivered to the company in the year. An adjusted beet tonne, defined in the inter-professional agreement of 3 October 1983, as amended on 30 November 1984, between British Sugar plc and the National Farmers' Union is a conversion of actual beet tonnes by reference to the sugar content. The total contribution from growers and British Sugar plc amounted to £1,873,640; this is an increase of £163,708 compared with the previous year.

The net cost of the 1988–89 Research and Education Programme, together with related administrative expenses, came to £1,749,557, £32,570 less than the estimated expenditure of £1,782,127 set out in the Schedule to the Statutory Instrument (1988 No. 336). As at 31 March 1989, £2,606,521 was available to meet the Fund's known liabilities and the cost of the 1989–90 programme until the statutory contributions become due around December 1989.

Home Grown Sugar Beet (Research and Education) Fund

INCOME AND EXPENDITURE ACCOUNT FOR THE YEAR ENDED 31 MARCH 1989

	Notes	Year to 31 March 1989 £		Year to 31 March 1988 £
INCOME				
Income from statutory contributions	2		**1,873,640**	1,709,932
			1,873,640	1,709,932
EXPENDITURE				
Net payments to Research Establishments	3	**1,291,152**		1,178,309
Net payments to British Sugar plc	4	**326,247**		337,549
Depreciation	8	**123,618**		136,734
Administrative expenses	5	**64,616**		45,484
			(1,805,633)	
OPERATING SURPLUS			**68,007**	11,856
Interest receivable	6	**182,039**		107,188
Other receipts	7	**93,839**		125,219
Profit on sale of fixed assets		**627**		995
Amounts written off investments		**(4,823)**		(104)
Amounts written off fixed assets		**(60)**		
			271,622	
SURPLUS FOR YEAR			**£339,629**	£245,154

Home Grown Sugar Beet (Research and Education) Fund

BALANCE SHEET AS AT 31 MARCH 1989

	Notes	Year ended 31 March 1989 £	Year ended 31 March 1988 £
FIXED ASSETS			
Fixed assets at net book value	8	**1,195,114**	1,252,178
Investments (cash on deposit)		**2,604,074**	2,359,036
		3,799,188	3,611,214
CURRENT ASSETS			
Debtors	10	**187,487**	24,521
Cash at bank and in hand		**2,447**	2,555
		189,934	
CREDITORS: amounts falling due within one year	11	**(405,295)**	(394,092)
NET CURRENT ASSETS		**(215,361)**	
TOTAL ASSETS LESS CURRENT LIABILITIES		**£3,583,827**	£3,244,198
FINANCED BY:			
General Fund as at 1 April		**3,244,198**	2,999,044
Surplus for the Year		**339,629**	245,154
		£3,583,827	£3,244,198

D H Andrews
Accounting Officer

Ministry of Agriculture, Fisheries and Food
13 October 1989

Notes to the Account

1. Principal Accounting Policies

a. *Accounting Principles*

The income and expenditure account is prepared in accordance with standard accounting conventions governing accounts. The account last year was prepared as a Receipts and Payments Account and the adjusted figures are shown as a comparison. All figures are rounded to the nearest pound.

b. *Fixed Assets*

i. When capital assets surplus to requirements are sold the profit arising from disposal is shown in the account albeit that the cash receipts are actually offset against the grant payable.

ii. Only capital items with an initial cost price of £50 or more are included as fixed assets.

iii. Depreciation is normally provided on fixed assets at rates calculated to write off the cost of the assets evenly over its expected useful life.

Laboratory and field equipment	— over 10 years
Office equipment	— over 10 years
Farm equipment	— over 5 years
Vehicles	— over 4 years

2. Income from statutory contributions

Statutory contributions are raised through a levy paid equally by growers and British Sugar plc on every adjusted tonne of beet delivered to British Sugar plc.

	£	£
Statutory Contributions from growers	936,820	
from British Sugar plc	936,820	
		£1,873,640

3. Payments to Research Establishments

Grants to research establishments are usually paid in four instalments, three of which are paid before the end of the year, the balance is payable on receipt of the audited statement of account. The exception is Broom's Barn Experimental Station where three-quarters of the final instalment is payable before the end of the financial year.

	£
Payments to Research Establishments 1988–89 (including income retained)	1,309,228
Less:	
For fixed asset expenditure (see Note 9)	67,542
Final instalment of grant 1987–88	52,460
Plus:	
Final instalment of grant 1988–89 (see Note 11)	77,405
Payment to Broom's Barn 1987–88	24,521
As per Income and Expenditure Account (see Note 9)	**£1,291,152**

4. Payments to British Sugar plc   The only payment made to British Sugar plc relates to expenditure incurred in the previous financial year.

Payments made to British Sugar plc in 1988–89 comprised:

	£	£
Payments for expenditure incurred in 1987–88 as follows:		
British Sugar Beet Review	20,651	
Films and photography	693	
Weed Beet warning schemes	8,302	
Demonstrations	308,291	
Audit Fee	1,495	
		£339,432
Total payment made to British Sugar plc for 1988–89 will be:		
Education programme 1988–89		**325,290**
Balance of refund on sale of equipment		**957**
As per Income and Expenditure Account		**£326,247**

5. Administrative Expenses

IIRB Subscriptions	9,864	
(Less recoverable subscriptions)	1,630	
		8,234
IIRB Expenses and visits		**12,323**
Contingencies		**4,785**
Committee travel and subsistence expenses (a)		**15,452**
MAFF Administration fee		**19,172**
NILO Management fees		**2,050**
Audit fee for 1987–88 account		**2,200**
		£64,216
Less:		
Audit Fee 1987–88		**2,200**
Plus:		
Audit Fee 1988–89		**2,600**
		£64,616

NB: IIRB—Institut International de Recherches Betteravieres.
      NILO—National Investments and Loans Office.

(a) This includes £8,341 expenses for foreign travel for scientific studies.

6. Interest   Funds which are not required immediately are invested with the National Investments and Loans Office. Interest received during 1988–89 amounted to £182,039.

7. Other Receipts

	£	£
Broom's Barn Farm:		
Total receipts for 1988–89	93,232	
Less: proceeds from disposal of assets	1,550	
		91,682
National Institute of Agricultural Botany		**1,200**
British Sugar plc		**957**
Other receipts		**£93,839**

7

8. Fixed Assets The fixed assets with a net book value of £1,195,114 as at 31 March 1989 comprise:

	Land and Buildings	Vehicles and Farm Equipment	Laboratory Field and Office Equipment	Total
Cost	£	£	£	£
At 1 April 1988	852,052	594,374	339,057	1,785,483
Adjustment (a)	—	(3)	(57)	(60)
Sub Total	852,052	594,371	339,000	1,785,423
Additions (see Note 9)	—	9,694	57,848	67,542
Disposals	—	(7,707)	(1,602)	(9,309)
At 31 March 1989	852,052	596,358	395,246	1,843,656
Depreciation	£	£	£	£
At 1 April 1988	—	379,511	153,794	533,305
Provided during year	—	87,133	36,485	123,618
Disposals	—	(7,201)	(1,180)	(8,381)
		459,443	189,099	648,542
Net Book Value				
At 1 April 1988	£852,052	£214,863	£185,263	£1,252,178
At 31 March 1989	£852,052	£136,915	£206,147	£1,195,114

(a) Adjustment in respect of reassessment of fixed assets due to new format of the account.

9. Research Establishments Expenditure

Capital Expenditure (see Note 3)

	£	£
Broom's Barn Experimental Station	60,525	
National Institute of Agricultural Botany	5,147	
Norfolk Agricultural Station	1,870	
		67,542
Current Expenditure (see Note 3)		1,291,152
Gross Expenditure 1988–89		£1,358,694

10. Debtors

	£	£
Payments of levy not yet received	187,364	
Receipts from sale of asset Institute of Engineering Research	5	
Overpayment of MAFF administration charge	118	
		£187,487

11. Creditors

	£	£
British Sugar plc	325,290	
Balance of grant to Research Establishments	77,405	
National Audit Office	2,600	
		£405,295

Certificate and Report of the Comptroller and Auditor General

I certify that I have examined the financial statements on pages 3 to 8 in accordance with the Food Act 1984 Section 68 and the National Audit Office auditing standards.

In my opinion the financial statements give a true and fair view of the state of affairs of the Home Grown Sugar Beet (Research and Education) Fund at 31 March 1989 and of its surplus and source and application of funds for the year then ended and have been properly prepared in accordance with the provisions of the Food Act 1984 and the directions made thereunder by the Minister of Agriculture, Fisheries and Food.

I have no observations to make on these financial statements.

John Bourn
Comptroller and Auditor General

National Audit Office
1 December 1989

Case 3
Performance Indicators

OBJECTIVES

1. To explain and illustrate the nature of performance indicators.
2. To explore the use, and possible abuse, of performance indicators.

MATERIALS

1. *The Government's Expenditure Plans 1990–91 to 1992–93*, chapter 14: Department of Social Security (Cm. 1014) (London: HMSO, 1990), paragraphs 85–88 and tables 14.31–14.34 (Exhibit 3.1).
2. Table of examples of performance indicators from P. Jackson and B. Palmer, *First Steps in Measuring Performance in the Public Sector: A Management Guide* (Public Finance Foundation, 1989) (Exhibit 3.2).

INTRODUCTION

A profit-seeking private sector organization measures its performance primarily in terms of its profitability. Public sector organizations cannot generally do this, partly because they do not charge for their outputs, or at any rate do not charge a price intended to reflect purely 'what the market will bear', and partly because, even if they did, it would not necessarily be appropriate to measure their performance in terms of the gap between charges for output and the market prices they pay for their inputs.

How then should their performance be measured, assuming that we are unwilling simply to have faith that public sector managers will be achieving the best that can be done? One response to the problem which has received widespread attention in the last decade is the development of 'performance indicators'. These are quantified measures designed to reflect some aspect of the operational performance of an entity. Two points need to be emphasized: performance indicators are inevitably *partial* in the sense that they do not claim to provide, as profitability does in the profit-seeking sector, a comprehensive measure of overall performance; and they are usually imprecise, because of the difficulty of measuring inputs and outputs. It is often suggested that the use of the word 'indicator' reflects the partiality and imprecision associated with performance measurement in the public sector although some of the literature pays little more than lip-service to the need to interpret performance indicators with caution.

Again, some of the literature on performance indicators applies the term to almost any statistical measurement of the entity's operations, including quite straightforward activity measures covering inputs (such as expenditure on salaries and wages or the number of staff employed), throughputs (pupils in education) or outputs (number of miles of road built). This undermines the meaningfulness of the concept: the term is better kept for measures which reflect efficiency or effectiveness rather than simply volume of operations.

The materials for this case provide performance indicators covering the administration of the main social security benefits by the Department of Social Security's network of local offices. A list of examples of performance indicators is also provided: note that the classification in this list does not correspond precisely to that employed in the analysis section of this case.

ANALYSIS

The performance of a public sector organization can be broken down into two main elements: *efficiency*, the rate at which inputs are converted into outputs; and *effectiveness*, the relationship between outputs achieved and the desirable level of output.

Efficiency is measured as the ratio between outputs achieved and inputs consumed: the higher the ratio, the more efficient the organization. Thus, a refuse collection service might measure its efficiency by the number of households serviced per member of staff or per team: the higher the number of households serviced the more efficient the operation. This immediately introduces us to one of the problems associated with performance measurement: the difficulty of measuring inputs and outputs precisely. In this case, if the number of households serviced is increased but the teams spill waste or leave sacks uncollected, output may not in fact have increased and indeed the ultimate outcome being pursued, public hygiene, may actually be impaired. Even inputs, which are usually easier to measure, cause problems: thus if the team is provided with new vehicles, which have much more elaborate equipment but are much more expensive, but do not achieve any increase in productivity, performance will appear stable but efficiency will actually have diminished because the use of 'teams' as a measure of inputs does not completely reflect the volume of resources being consumed.

Efficiency in procurement, that is, obtaining inputs as cheaply as possible, is often referred to as *economy* and treated as a separate aspect of performance although it is really only an aspect of efficiency, namely the ratio of real resource inputs to money inputs.

Effectiveness, the relationship between outputs achieved and the desirable level of output, is usually more difficult to measure than efficiency, because of the difficulty of specifying the desirable level of output. In practice, many measures of effectiveness focus on *quality of service* or *take-up rate*. The latter identifies the target population which it is considered desirable to have use the service (for example, it might be considered that all eligible people should in fact claim retirement pensions so that a take-up rate of less than 100 per cent would be undesirable).

Quality of service focuses on either a given level of service (such as 95 per cent of trains arriving within five minutes of the timetabled time) or the level of consumer satisfaction with the service received. The same problems of measuring output arise as with efficiency, and the relationship between the measure of desirable output used in the indicator and the underlying need of the population may be problematic. For example, measuring the effectiveness of a railway in terms of a given target of trains arriving on time may mean that holding up the inter-city express with hundreds of passengers on board so that a dozen local services travelling almost empty get through on time appears to increase the effectiveness of the operation; equally, as consumers of a service develop higher and higher expectations they may come to regard a given level of service as unacceptable when they previously regarded it as acceptable.

The direct outputs of public sector bodies frequently do not reflect the final outcome or impact which the body is seeking: thus, for example, the outputs of the National Health Service may be taken to be operations performed or patients successfully treated, but the final outcome to be pursued is a healthy population. Hence, if spending on preventive care were reduced with the result that more people suffered illness and had to be cured the output of the service might appear to be increasing, and if this were achieved with a given level of inputs, efficiency would appear to be improving. It is sometimes possible to measure impact as a further aspect of performance although it is usually difficult to measure such abstractions as 'the nation's health' or the 'well-rounded citizen' schooling is supposed to produce with any precision and even more difficult to determine to what extent changes are due to the activities of public sector bodies.

Looking at a single figure for a performance indicator will often tell us very little about performance. To learn anything of value it is necessary to compare the figure with others, for example looking at previous figures for the same operation (trend analysis), figures for other, broadly comparable operations, or a previously specified target. In the case of central government, however, it will often be difficult to identify comparable operations. The social security indicators in this case use past trends (table 14.31) and targets (table 14.33).

QUESTIONS

1. The performance indicators in the materials for this case covering social security benefits concentrate on only one aspect of performance. Which? Explore the possible problems which might arise in interpreting the indicators as a result of the partiality of their coverage.
2. Taking any public sector operation with which you are familiar (such as higher education), construct at least three performance indicators for each of the following elements of performance:

   (a) efficiency;
   (b) quality of service;

(c) take-up;
(d) impact.

3. Show how the performance indicators constructed in question 2 could be used to improve the performance of the operation.
4. Show how the performance indicators constructed in question 2 could be manipulated to show an improvement in performance when none had in fact taken place.

FURTHER READING

Flynn, A., Gray, A., Jenkins, W. and Rutherford, B. A. (1988) Making indicators perform, *Public Money and Management*, Winter, pp. 35–41.

Jackson, P. and Palmer, B. (1989) *First Steps in Measuring Performance in the Public Sector: A Management Guide*, Public Finance Foundation, London.

Rutherford, B. A. (1983) *Financial Reporting in the Public Sector*, Butterworths, London, chapter 14.

Exhibit 3.1 *The Government's Expenditure Plans 1990–91 to 1992–93,* chapter 14: Department of Social Security, paragraphs 85–88 and tables 14.31–14.34. (Reproduced by permission of the Controller of Her Majesty's Stationery Office.)

Table 14.30   Benefit claims and payments statistics

	1984–85	1985–86	1986–87	1987–88	1988–89
Benefit claims (thousands)					
Retirement pension([1])	810	860	760	710	700
Widows' benefit	70	70	60	60	60
Unemployment benefit	5,290	5,480	5,260	4,640	4,080
Sickness and invalidity benefits	1,410	1,470	980	990	1,000
Maternity benefits([2])	660	720	610	160	130
Attendance allowance	220	250	300	350	395
Mobility allowance	130	150	170	220	230
Income support/supplementary benefit([3])	6,180	5,880	5,440	4,640	3,730
IS/supplementary benefit reassessments due to changes of circumstances	12,410	13,470	16,300	13,460	9,670
Child benefit	660([5])	720	720	780	860
Family credit/family income supplement([4])	400	400	410	420	670
Social Fund:					
Maternity payments	—	—	—	—	210
Funeral payments	—	—	—	—	50
Community care grants	—	—	—	—	320
Budget loans	—	—	—	—	930
Crisis loans	—	—	—	—	500
Cold weather payments	—	—	—	—	1
Other local office statistics					
IS/supplementary benefits home visits made([3])	3,000	2,360([6])	1,580	1,230	960
IS/supplementary benefit appeals heard by tribunals	100	110	130	180	150
Callers at local offices	22,580	22,610	22,780	21,990	21,070
Benefit payments (millions)					
By order book	827	830	839	840	26
By girocheque	114	119	112	94	80
By automated credit transfer	10	15	20	23	31
By payable order	5	9	10	9	10

([1])*Including non-contributory retirement pension.*
([2])*Maternity grant and maternity allowance up to 1986–87. Maternity grant was abolished in April 1987. The fall in numbers in 1987–88 and 1988–89 reflects the introduction of statutory maternity pay in April 1987.*
([3])*Income support in 1988–89.*
([4])*Family credit in 1988–89.*
([5])*Figures affected by industrial action at Newcastle Central Office.*
([6])*The fall in the number of home visits made reflects the extension of postal claims procedures from May 1985.*

85. DSS has a well established management information system which includes a range of output measures and performance indicators covering the administration of all the major benefits. Performance indicators provide a measure of how quickly and how accurately claims are handled. **Table 14.31** shows the national level of performance in 1988–89 as measured by these indicators compared with the results achieved in previous years. Performance on income support in 1988–89 was maintained or improved in all areas with the exception of visiting.

Table 14.31   Social security performance indicators

	1984–85 [1]	1985–86 [1]	1986–87	1987–88	1988–89
Clearance time (in days)					
Retirement pension claims[2]	47	31	27	25	22
Sickness/invalidity benefit claims	11	10	10	10	10
Maternity benefit claims	15	13	12	17	15
Attendance allowance claims	45	42	44	41	38
Mobility allowance claims	53	46	40	40	40
Family credit					17
Income support claims[3]					5
Supplementary benefit claims (excluding caller claims)[4]	6	8	7	6	
Supplementary benefit caller claims	2	2	2	2	
Income support visits (all grades)					11
Supplementary benefit home visits by executive officers[5]	10	10	9	10	
IS/supplementary benefit assessments reviewed[6]	2	2	2	2	2
Income support appeals					20
Supplementary benefit appeals[7]	–	18	21	23	
Child benefit: straightforward claims	4	6	4	6	4
One parent benefit claims	9	18	11	11	10
Error rates (percentage of payments incorrect)					
Short term contributory benefits	3·2	3·9	3·9	4·1	4·0
Attendance allowance	4·2	3·1	3·5	0·8	0·7
Mobility allowance	1·6	1·1	1·5	1·1	2·6
Family credit					8·6
IS/supplementary benefit[6]	9·6	10·5	10·4	11·6	9·1
Child benefit	0·9	0·8	0·7	1·1	1·1
One parent benefit	5·6	4·5	3·8	4·0	4·1

[1] *Results in 1984–85 and 1985–86 were affected by civil service industrial disputes.*
[2] *The process of claiming retirement pension allows a total of some 120 days from the outset to the date payment becomes due.*
[3] *Includes both caller and non-caller claims.*
[4] *For 1985–86 only, a revised basis for statistical recording lengthened average clearance times shown for non-caller claims.*
[5] *Clearance time since visit initiated.*
[6] *Income support for 1988–89.*
[7] *New performance indicator introduced in July 1985 which measures the time taken from the receipt of an appeal at the local office to submission to a tribunal.*

86.   The reform of the social security system in April 1988 made it easier to understand and brought significant improvements in service. For example, clearance times for income support claims in 1988–89 were, on average, 22 per cent better than those for its predecessor, supplementary benefit, in 1987–88. **Table 14.32** illustrates the improvements in claims clearance and accuracy of payments in the main benefit areas.

Table 14.32   Improvements in clearance times and accuracy rates

	1987–88		1988–89
Supplementary benefit claims (Time to clear)	6·3 days	Income support claims (Time to clear)	4·9 days
Supplementary benefit error rate	11·6%	Income support error rate	9·1%
Callers: total time in LOs			
Supplementary benefit	25·9 mins	Income support	19·6 mins
Retirement pension claims	24·7 days		22·0 days

87. **Table 14.33** sets out the Department's national performance targets for key benefits during 1989–90. For those benefits administered through the Department's local office network the local target values can be spread either side of the national target. Reporting systems establish the extent to which individual office performance meets defined minimum, or tolerable, standards—thereby enabling management attention to be concentrated towards improving poorly performing offices.

Table 14.33   Performance targets 1989–90

	Clearance time	Error rate ceiling (per cent)
Retirement pension		
– Regional Organisation	24 days	
– Claims reserved to Central Pensions Branch	91 per cent in 30 days	3·0
Sickness/Invalidity benefit	10 days	3·7
Income Support		
i. claims	5 days }	
ii. assessment review	3 days }	9·0
Social Fund		
i. crisis loans	1 day	
ii. community care grants	8 days	
iii. budgeting loans	8 days	
Family credit	18 days	7·0
Attendance allowance	37 days	1·0
Mobility allowance	37 days	1·5
Invalid care allowance	50 days	4·0
War pension	24 weeks	3·3
Child benefit		
i. straightforward claims	80 per cent in 5 days	0·0
ii. non-straightforward claims	80 per cent in 16 days	2·5
One parent benefit	80 per cent in 12 days	4·0

88. As part of the commitment to improve service to the public all local offices measure the quality of their service in important areas. Managers also carry out a postal customer opinion survey each year to find out what their customers think of the service. **Table 14.34** summarises the results for 1988–89.

Table 14.34   Quality of service statistics 1988–89

	Income support/ Social Fund	Contributory benefits
(i) Caller times		
Pre-reception waiting times (average)	11·6 minutes	7·9 minutes
Total time spent in the office (average)	19·6 minutes	14·5 minutes
Satisfactory standard of interview achieved	92 per cent	93 per cent
(ii) Visits		
Satisfactory standard of interview achieved	89 per cent	—
(iii) Outgoing mail		
Satisfactory standard achieved	45 per cent	74 per cent

Exhibit 3.2   Table of examples of performance indicators from P. Jackson and B. Palmer, *First Steps in Measuring Performance in the Public Sector: A Management Guide*

Indicators	Examples
Cost indicators (economy)	Annual cost per aged person in residential home.
Productivity indicators (efficiency)	Number of library books issued per library assistant per hour.
	Yield per VAT visit.
	Ratio of laboratory technicians to clinicians.
Time targets (efficiency/effectiveness)	Turnround time for dealing with applications for government grant.
Volumes of service (crude measure of efficiency/effectiveness)	Number of housing repairs.
	Number of vehicle licensing applications processed.
	Battalion training days.
Quality of service indicators (effectiveness)	Percentage of library users satisfied with library services.
	Number of complaints received from public on street cleaning.
	Speed of completing housing repairs.
Demand (or take-up rate) for service indicators (effectiveness)	Acres of recreation land per 1,000 population.
	Number of bathers in municipal pools.
	Additionality created by government grant.
Availability of services (effectiveness/equity)	Availability of library services to all locations/age groups.
Outcome (or impact) of policy indicators	Reduction of unemployment levels through vocational training scheme.

Case 4
Supply Estimates

OBJECTIVES

1. To examine the supply procedure and the terminology associated with that procedure.
2. To investigate the nature of cash budgeting.
3. To consider how supply estimates should be interpreted.

MATERIALS

Supply Estimates 1988–89: Class XII: Department of Education and Science: Vote 1: Schools, Further Education and Other Educational Services (Part) (Supply Estimates: 1988–89: Class XII: Department of Education and Science, HC 1987–88 339-XII, HMSO, pp. 9–12) (Exhibit 4.1).

INTRODUCTION

The supply procedure is the means by which the government seeks formal parliamentary approval for its expenditure for the coming year. The government gives some indication of its intentions in a variety of documents and at various points in time: the plans for a given year grow more detailed as the beginning of the year approaches. Supply procedure is the final phase in this cycle and although the details change from time to time the basic system has operated in much the same way for many years.

The structure of the central government accounting system was examined in Case 1. The vote used here is the same as that featured in Case 1, so that we are now examining the budget for the cash we saw being spent in Case 1.

ANALYSIS

The main estimates are presented to Parliament shortly before the beginning of the financial year on 1 April. They constitute a request for funds and the request is approved by means of an Appropriation Act. If additional funds are needed supplementary estimates are presented, usually in groups in June, November and February. Debate on estimates in the full House of Commons is rather limited and usually focuses on a few items; the system of parliamentary select committees shadowing departments permits fuller debate by smaller groups of MPs.

Supply estimates take a standard format although the supplementary information given differs from vote to vote. An introduction (omitted from the case material) gives a brief commentary. Part I of the estimate itself gives the 'ambit' of the vote, that is, a formal description of the services to be financed, the net amount of money sought, and the department or person with official responsibility for accounting for that money. The ambit plays a key role in accountability because it indicates the legal limit on the nature of the expenditure which can be financed from the funds obtained; it is thus the starting point in testing the 'propriety and regularity' of the subsequent expenditure.

Because the approval of expenditure by Parliament does not take place until part-way through the year funds have to be advanced to departments as a 'vote on account' to enable them to operate until approval is received. The estimate indicates how much of the sum for which approval is sought has been advanced in this way and what amount is left as the 'balance to complete'.

Parts II and III of the estimate give supporting detail but are not included in the relevant Appropriation Act and thus have no statutory authority – this means that the department can transfer ('vire') sums within (but not between) votes. Part II sets out the gross provision and the net sum sought (after applying appropriations in aid) broken down by functions and subheads within functions. The subhead details include further subdivisions and a narrative explanation of the purpose for which the funds are required and any unusual points about the way the funds are controlled. The right-hand column gives the provision sought for the relevant year while on the left are columns giving the provision sought for the preceding year and the actual expenditure (outturn) for the year before that, which is the latest year actually completed at the point at which the main estimates are prepared. Note that sections H and I of the subhead detail have been omitted from the case material.

Part III of the estimate (omitted from the case material) gives details of expected incidental receipts which are not to be used as appropriations in aid.

QUESTIONS

1. Explain, giving examples from the case material where appropriate, what is meant by each of the following:

    (a) supply estimate;
    (b) main estimate;
    (c) supplementary estimate;
    (d) ambit of the vote;
    (e) subhead;
    (f) vote on account;
    (g) balance to complete.

2. Examine the strengths and weaknesses of a budgeting and control system based on cash payments.

3. How useful to Parliament is it to know that it is proposed to pay to schoolchildren of Polish ex-servicemen who served with HM forces

during the Second World War allowances amounting to £1,000 (G5(1)) out of the £464 million requested for the vote?

FURTHER READING

Henley, D., Holtham, C., Likierman, A. and Perrin, J. (1986) *Public Sector Accounting and Financial Control*, 2nd edition, Van Nostrand Reinhold, Wokingham, chapter 2.

Jones, R. and Pendlebury, M. (1988) *Public Sector Accounting*, 2nd edition, Pitman, London, chapters 2, 3 and 8.

Rutherford, B. A. (1983) *Financial Reporting in the Public Sector*, Butterworths, London, chapters 5 and 9.

HM Treasury (1988) *Central Government: Financial Accounting and Reporting Framework*, HM Treasury, London.

HM Treasury (1990) *Supply Estimates 1990–91: Summary and Guide*, Cm. 980, HMSO, London.

Exhibit 4.1 Supply Estimates 1988–89: Class XII: Department of Education and Science: Vote 1: Schools, Further Education and Other Educational Services (part)

SCHOOLS, FURTHER EDUCATION AND OTHER EDUCATIONAL SERVICES

Part I	£463,655,000

Amount required in the year ending 31 March 1989 for expenditure by the Department of Education and Science on schools, further education, teacher training, adult education and miscellaneous educational services and research, including grants in aid and international subscriptions.

The **Department of Education and Science** will account for this Vote.

	£
Net total	463,655,000
Allocated in the Vote on Account (HC 105)	169,642,000
Balance to complete	294,013,000

Part II **Summary and subhead detail**

Summary

1986–87	1987–88		1988–89		
Net outturn £'000	Total net provision £'000		Gross provision £'000	Appropriations in aid £'000	Net provision £'000
54,886	61,763	**Schools (Sections A to C)**	**97,769**	**3,977**	**93,792**
107,351	117,234	**Higher and further education (Sections D and E)**	**125,846**	**5,372**	**120,474**
(−40	−50	of which: net contributions to the European Communities		1	−1)
27,021	30,952	**Miscellaneous educational services, research and administration (Sections F to H)**	**39,797**	**408**	**39,389**
51,334	169,000	**Other (non-public) expenditure (I)**	**210,000**	**–**	**210,000**
240,592	378,949	**Total**	**473,412**	**9,757**	**463,655**
	Forecast outturn £'000 366,300				

Subhead detail

1986–87	1987–88		1988–89
	Total		
Outturn	provision		Provision
£'000	£'000		£'000

Schools (Sections A to C)
Section A: Primary and secondary

741	675	**A1 Grants to special schools: capital**	692
		Grants towards the cost of approved building schemes at non-maintained special schools catering for pupils with special educational needs.	
51,400	57,990	**A2 Aided and special agreement schools: building grants and loans**	74,618
	57,485	(1) Grants of 85% of the cost of repairs and approved capital works.	74,100
	505	(2) Discretionary loans towards certain approved capital works.	518
52,141	58,665	**Gross total**	75,310
		Less:	
211	3,973	**AZ Appropriations in aid**	3,977
	173	(1) Repayment of grants overpaid in previous years.	177
	3,800	(2) Repayment of loans under subhead A2(2)	3,800
51,930	54,692	**Net total**	71,333

Section B: Supporting services and fees at non-maintained schools

55	30	**B1 Grants to direct grant schools**	15
		Grants paid in respect of two nursery schools and pupils at the Royal Hospital School, Holbrook.	
2,901	3,441	**B2 Grants to music and ballet schools**	3,744
		Fee remission and incidental expenses for aided pupils at five specialist schools.	
2,956	3,471	**Total**	3,759

Section C: City Technology Colleges

–	3,600	**C1 City Technology Colleges**	18,700
		Grants to be paid for expenditure associated with the planning, establishment and recurrent costs of City Technology Colleges.	

Higher and further education (Sections D and E)
Section D: Voluntary and direct grant

1986–87	1987–88		1988–89
	Total		
Outturn	provision		Provision
£'000	£'000		£'000
77,031	82,262	**D1 Grants for further education: grant-aided colleges** Grants for current expenditure to voluntary and other colleges directly funded by the DES. Provision includes grants towards the cost of redundancies and premature retirement compensation arising from restructuring at colleges. Payments in support of the National Advisory Body for Public Sector Higher Education and the Voluntary Sector Consultative Council.	83,389
2,609	4,070 3,970	**D2 Grants and loans for further education-capital** (1) Grant-aided colleges. Grants of up to 100 per cent of the cost of capital building work (normally up to 85% in respect of voluntary colleges) and equipment costing more than £6,500 and discretionary loans to Governors for the balance of costs.	3,419 3,365
	100	(2) Establishments for the handicapped. Grants of up to 100 per cent of the cost of approved capital works, for which independent and non-maintained establishments of further education are eligible to apply.	54
5,677	5,703	**D3 Royal College of Art: grant in aid** On advice from the Visiting Committee grant in aid is provided for recurrent expenditure, bursaries and minor capital works.	6,156
1,057	3,644	**D4 Royal College of Art: grant for capital expenditure** Major capital works at the College's accomodation in South Kensington.	2,513
7,771	8,264	**D5 Cranfield Institute of Technology: grant in aid** On advice from the Visiting Committee grant in aid is provided for recurrent expenditure and minor capital works.	8,648
753	717	**D6 Cranfield Institute of Technology: grant for capital expenditure** Major capital works at the Institute.	581
–	120	**D7 Cranfield Information Technology Institute: grant** The Institute provides degree courses in information technology. The grant provides for recurrent expenditure and minor capital works.	300
514	316	**D8 Courses for teachers: grants** Grants for a programme of short in-service training courses and conferences organized by HM Inspectorate and for bursaries for European teachers attending the courses, under a scheme run by the Council of Europe.	323

1986–87	1987–88		1988–89
Outturn £'000	Total provision £'000		Provision £'000
1,354	2,449	**D9 Teacher training: Bursaries and grants for the training of teachers in shortage subjects** Bursary scheme for trainee teachers in mathematics, physics and CDT.	2,979
96,766	107,545	**Gross total**	108,308
		Less:	
4,710	6,038	**DZ Appropriations in aid**	5,372
	4,584	(1) Payments by the governments of the Isle of Man and the Channel Islands for students attending higher education institutions in the United Kingdom.	4,699
	50	(2) Reimbursement from the European Agricultural Guidance and Guarantee Fund of 25 per cent of the costs of certain vocational training and retraining courses in agriculture and horticulture.	1
	1,404	(3) Royal College of Art receipts. Proceeds from the sale of property owned by the RCA to be reinvested in the rationalization of the College's accommodation.	672
92,056	101,507	**Net total**	102,936
		Section E: Adult education	
15,295	15,727	**E1 Adult education**	17,538
	15,687	(1) Current Grants towards the recurrent costs of certain bodies which provide liberal adult education, and some national associations; expenditure on adult education bursaries, the REPLAN programme and the training of trade union and health and safety representatives.	17,497
	40	(2) Capital Grants towards major capital works at the long-term residential colleges.	41
15,295	15,727	**Total**	17,538
		Miscellaneous educational services, research and administration (Sections F to H)	
		Section F: Youth service	
3,592	3,687	**F1 Current expenditure: grants** Grants for work in the youth service; including two organizations for training of youth leaders and various national voluntary youth organizations.	3,981
536	549	**F2 Capital expenditure: grants** Grants towards capital projects of national significance carried out by the voluntary youth service.	463
4,128	4,236	**Total**	4,444

Subhead detail (contd)

1986–87	1987–88		1988–89
	Total		
Outturn	provision		Provision
£'000	£'000		£'000

Section G: International services

2,207	2,550	**G1 The European schools** UK contribution to teaching staff costs of the nine European Schools (and for capital expenditure at the one at Culham, Oxfordshire) which provides education mainly for children of staff of European Community institutions.	2,905
714	931	**G2 Teachers on interchange grants** Grants to teachers in England and Wales on study visits and exchange schemes in other countries.	938
1,451	1,483	**G3 Organizations concerned with the interchange of teachers and students: grants** The administration expenses of the Central Bureau for Educational Visits and Exchanges (CBEVE) and the League for the Exchange of Commonwealth Teachers (LECT)	1,526
277	308	**G4 Joint United States–United Kingdom Educational Commission (Fulbright Commission): grants** The sterling equivalent of the one third of the cost of administering the Fulbright Scholarship and Student Awards. The United States government meets the remaining two thirds.	300
6	9 1 8	**G5 Miscellaneous services** (1) Allowances paid to schoolchildren of Polish ex-servicemen who served with HM Forces during the 1939–45 war. (2) International conferences held in England and Wales organized by outside bodies, which are considered to be of special value to the education service.	25 1 24
4,655	5,281	**Total**	5,694

LOCAL
GOVERNMENT

Case 5
Local Authority Annual Budget

OBJECTIVES

1. To examine the 1989–90 estimates for the London Borough of Tower Hamlets in the context of political, administrative and financial decentralization.
2. To evaluate the usefulness of local authority annual budgets for decision-making and accountability.

MATERIALS

Extracts from the London Borough of Tower Hamlets Estimates for the General Rate for the Year 1989–90: Summary pp. i–ii; Bethnal Green pp. 1–1a; Bow pp. 1–1a; Globe Town pp. 1–1a; Isle of Dogs pp. 1–1a; Poplar pp. 1–1a; Stepney pp. 1–1a; Wapping pp. 1–1a; Central Services pp. 1, 25 and 52 (Exhibit 5.1).

INTRODUCTION

There is no legal requirement for local authorities to prepare annual budgets although such a requirement is implicit in the Local Government Act 1972. Section 5 states that 'every local authority shall make proper arrangements for the administration of their financial affairs and shall secure that one of their officers has responsibility for the administration of those affairs'. Moreover, each local authority must set a legal community charge once a year and, since this is usually determined as the difference between estimated receipts, in the form of grants from central government or income from trading, and desired expenditure on services, it is in effect impossible to set the community charge without preparing an annual budget.

In common with most public and private sector organizations the annual budget performs several roles in the planning and control process. Once the budget is approved at the council meeting in February or March it sets the limit for expenditure on each of the main services provided by the local authority. Planning and control decisions concerning each service are the responsibility of the appropriate committee, for example the Housing Committee or the Social Services Committee. The membership of the committees is drawn from the elected councillors, who are given administrative support and advice by officials in the relevant departments. It is not normally possible for a committee to spend more than it has been authorized to do by the annual budget. However, it is legitimate and quite common practice for overspending to occur on some individual services within the responsibility of a committee provided that there are corresponding savings or underspendings on other individual services. For example, a Social Services Committee can use savings on the home help service to fund additional expenditure on children's homes. This procedure is known as virement and, as local authorities move towards decentralization and financial delegation, both the scope and use of virement will increase.

In addition to setting limits on total expenditure the annual budget gives an indication of the priorities attached to different services for the coming year and any new projects and programmes that have been approved. In this way the budget becomes a statement of the expectations of the individual committees and the local authority as a whole. Furthermore, the annual budget can be used by stakeholders as the benchmark for comparing and evaluating the actual performance of the local authority. The budget, therefore, has a political, as well as an organizational and managerial role. The local authority can be made accountable to both those who receive local authority services and those who fund those services through local taxation, in part at least, by the annual budget. Indeed, the timing of local elections in early May means that the annual budget provides the most up-to-date financial information about the activities of the local authority.

The traditional presentation of a local authority budget is on a line-by-line basis. For each committee the estimated expenditure will be set out under functional headings such as employees, premises, transport and supplies. This presentation is heavily influenced by the needs of the financial accounting system and hence is consistent with the way the financial accounts are prepared.

It has the disadvantage of encouraging incremental budgeting, however, whereby this year's budget is largely determined by last year's budget adjusted for estimated price level changes. This may mean that expenditure continues to be authorized on projects which are no longer achieving the objectives originally set for them, and that too little money is available for new projects which would achieve the same objectives more efficiently and effectively. One way of avoiding these undesirable consequences is to use an alternative method known as zero-base budgeting (ZBB), in which each item of expenditure has to be annually rejustified. The aim of ZBB is to identify the effort and related cost associated with different levels of service or activity so that informed decisions can be taken on what level of effort to provide or even on whether that service or activity should continue to operate.

In addition, and perhaps of more concern, is that it is difficult, if not impossible, to identify the overall cost of specific projects and programmes, for example the total cost of maintaining an individual housing estate or running a leisure centre. In order to provide cost information by project rather than by functional heading it has been suggested that local authorities adopt a planning, programme and budgeting system (PPBS). The emphasis in PPBS is on the policy objectives of the local authority and the outputs necessary to achieve those objectives. A PPBS budget is structured in such a way that the total resources and activities required to achieve an objective can be identified, even if they are supplied by different departments of the local authority. For example, the establishment of a women's refuge may require resources and services from social services, housing, transport and education, and PPBS enables planning to take place across conventional departmental boundaries. PPBS also provides analyses of the costs and benefits of each programme so that choices can be made between competing demands for scarce resources. A good example of this would be the evaluation of alternative programmes to alleviate the problems of homelessness in a local authority. One programme might involve the purchase of large old properties and converting them into smaller units of accommodation. An alternative might be to provide incentives to increase the supply of private rented accommodation in the area. PPBS can provide a very useful method for choosing between these two programmes.

ANALYSIS

The general rate estimates for Tower Hamlets for 1989–90 (Exhibit 5.1) are both a typical and a unique example of a local authority budget. They are typical because they are presented in the conventional line-by-line format, with expenditure grouped under the usual department or committee headings. They are also unique because they consist of a summary set of estimates for the local authority as a whole and detailed sets of estimates for the seven neighbourhoods (hamlets) which make up the authority.

When the Liberal Party gained control of Tower Hamlets in 1986 it implemented a radical manifesto proposal to give power to the hamlets through a programme of financial, administrative and political decentralization. The Borough of Tower Hamlets was divided into seven neighbourhoods, as shown in Figure 5.1. Each neighbourhood is managed by its own standing neighbourhood committee made up of councillors elected in the area and responsible for the delivery of all services in the neighbourhood. The decentralization of services was implemented in two main stages. Within two years most of the authority-wide service delivery committees and departments had been abolished and their functions delegated to equivalent neighbourhood committees. For example, there are no central committees for housing, planning and development or leisure and recreation. For legal reasons there is a central Social Services Committee and Director of Social Services, but the delivery of social services is the responsibility of the seven neighbourhood social services managers. The second phase of the decentralization process saw the delegation of some of the central support departments to the neighbourhoods, for example personnel and management services, legal services and trading standards. Some of the finance functions, for example staff payroll, have also been decentralized and each neighbourhood has an administration and finance manager who, along with the other neighbourhood managers, reports to the neighbourhood chief executive. The

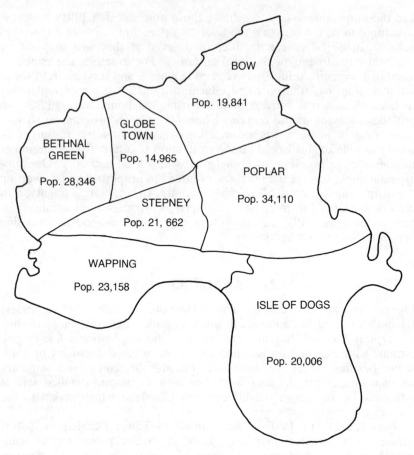

Figure 5.1   The neighbourhoods of Tower Hamlets
Population figures are estimates derived from the London Research Centre's Population
Estimate and Forecast for Wards in Greater London, 1991.

formal organization of one of the neighbourhoods, Globe Town, is shown
in Figure 5.2.

There is still a level of centralized decision-making in the form of a
Policy and Strategy Committee, contolled by the Liberal Democrats,
a General Manager for Finance and Performance Monitoring and a
General Manager for Strategic Services. Nevertheless, the essence of the
system is that the neighbourhoods do have considerable decision-making
and administrative autonomy, as an analysis of the estimates shows. The
centre allocates each neighbourhood an annual budget based mainly on
needs assessment. The neighbourhoods are then allowed to spend the
allocated budget as they wish, including the freedom to vire between any
budget heads. Neighbourhoods decide for themselves the size of their
staff establishment and their policy on filling vacancies. Neighbourhoods
are also allowed to sell assets and use the receipts to support building or
renewal projects.

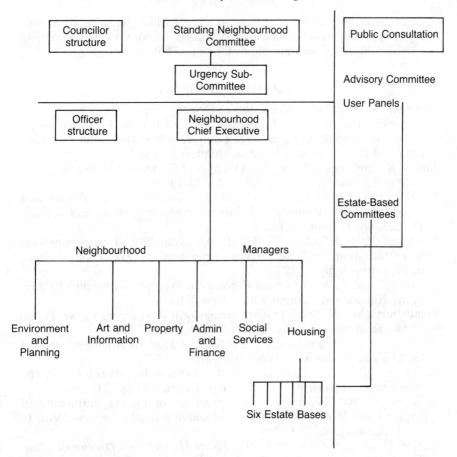

Figure 5.2 Globe Town's formal organization structure

The considerable financial autonomy given to neighbourhoods does create some of its own problems. For example, there is less opportunity to take advantage of economies of scale and there are difficulties where the services of one neighbourhood are consumed by the residents of an adjacent neighbourhood, for example libraries. Notwithstanding these problems the Tower Hamlets experiment in decentralization can be said to be a success. In 1990 the Liberal Democrats were returned to power with an increased majority.

QUESTIONS

1. Discuss the usefulness of the annual budget for planning and control decisions in a local authority.
2. What are the advantages and disdavantages of delegating financial responsibility to the neighbourhoods in Tower Hamlets?

3. Compare and contrast functional line-by-line budgets with programme budgeting. Which type of budget is more useful for making local authorities accountable to their stakeholders?

FURTHER READING

Danziger, J. M. (1978) *Making Budgets*, Sage, London.

Henley, D., Holtham, C., Likierman, A. and Perrin, J. (1989) *Public Sector Accounting and Financial Control*, 3rd edition, Van Nostrand Reinhold (International) London, chapters 3, 5 and 6.

Jones, R. and Pendlebury, M. (1988) *Public Sector Accounting*, 2nd edition, Pitman, London, chapters 2, 3, 4 and 5.

Lowndes, V. and Stoker, G. (1992) An evaluation of neighbourhood decentralization: customer and citizen perspectives, *Policy and Politics*, Vol. 26, no. 1, January, pp. 47–61.

Lowndes, V. and Stoker, G. (1992) An evaluation of neighbourhood decentralization: staff and councillor perspectives, *Policy and Politics*, April, forthcoming.

Novick, D. (ed.) (1973) *Current Practices in Program Budgeting (PPBS)*, Crane Russak and Company Inc., New York.

Pendlebury, M. W. (ed.) (1989) *Management Accounting in the Public Sector*, Heinemann Professional, London, chapter 1.

Phyrr, P. A. (1973) *Zero-Base Budgeting – A Practical Management Tool for Evaluating Expenses*, Wiley, Chichester.

Schick, A. (1966) The road to PPB: the stages of budget reform, *Public Administration Review*, Vol. 26, no. 4, December, pp. 243–58.

Skousen, C. R. (1990) Budgeting practices in local governments of England and Wales, *Financial Accountability & Management*, Vol. 6, no. 3, Autumn, pp. 191–208.

Stoker, G. and Lowndes, V. (1991) *Tower Hamlets and Decentralisation: The Experience of Globe Town Neighbourhood*, Local Government Management Board, Luton.

Wildavsky, A. (1975) *The Politics of the Budgetary Process*, 2nd edition, Little Brown, Boston, Mass.

Exhibit 5.1 Extracts from the London Borough of Tower Hamlets Estimates for the General Rate for the Year 1989–90

LONDON BOROUGH OF TOWER HAMLETS   PAGE i

GENERAL RATE ESTIMATES 1989/90   ESTIMATED SUMMARY OF RATE REQUIREMENTS

	DETAILS	1988/89			1989/90	
		RATE LEVY	ESTIMATE	REVISED ESTIMATE	ESTIMATE	RATE LEVY
1.	TOTAL EXPENDITURE	229.15	126,033,000	126,033,000	125,033,000	208.39
2.	LESS : BLOCK GRANT	104.41	57,424,000	58,392,000	73,960,000	123.27
3.	PROVISION FOR LOSS OF BLOCK GRANT	(9.97)	(5,482,000)	0	0	.00
4.	LONDON RATE EQUALISATION SCHEME	20.46	11,254,600	11,254,600	11,758,000	19.60
5.	CONTRIBUTION TO BALANCES	(8.96)	(4,930,000)	(11,380,000)	0	.00
6.	TOTAL NET EXPENDITURE BEFORE PRECEPTS	123.21	67,766,400	67,766,400	39,315,000	65.53
	ADD : PRECEPTS					
7.	INNER LONDON EDUCATION AUTHORITY	81.80	44,990,000	44,990,000	47,052,000	78.42
8.	METROPOLITAN POLICE	17.24	9,482,000	9,482,000	11,868,000	19.78
9.	LONDON FIRE AND CIVIL DEFENCE AUTHORITY	8.07	4,438,500	4,438,500	4,620,000	7.70
10.	DEPARTMENT OF TRANSPORT	6.07	3,340,500	3,340,500	5,436,000	9.06
11.	PRECEPTING BODIES REQUIREMENTS (Lines 7 to 10)	113.18	62,251,000	62,251,000	68,976,000	114.96
12.	TOTAL RATE REQUIREMENTS (Lines 6 and 11)	236.39	130,017,400	130,017,400	108,291,000	180.49
13.	PRODUCT OF A PENNY RATE	1.00	550,000	550,000	600,000	1.00

SUMMARY OF NET EXPENDITURE CHARGEABLE TO RATE

SERVICE	1988/89		1989/90
	ESTIMATE	REVISED ESTIMATE	ESTIMATE
	£	£	£
NEIGHBOURHOOD COMMITTEES :-			
BETHNAL GREEN	14,315,200	14,834,700	14,693,400
BOW	11,970,900	12,344,900	12,624,800
GLOBE TOWN	9,752,100	10,031,100	10,581,200
ISLE OF DOGS	10,365,600	10,676,500	10,483,800
POPLAR	19,602,400	19,797,900	19,156,700
STEPNEY	11,006,000	11,213,200	11,432,000
WAPPING	12,016,100	11,824,300	11,658,800
TOTAL : NEIGHBOURHOODS	89,028,300	90,722,600	90,630,700
CENTRAL DEPARTMENTS :-			
CHIEF EXECUTIVE	14,889,800	11,974,300	11,938,600
BOROUGH SECRETARY	5,427,700	5,195,600	3,774,200
ORGANISATIONAL DEVELOPMENT	4,201,900	4,057,800	5,114,400
BOROUGH TREASURER	170,400	1,137,800	5,731,000
BOROUGH BUILDING SERVICES	472,800	236,400	0
BOROUGH VALUER	1,051,400	525,700	0
BOROUGH ENGINEER	7,464,400	9,512,500	3,170,300
SOCIAL SERVICES	1,939,700	1,283,700	3,595,800
TOTAL : CENTRAL DEPARTMENTS	35,618,100	33,923,800	33,324,300
SUB-TOTAL : ALL COMMITTEES AND DEPARTMENTS	124,646,400	124,646,400	123,955,000
PRECEPTS AGAINST L.B.T.H. BLOCK GRANT :-			
LEE VALLEY REGIONAL PARK AUTHORITY	105,100	105,100	125,200
LONDON WASTE REGULATORY BODY	70,000	70,000	78,600
LONDON RESIDUARY BODY LEVY	388,000	388,000	0
THAMES WATER AUTHORITY LEVY	823,500	823,500	874,200
TOTAL : PRECEPTS	1,386,600	1,386,600	1,078,000
TOTAL : ALL COMMITTEES, DEPARTMENTS, AND PRECEPTS	126,033,000	126,033,000	125,033,000

Bethnal Green Neighbourhood: Estimates for the general rate for the year 1989–90

GENERAL RATE ESTIMATES 1989/90   BETHNAL GREEN NEIGHBOURHOOD COMMITTEE

		1988/89		1989/90
SERVICE SUMMARY	PAGE NO.	ORIGINAL ESTIMATE	REVISED ESTIMATE	ESTIMATE
ADMINISTRATION				
Neighbourhood Administration	2	1,223,000	1,641,400	1,199,400
Legal Services	3	0	64,600	129,600
1st Stop Shop (L.E.B.)	4	22,100	22,100	75,400
Cambridge Heath Complex	5	631,300	633,300	645,700
Rushmead	6	203,900	186,000	129,900
Total : Neighbourhood Administration		2,080,300	2,547,400	2,180,000
HEALTH AND CONSUMER SERVICES				
Environmental Health	7	101,500	292,500	473,600
Street Trading	8	(196,900)	(130,100)	(129,300)
Total : Health and Consumer Services		(95,400)	162,400	344,300
HIGHWAYS				
Highways and Works	9	851,500	740,300	1,558,100
HOUSING				
General Management	10	790,900	739,300	487,700
Estate Management	11	3,174,200	3,213,200	3,301,900
Other Housing Services	12	1,773,400	1,272,200	901,300
Surveying and Engineering Services	13	114,400	114,400	102,700
Proj. Mngmt. and Architectural Services	14	0	0	0
Total : Housing		5,852,900	5,339,100	4,793,600
LEISURE AND RECREATION				
Leisure Administration	15	97,700	85,700	48,800
Whitechapel and Cheshire St. Baths	16	453,500	459,600	406,400
Kobi Nazrul and Brady Centres	17	146,400	150,800	152,800
Parks and Open Spaces	18	475,600	426,500	343,200
Playleaders and 1 O'Clock Clubs	19	0	0	64,300
Community Action Sports	20	0	0	49,700
Libraries	21	334,100	392,400	343,400
Total : Leisure and Recreation		1,507,300	1,515,000	1,408,600
PLANNING AND DEVELOPMENT				
Development Control	22	108,900	135,900	161,600
PROPERTY MANAGEMENT				
Property Management	23	69,700	271,600	321,200
TOTAL CARRIED FORWARD TO PAGE 1a		10,375,200	10,711,700	10,767,400

GENERAL RATE ESTIMATES 1989/90   BETHNAL GREEN NEIGHBOURHOOD COMMITTEE

SERVICE SUMMARY	PAGE NO.	1988/89		1989/90
		ORIGINAL ESTIMATE	REVISED ESTIMATE	ESTIMATE
TOTAL BROUGHT FORWARD FROM PAGE 1a		10,375,200	10,711,700	10,767,400
OTHER SERVICES				
Economic Development	24	283,500	468,300	409,000
SOCIAL SERVICES				
Social Services Administration	25	396,400	310,500	328,100
Nelson Gardens Childrens Home	26	234,000	231,400	248,400
Children : Other Accommodation	27	251,600	251,600	0
Boarded Out Children	28	197,600	197,600	209,900
Mary Hughes Day Nursery	29	334,500	278,200	258,100
Playgroups and Childminders	30	20,200	10,200	19,600
Children : Preventive and Support	31	36,000	36,000	35,800
Sarel House	32	334,200	321,300	260,200
Mandela & Peachy Edwards House	33	17,700	26,100	125,200
Other Accommodation for Adults	34	184,300	184,300	193,700
Home Help Service	35	405,400	443,600	452,100
St Matthew's Day Centre	36	0	15,000	50,400
Meals in the Home	37	135,100	66,600	63,900
St Hilda Hollybush & Toynbee Lunch Clubs	38	31,600	19,100	17,500
Elderly : Travel Permits	39	315,700	324,400	356,800
Sheltered Workshops	40	18,100	18,100	17,700
Aids and Adaptations	41	14,300	14,300	13,800
Physically Handicapped : Travel Permits	42	56,100	49,300	54,200
Pritchards Road Day Centre	43	196,400	164,100	184,700
Fieldwork Services	44	477,300	562,900	497,600
Total : Social Services		3,656,500	3,524,600	3,387,700
TOTAL: ALL SERVICES		14,315,200	14,704,600	14,564,100
less : Transfer to statutory Street Trading Account		-	(130,100)	(129,300)
TOTAL: NEIGHBOURHOOD BUDGET		14,315,200	14,834,700	14,693,400

Bow Neighbourhood: Estimates for the general rate for the year 1989−90

GENERAL RATE ESTIMATES 1989/90   BOW NEIGHBOURHOOD COMMITTEE

		1988/89		1989/90
SERVICE SUMMARY	PAGE NO.	ESTIMATE	REVISED ESTIMATE	ESTIMATE
ADMINISTRATION				
Neighbourhood Administration	2	985,900	1,056,900	1,241,100
1st Stop Shop (Roman Road)	3	22,500	82,700	90,600
Vernon Hall & Neighbourhood Centre	4	65,300	43,700	205,100
Bow House	5	416,100	346,500	289,600
Total : Neighbourhood Administration		1,489,800	1,529,800	1,826,400
HEALTH AND CONSUMER SERVICES				
Area Improvements	6	0	28,700	60,600
Environmental Health	7	76,000	180,400	346,800
Street Trading	8	51,600	19,800	29,900
Total : Health and Consumer Services		127,600	228,900	437,300
HIGHWAYS AND WORKS				
Highways	9	652,600	745,100	513,800
Refuse Collection	10	0	10,700	448,500
Street Sweeping	11	0	126,700	293,500
Total : Highways and Works		652,600	882,500	1,255,800
HOUSING				
General Management	12	565,000	642,500	679,700
Surveying Services	13	0	49,900	50,200
Estate Management	14	2,886,900	2,623,800	2,864,700
Other Housing Services	15	402,600	454,700	(757,100)
Total : Housing		3,854,500	3,770,900	2,837,500
LEISURE AND RECREATION				
Swimming Pools(Victoria Park Lido)	16	120,200	22,600	30,000
Swimming Pools(Bow Baths)	17	6,700	30,700	51,800
Sutherland Road	18	-	-	50,000
Parks and Open Spaces	19	608,900	457,600	451,200
Victoria Park	20	633,100	728,900	1,331,500
Entertainment and arts activities	21	98,900	23,400	49,100
Libraries	22	260,600	190,500	212,700
Total:Leisure and Recreation		1,728,400	1,453,700	2,176,300
PLANNING AND DEVELOPMENT				
Development Control	23	73,400	103,000	139,800
Management of Industrial and - - Commercial Land and Buildings	24	15,300	64,100	67,600
Total : Planning and Development		88,700	167,100	207,400
TOTAL CARRIED FORWARD TO PAGE 1a		7,941,600	8,032,900	8,740,700

GENERAL RATE ESTIMATES 1989/90   BOW NEIGHBOURHOOD COMMITTEE

SERVICE SUMMARY	PAGE NO.	1988/89		1989/90
		ESTIMATE	REVISED ESTIMATE	ESTIMATE
TOTAL BROUGHT FORWARD FROM PAGE 1		7,941,600	8,032,900	8,740,700
PROPERTY SERVICES				
Property Services				
Total : Property Services	25	-	171,500	155,700
OTHER SERVICES				
Community Relations	26	96,000	217,200	129,600
Miscellaneous	27	548,700	587,600	317,200
Total : Other Services		644,700	804,800	446,800
SOCIAL SERVICES				
Social Services Administration	28	265,400	220,700	191,200
Transport	29	-	74,300	152,400
Community Homes for Children	30	99,900	178,000	179,500
Reception and Observation	31	292,600	320,200	314,800
Children : Other Accommodation	32	186,100	186,100	0
Boarded Out Children	33	146,100	146,100	116,900
Day Nurseries	34	294,000	296,400	304,600
Playgroups and Childminders	35	19,300	17,400	17,600
Children : Preventive and Support	36	20,600	20,900	22,100
Homes for the Elderly	37	369,200	370,200	366,500
Sheltered Accommodation	38	102,200	100,300	102,700
Other Accommodation for Adults	39	143,200	143,200	142,100
Home Help Service	40	297,000	297,200	297,200
Day Centres	41	53,100	29,600	29,700
Meals in the Home	42	113,000	55,400	110,800
Luncheon and Social Clubs	43	26,200	25,400	26,300
Elderly : Travel Permits	44	253,900	260,700	287,000
Sheltered Workshops	45	7,700	8,200	8,900
Aids and Adaptations	46	13,500	13,500	13,500
Physically Handicapped : Travel Permits	47	47,600	41,700	45,900
Home for the Mentally Handicapped	48	119,200	119,500	120,600
Home for the Mentally Ill	49	9,000	1,000	1,000
Mentally Handicapped : Training Centres	50	59,300	75,300	79,100
Fieldwork Services	51	446,500	354,200	381,100
Total : Social Services		3,384,600	3,355,500	3,311,500
TOTAL: ALL SERVICES		11,970,900	12,364,700	12,654,700
less : Transfer to statutory Street Trading Account		-	19,800	29,900
TOTAL : NEIGHBOURHOOD BUDGET		11,970,900	12,344,900	12,624,800

Globe Town Neighbourhood: Estimates for the general rate for the year 1989–90

GENERAL RATE ESTIMATES 1989/90   GLOBE TOWN NEIGHBOURHOOD COMMITTEE

SERVICE SUMMARY	PAGE NO.	1988/89		1989/90
		ESTIMATE	REVISED ESTIMATE	ESTIMATE
ADMINISTRATION				
Neighbourhood Administration	2	962,000	934,800	1,164,600
Chief Executive	3	0	543,600	407,300
Russia Lane	4	67,500	74,800	70,900
Bacton House	5	104,600	173,700	210,500
Cornwall Avenue	6	64,900	78,800	88,000
Total : Neighbourhood Administration		1,199,000	1,805,700	1,941,300
ENVIRONMENTAL DEVELOPMENT				
Environ. Health and Trading Stnds	7	61,300	74,300	153,800
Municipal Markets	8	45,300	45,300	44,900
Street Trading	9	11,900	11,900	11,900
Engineering: Highways and Works	10	489,200	406,400	430,700
Client Services : Pools & Laundries	11	602,600	749,300	784,600
Client Services : Parks & Open Spaces	12	375,200	288,300	305,600
Clients Services : Clnsng/Inspection	13	0	102,200	600,900
Planning and Economic Development	14	76,900	79,700	118,700
Total : Environmental Development		1,662,400	1,757,400	2,451,100
HOUSING				
General Management	15	444,300	488,000	512,800
Estate Management	16	1,771,900	1,871,600	1,798,400
Other Housing Services	17	1,283,300	1,043,300	613,100
Total : Housing		3,499,500	3,402,900	2,924,300
ARTS AND INFORMATION				
Other Recreational and Arts Activities	18	48,300	10,800	28,400
Libraries	19	777,900	851,400	385,600
Total : Arts and Information		826,200	862,200	914,000
PROPERTY SERVICES				
Management of Industrial and -				
Commercial Buildings	20	10,900	31,800	28,800
Valuation and Right to Buy	21	0	29,400	123,600
Building Services - Holding Account	22	0	0	0
Total : Property Services		10,900	61,200	152,400
TOTAL CARRIED FORWARD TO PAGE 1a		7,198,000	7,889,400	8,383,100

GENERAL RATE ESTIMATES 1989/90   GLOBE TOWN NEIGHBOURHOOD COMMITTEE

SERVICE SUMMARY	PAGE NO.	1988/89		1989/90
		ESTIMATE	REVISED ESTIMATE	ESTIMATE
TOTAL BROUGHT FORWARD FROM PAGE 1		7,198,000	7,889,400	8,383,100
OTHER SERVICES				
Community Relations	23	86,300	0	0
Miscellaneous	24	411,400	0	0
Total : Other Services		497,700	0	0
SOCIAL SERVICES				
Social Services Administration	25	216,200	232,100	268,500
Services for Adolescents	26	2,300	0	0
Children : Other Accommodation	27	114,700	114,700	0
Boarded out Children	28	90,000	90,000	92,500
Day Nurseries	29	246,000	235,700	237,400
Playgroups and Childminders	30	19,300	1,100	25,500
Children : Preventive and Support	31	24,600	22,500	24,600
Sheltered Accommodation	32	15,500	13,500	19,800
Other Accommodation for Adults	33	126,000	126,000	132,600
Home Help Service	34	266,500	276,800	287,500
Meals in the Home	35	83,700	89,600	99,600
Luncheon and Social Clubs	36	11,700	11,700	12,300
Cafeterias	37	7,300	43,200	43,400
Elderly : Travel Permits	38	230,700	237,100	260,800
Aids and Adaptions	39	10,700	15,800	11,300
Physically Handicapped : Travel Permits	40	31,800	28,000	30,900
Centres For The Mentally Ill	41	62,400	58,500	59,800
Fieldwork Services	42	487,500	553,300	603,300
Surplus Buildings	43	9,500	4,000	200
Total : Social Services		2,056,400	2,153,600	2,210,000
TOTAL : ALL SERVICES		9,752,100	10,043,000	10,593,100
less : Transfer to statutory Street Trading Account		-	11,900	11,900
		9,752,100	10,031,100	10,581,200

Isle of Dogs Neighbourhood: Estimates for the general rate for the year 1989–90

GENERAL RATE ESTIMATES 1989/90   ISLE OF DOGS NEIGHBOURHOOD COMMITTEE

SERVICE SUMMARY	PAGE NO.	1988/89 ORIGINAL ESTIMATE	1988/89 REVISED ESTIMATE	1989/90 ESTIMATE
ADMINISTRATION				
Neighbourhood Administration	2	1,017,400	1,128,300	1,063,600
Great Eastern D	3	164,600	247,800	239,200
Woodstock Terrace	4	105,000	77,400	74,300
Great Eastern B	5	0	0	146,700
Total : Neighbourhood Administration		1,287,000	1,453,500	1,523,800
HEALTH AND CONSUMER SERVICES				
Environmental Protection	6	745,000	616,700	621,900
Street Cleansing & Refuse Collection	7	0	0	488,300
Total : Health and Consumer Services		745,000	616,700	1,110,200
HOUSING				
General Management	8	447,100	599,200	347,800
Estate Management	9	1,754,700	1,793,600	2,143,900
Other Housing Services	10	1,568,800	1,374,600	571,500
Total : Housing		3,770,600	3,767,400	3,063,200
LEISURE AND RECREATION				
Swimming Pools and Laundries	11	368,500	431,000	404,700
Sports Halls and Leisure centres	12	93,400	119,300	113,000
Parks and Open Spaces	13	499,000	516,500	531,800
Arts Centre	14	107,400	163,100	171,000
Other Recreational and Arts Activities	15	53,000	60,300	59,000
Water Activities	16	37,900	40,800	41,900
Libraries	17	104,500	117,600	116,300
Total : Leisure and Recreation		1,263,700	1,448,600	1,437,700
PLANNING AND DEVELOPMENT				
Development Control	18	105,800	144,200	195,500
Landscape Architects	19	0	9,900	19,800
Management of Industrial and -				
- Commercial Land and Buildings	20	184,800	238,300	249,100
Total : Planning and Development		290,600	392,400	464,400
NEIGHBOURHOOD BUILDING SERVICES				
Administration	21	0	15,200	34,700
Architecture	22	0	0	0
Total : N.B.S.		0	15,200	34,700
SURVEYING SERVICES				
Surveying Services	23	0	0	0
TOTAL CARRIED FORWARD TO PAGE 1a		7,356,900	7,693,800	7,634,000

GENERAL RATE ESTIMATES 1989/90   ISLE OF DOGS NEIGHBOURHOOD COMMITTEE

SERVICE SUMMARY	PAGE NO.	1988/89		1989/90
		ORIGINAL ESTIMATE	REVISED ESTIMATE	ESTIMATE
TOTAL BROUGHT FORWARD FROM PAGE 1		7,356,900	7,693,800	7,634,000
CENTRAL POLICY				
Policy Unit	24	100,200	138,800	230,500
Legal Services	25	0	40,500	77,500
Total : Central Policy		100,200	179,300	308,000
OTHER SERVICES				
Miscellaneous	26	349,500	214,100	175,400
SOCIAL SERVICES				
Social Sevices Administration	27	299,900	237,800	220,500
Community Homes for Children	28	329,700	326,600	318,200
Children : Other Accomodation	29	170,800	170,800	0
Boarded Out Children	30	134,200	134,200	163,100
Day Nurseries	31	378,600	392,500	386,700
Playgroups & Childminders	32	18,800	17,000	17,200
Intermediate Treatment	33	111,100	120,700	108,400
Children : Preventative & Support	34	21,900	28,200	21,900
Sheltered Accomodation	35	16,200	18,100	16,100
Other Accomodation for Adults	36	78,200	78,200	63,800
Home Help Service	37	161,800	206,800	179,400
Day Centres	38	156,700	200,400	211,900
Meals in the Home	39	74,700	77,100	83,300
Luncheon and Social Clubs	40	36,500	37,700	39,400
Elderly : Travel Permits	41	146,300	153,800	169,200
Aids and Adaptations	42	10,400	10,400	10,400
Physically Handicapped : Travel Permits	43	38,200	34,500	37,900
Fieldwork Services	44	375,000	344,500	319,000
Total : Social Services		2,559,000	2,589,300	2,366,400
		10,365,600	10,676,500	10,483,800

Poplar Neighbourhood: Estimates for the general rate for the year 1989–90

GENERAL RATE ESTIMATES 1989/90   POPLAR NEIGHBOURHOOD COMMITTEE

SERVICE SUMMARY	PAGE NO.	1988/89 ESTIMATE	1988/89 REVISED ESTIMATE	1989/90 ESTIMATE
ADMINISTRATION				
Neighbourhood Administration	2	1,448,300	1,798,600	1,685,400
Legal Services	3	0	59,200	126,500
Bromley Public Hall	4	37,900	39,300	30,200
86 Bow Road	5	55,300	52,600	42,400
723 Commercial Road	6	176,400	71,000	87,500
Total : Neighbourhood Administration		1,717,900	2,020,700	1,972,000
HEALTH AND CONSUMER SERVICES				
Environmental Health	7	41,200	84,300	122,000
Gypsy Liaison	8	44,100	43,200	43,900
Trading Standards	9	0	34,800	76,500
Municipal Markets	10	(120,000)	(108,300)	(107,900)
Street Trading	11	68,900	65,200	62,500
Total : Health and Consumer Services		34,200	119,200	197,000
HIGHWAYS				
Highways and Works	12	664,000	814,500	744,600
CLIENT SERVICES				
Street Cleansing and Refuse	13	0	6,200	724,800
BUILDING SERVICES				
Infrastructure Group	14	0	0	0
HOUSING				
General Management	15	897,600	1,034,700	848,000
Estate Management	16	4,989,300	5,279,200	5,234,400
Other Housing Services	17	2,322,200	1,797,300	568,700
Total : Housing		8,209,100	8,111,200	6,651,100
LEISURE AND RECREATION				
Swimming Pools and Laundries	18	18,200	19,400	19,800
Sports Halls and Leisure Centres	19	125,100	123,000	122,100
Parks and Open Spaces	20	669,700	636,400	639,900
Other Recreational and Arts Activities	21	48,200	95,600	132,300
Libraries	22	298,900	365,400	357,500
Total : Leisure and Recreation		1,160,100	1,239,800	1,271,600
PLANNING AND DEVELOPMENT				
Development Control	23	83,700	133,900	127,100
Valuation	24	0	56,800	186,200
Management of Industrial and - - Commercial Land and Buildings	25	14,400	35,200	56,100
Total : Planning and Development		98,100	225,900	369,400
OTHER SERVICES				
Community Relations	26	90,000	47,900	114,100
Miscellaneous	27	665,900	244,300	710,400
Total : Other Services		755,900	292,200	824,500
TOTAL CARRIED FORWARD TO PAGE 1a		12,639,300	12,829,700	12,755,000

GENERAL RATE ESTIMATES 1989/90   POPLAR NEIGHBOURHOOD COMMITTEE

SERVICE SUMMARY	PAGE NO.	1988/89 ESTIMATE	1988/89 REVISED ESTIMATE	1989/90 ESTIMATE
TOTAL BROUGHT FORWARD FROM PAGE 1a		12,639,300	12,829,700	12,755,000
SOCIAL SERVICES				
Social Services Administration	28	542,900	625,400	600,400
Community Homes for Children	29	309,300	331,400	326,800
Reception and Observation	30	100,800	104,100	105,300
Children :Other Accommodation	31	299,200	349,000	0
Boarded Out Children	32	234,700	234,700	261,000
Day Nurseries	33	185,100	195,400	189,600
Family Centre	34	140,800	158,500	155,600
Playgroups and Childminders	35	19,800	21,700	21,000
Children : Preventive and Support	36	39,200	40,000	45,000
Homes for the Elderly	37	1,068,700	1,075,400	828,600
Sheltered Accommodation	38	53,100	48,500	48,500
Other Accommodation for Adults	39	185,200	185,200	196,500
Work Centre for the Elderly	40	161,400	125,300	67,400
Home Help Service	41	390,900	390,900	528,600
Day Centres	42	356,600	250,600	110,800
Meals in the Home	43	143,700	171,600	312,900
Luncheon and Social Clubs	44	54,300	44,300	22,500
Elderly : Travel Permits	45	379,900	390,400	429,400
Home for the Physically Handicapped	46	334,800	323,800	309,300
Social Rehabilitation Centres	47	247,600	223,000	170,100
Sheltered Workshops	48	33,500	33,500	44,400
Aids and Adaptations	49	16,300	16,800	16,800
Physically Handicapped : Travel Permits	50	105,000	92,500	101,700
Home for the Elderly Mentally Ill	51	403,300	454,800	459,500
Centres for the Mentally Ill	52	72,700	0	0
Home for the Mentally Handicapped	53	160,900	175,000	188,700
Mentally Handicapped : Training Centres	54	408,600	374,700	365,900
Fieldwork Services	55	514,800	596,900	557,900
Total : Social Services		6,963,100	7,033,400	6,464,200
TOTAL : ALL SERVICES		19,602,400	19,863,100	19,219,200
less : Transfer to statutory Street Trading Account		-	65,200	62,500
TOTAL : NEIGHBOURHOOD BUDGET		19,602,400	19,797,900	19,156,700

Stepney Neighbourhood: Estimates for the general rate for the year 1989–90

GENERAL RATE ESTIMATES 1989-90   STEPNEY NEIGHBOURHOOD COMMITTEE

		1988/89		1989/90
SERVICE SUMMARY	PAGE NO.	ORIGINAL ESTIMATE	REVISED ESTIMATE	ESTIMATE
ADMINISTRATION				
Neighbourhood Administration	2	1,045,500	1,048,100	1,249,500
Cheviot House	3	379,300	398,900	410,200
Jubilee Street	4	171,800	54,600	53,000
Oceanair House	5	0	0	115,300
Other Buildings	6	0	19,800	64,700
Total : Neighbourhood Administration		1,596,600	1,521,400	1,892,700
HEALTH AND CONSUMER SERVICES				
Environmental Health	7	64,300	84,400	156,500
Trading Standards	8	0	20,300	61,400
Street Trading	9	(1,700)	900	1,400
Total : Health and Consumer Services		62,600	105,600	219,300
TECHNICAL SERVICES				
Administration	10	0	54,000	31,300
Street Cleansing and Refuse Collection	11	0	0	503,900
Highways and Works	12	625,300	477,400	445,300
Architectual Services	13	0	2,600	600
Surveying Services	14	0	0	0
Total : Technical Services		625,300	534,000	981,100
HOUSING				
General Management	15	691,300	627,300	621,500
Estate Management	16	1,834,900	2,124,300	2,089,800
Other Housing Services	17	2,023,200	1,531,100	926,800
Aims Team	18	0	60,100	102,000
Total : Housing		4,549,400	4,342,800	3,740,100
LEISURE AND RECREATION				
Parks and Open Spaces	19	331,000	389,600	323,300
Other Recreation and Arts Activities	20	80,000	103,700	110,300
Libraries	21	74,100	94,700	84,900
Total : Leisure and Recreation		485,100	588,000	518,500
TOTAL : CARRIED FORWARD TO PAGE 1a		7,319,000	7,091,800	7,351,700

GENERAL RATE ESTIMATES 1989-90   STEPNEY NEIGHBOURHOOD COMMITTEE

SERVICE SUMMARY	PAGE NO.	1988/89		1989/90
		ORIGINAL ESTIMATE	REVISED ESTIMATE	ESTIMATE
TOTAL : BROUGHT FORWARD FROM PAGE 1		7,319,000	7,091,800	7,351,700
PLANNING AND DEVELOPEMENT				
Economic/Developement Control	22	94,300	116,100	140,400
Management of Industrial and Commercial Land and Buildings	23	14,600	14,600	12,200
Valuation Services	24	0	13,700	42,100
Total : Planning and Developement		108,900	144,400	194,700
OTHER SERVICES				
Community Relations	25	158,000	0	0
Miscellaneous	26	367,100	614,100	691,600
Total : Other Services		525,100	614,100	691,600
SOCIAL SERVICES				
Social Services Administration	27	215,900	227,200	213,300
Transport Holding Account	28	0	22,800	33,300
Children : Other Accommodation	29	170,700	159,000	0
Fostering and Adoption	30	134,100	222,900	223,700
Day Nurseries	31	72,000	72,000	80,000
Playgroups and Childminders	32	18,800	8,300	14,000
Children : Preventive and Support	33	26,600	23,600	26,000
Homes for the Elderly	34	442,100	466,800	467,800
Other Accommodation for Adults	35	141,700	130,100	173,300
Home Help Service	36	294,000	363,300	351,700
Meals in the Home	37	84,600	79,700	76,400
Luncheon and Social Clubs	38	45,400	42,700	41,600
Elderly : Cafeterias	39	57,400	66,300	73,800
Elderly : Travel Permits	40	289,000	304,100	334,500
Social Rehabilitation Centre	41	138,400	149,100	136,900
Aids and Adaptations	42	80,800	99,100	90,800
Physically Handicapped : Travel Permits	43	49,700	44,700	49,200
Fieldwork Services	44	791,800	882,100	809,100
Total : Social Services		3,053,000	3,363,800	3,195,400
TOTAL : ALL SERVICES		11,006,000	11,214,100	11,433,400
less : Transfer to statutory Street Trading Account		-	900	1,400
TOTAL : NEIGHBOURHOOD BUDGET		11,006,000	11,213,200	11,432,000

Wapping Neighbourhood: Estimates for the general rate for the year 1989–90

GENERAL RATE ESTIMATES 1989/90   WAPPING NEIGHBOURHOOD COMMITTEE

SERVICE SUMMARY	PAGE NO.	1988/89 ORIGINAL ESTIMATE	1988/89 REVISED ESTIMATE	1989/90 ESTIMATE
ADMINISTRATION				
Neighbourhood Administration	2	1,002,000	1,176,000	1,165,500
1st Stop Shop	3	21,700	55,700	72,300
Limehouse Town Hall	4	79,900	85,800	84,800
Gem House	5	141,700	119,800	99,800
St Georges Town Hall	6	107,400	129,700	102,200
Total : Neighbourhood Administration		1,352,700	1,567,000	1,524,600
HEALTH AND CONSUMER SERVICES				
Health and Consumer Services	7	64,100	166,400	213,300
Municipal Markets	8	36,400	0	0
Street Trading	9	7,700	0	0
Total : Health and Consumer Services		108,200	166,400	213,300
HIGHWAYS				
Highways and Works	10	784,800	750,800	1,327,700
HOUSING				
General Management	11	618,900	804,800	728,400
Estate Management	12	2,606,700	2,486,100	2,851,800
Other Housing Services	13	1,039,100	594,000	396,400
Total : Housing		4,264,700	3,884,900	3,976,600
LEISURE				
Management	14	0	51,500	73,500
Swimming Pools and Laundries	15	589,500	593,500	598,600
Sports Halls and Leisure Centres	16	193,600	174,500	175,100
Parks and Open Spaces	17	492,400	592,800	604,000
Entertainments & Arts Activities	18	47,100	17,600	26,600
Libraries	19	507,100	557,000	630,400
Total : Leisure and Recreation		1,829,700	1,986,900	2,108,200
PLANNING AND DEVELOPMENT				
Planning and Development	20	98,700	72,500	90,800
Property Services	21	167,300	299,200	48,700
Total : Planning and Development		266,000	371,700	139,500
TOTAL CARRIED FORWARD TO PAGE 1a		8,606,100	8,727,700	9,289,900

GENERAL RATE ESTIMATES 1989/90   WAPPING NEIGHBOURHOOD COMMITTEE

SERVICE SUMMARY	PAGE NO.	1988/89		1989/90
		ORIGINAL ESTIMATE	REVISED ESTIMATE	ESTIMATE
TOTAL BROUGHT FORWARD FROM PAGE 1		8,606,100	8,727,700	9,289,900
OTHER SERVICES				
Community Relations	22	114,700	0	0
Miscellaneous	23	432,000	507,500	(2,800)
Total : Other Services		546,700	507,500	(2,800)
SOCIAL SERVICES				
Administration	24	181,900	183,100	184,400
Community Homes for Children	25	262,800	210,300	237,200
Children : Other Accommodation	26	192,100	192,100	0
Boarded Out Children	27	150,800	150,800	47,800
Day Nurseries	28	392,100	318,900	330,600
Children : Preventive and Support	29	27,300	27,300	27,300
Homes for the Elderly	30	464,900	502,300	521,000
Sheltered Accommodation	31	16,200	13,000	13,600
Other Accommodation for Adults	32	88,500	88,500	75,000
Home Help Service	33	324,800	193,200	218,400
Meals in the Home	34	82,700	49,000	49,000
Luncheon and Social Clubs	35	41,600	46,200	46,900
Elderly/Handicapped Services	36	219,800	224,300	220,300
Fieldwork Services	37	404,800	381,400	400,200
Furniture store	38	11,000	8,700	0
Residual costs : surplus buildings	39	2,000	0	0
Total : Social Services		2,863,300	2,589,100	2,371,700
TOTAL : NEIGHBOURHOOD BUDGET		12,016,100	11,824,300	11,658,800

Central Departments: Estimates for the general rate for the year 1989–90

GENERAL RATE ESTIMATES 1989/90   CENTRAL DEPARTMENTS

| SERVICE | EXPENDITURE VOTE NO. | 1988/89 | | 1989/90 |
		ORIGINAL ESTIMATE	REVISED ESTIMATE	ESTIMATE
CHIEF EXECUTIVE				
Public Relations	2	301,000	299,700	282,100
Central Policy Group	3	4,826,800	4,538,400	4,414,900
Special Projects Team	4	92,200	91,800	172,800
Housing Strategy	5	647,200	642,300	1,049,000
Homeless Families	6	8,671,700	6,053,600	5,410,600
Hostels	7	133,200	131,700	201,000
Rent Officer Service	8	0	0	0
Regstn. of Births,Deaths and Marriages	9	109,500	108,600	115,400
Canary Wharf Env. Health Team	10	0	0	200,000
102 Mile End Road	11	0	0	0
Mayfield House	12	4,300	4,300	4,700
Bethnal Green Town Hall	13	100,600	100,600	88,100
88 Roman Road	14	3,300	3,300	0
Branch Road	15	0	0	0
TOTAL : CHIEF EXECUTIVE		14,889,800	11,974,300	11,938,600

GENERAL RATE ESTIMATES 1988/89   CENTRAL DEPARTMENTS

SERVICE	EXPENDITURE VOTE NO.	1988/89		1989/90
		ORIGINAL ESTIMATE	REVISED ESTIMATE	ESTIMATE
BOROUGH TREASURER				
ADMINISTRATION				
EXPENDITURE				
Employees :-				
Salaries	815001	2,569,300	2,576,700	2,730,500
Other staff expenses	815005	30,000	28,100	31,500
Transport :-				
Direct transport	815020	118,400	112,800	107,900
Travelling and subsistence	815022	59,500	37,900	58,500
Supplies and services :-				
Equipment and furniture	815030	10,400	10,400	28,100
Printing,stationery & general office -expenses	815034	66,000	72,800	83,000
District Audit fees	815039	72,100	176,600	187,600
Audit stamp duty	-	57,800	-	-
Miscellaneous expenses	815066	4,000	4,200	6,200
Computer program (income)	815068	-	150,000	-
Contingency : Pay awards	-	155,100	-	-
		3,142,600	3,169,500	3,233,300
INCOME				
Recharged to other services :-				
D.L.O.	815082	62,500	62,500	65,600
Other grants,reimbursements & contributions	815086	126,500	142,000	146,000
Recharged to other funds :-				
Superannuation Fund	815090	180,300	190,300	197,400
Capital accounts	815098	55,000	55,000	55,000
		424,300	449,800	464,000
NET EXPENDITURE		2,718,300	2,719,700	2,769,300

GENERAL RATE ESTIMATES 1989/90   CENTRAL DEPARTMENTS

SERVICE	EXPENDITURE VOTE NO.	1988/89		1989/90
		ORIGINAL ESTIMATE	REVISED ESTIMATE	ESTIMATE
SOCIAL SERVICES				
Administration	53	909,400	752,200	993,900
Community Homes for Children	54	295,500	0	0
Reception and observation	55	110,000	28,000	110,000
Services for Adolescents	56	59,200	8,100	0
Children : Other Accomodation	57	0	0	1,835,200
Boarded Out Children	58	55,500	70,500	74,000
Teleshopping Service	59	20,000	40,000	60,000
Cafeterias	60	32,400	0	0
Holidays and Recreation	61	323,100	202,000	235,500
Holiday Home	62	61,100	123,700	19,000
T.B. and Alcohol Clients	63	2,300	2,300	2,300
Services for Mental Health	64	0	0	200,000
Surplus Buildings	65	50,700	62,900	59,600
Holiday Hotels	66	20,500	(6,000)	6,300
TOTAL : SOCIAL SERVICES		1,939,700	1,283,700	3,595,800

Case 6
Local Management of Schools

OBJECTIVES

1. To examine the annual budget and accounts for a local authority secondary school in the context of the local management of schools initiative.
2. To assess the usefulness of the information in the budget and the accounts for the management of schools.
3. To consider the consequences of delegating financial responsibility from the local education authority to the schools.

MATERIALS

1. Extracts from the 1991/92 Budget Statement and Allocation Summary for the Girls County High School, Colchester, Essex (Exhibit 6.1).
2. Interim Account Summary for eleven months ending 28 February 1991 (Exhibit 6.2).
3. Extracts from the Essex Scheme for Local Management of Schools, February 1990, pp. 6–16, 17–19 (Exhibit 6.3).

INTRODUCTION

The Education Reform Act 1988 introduced many changes in the organ-ization of schools and the delivery of education in the UK. The most important of these changes are open enrolment, the development of the National Curriculum, the provision for schools to opt out of local auth-ority control, and the implementation of financial delegation through the local management of schools (LMS). Although the subject of this case study is LMS, the other changes also have implications for the financial management of schools and it will be helpful to say a brief word about the financial implications of each of them.

Open enrolment means that local authorities are now not allowed to limit the number of pupils in a school below its maximum capacity. The aim of this provision is to allow popular schools to increase in size. Since the funding of schools under LMS is driven largely by pupil numbers there is every incentive for headteachers to expand exrolment to the limit of their schools' physical capacity.

The financial implications of the introduction of the National Curriculum relate primarily to staff costs. In particular, individual schools may not

have the correct balance of subject expertise to deliver the requirements
of the National Curriculum so that staff adjustments will be necessary,
perhaps in the form of retraining or severance. In addition, there is an
acute scarcity of teachers in some subjects and LMS may provide some
scope for schools to offer salary incentives.

The Education Reform Act makes provision for a school to opt out of
local authority control and receive its funding directly from the Department of Education and Science. These grant-maintained schools will
receive the funds that they would have received from the local authority
under LMS together with an amount which is deemed to cover its share
of the costs of the services retained and funded by the local education
authority (LEA). The effect of this will be to give a grant-maintained
school complete autonomy over which advisory and administrative services it should purchase and from where they should be bought.

ANALYSIS

Although local management of schools (LMS) was introduced by the
Education Reform Act 1988, several local authorities had been experi-
menting with financial delegation for schools throughout the 1980s.
Indeed, many of the detailed provisions of the Act can be traced to the
schemes introduced by, among others, Cambridgeshire and Solihull. The
basic idea of LMS is to devolve to schools the responsibility for managing
their own financial affairs. Under the previous financial regime almost all
spending decisions for a school were taken centrally by the LEA. This
meant that all expenditure on staffing and premises had to be authorized
by the Education Office and, with the exception of a few thousand
pounds for capitation-related items, headteachers had no discretion on
how funds for their schools were spent. Thus, it was not possible for
individual schools to take advantage of virement, whereby an underspending under one heading can be used to fund an overspending under
another heading.

Under LMS each school is given a global budget, which is held
centrally, but then has to be allocated by the school to a number of
subjective headings and spent according to the needs of the school. The
formal authority for spending decisions rests with the Governing Body,
which must ensure that expenditure is incurred only within the approved
budget. In practice, the expenditure powers of the Governing Body are
delegated to the headteacher, who is accountable to, and whose actions
are monitored and evaluated by, the Governing Body or its finance
subcommittee.

In determining the delegated budget to each school certain excepted
items are deducted from the general schools budget (GSB). Some of
these items are mandatory, for example capital expenditure and Government Grant related expenditure, while others are discretionary. Discretionary excepted items fall within two categories: those which are
not subject to any limit, for example central administration, and those
where the total amount held back by the LEA must not exceed 10 per
cent of the GSB, for example structural maintenance, special educational
needs and the educational psychology service. In this latter category, the

practice for whether or not items are delegated to schools varies among LEAs.

The Aggregated Schools Budget (GSB less excepted items) is allocated to each school on the basis of a formula determined by the LEA and approved by the Secretary of State. At least 75 per cent of the Aggregated Schools Budget (ASB) must be allocated on the basis of the number of pupils weighted by age. The remainder of the ASB is allocated on the basis of other 'reasonable' factors such as floor area, type of fuel used and off-site sports facilities. The determination of the total ASB and the basis of its allocation for the Essex County Council LMS Scheme is shown in Exhibit 6.3.

The amount allocated to each school is known as its budget share. The budget share for the Girls County High School in Colchester, Essex for 1991/92 is shown in Exhibit 6.1. The allocation for the year, £1,241,145, is shown at the foot of the first page of the exhibit. This allocation is itself determined in part by the use of the LEA's Formula Budget, with a weight of 40 per cent, and in part by the use of a base year spend calculation for the school, with a weight of 60 per cent. It is the intention of the Essex LEA to move to 100 per cent formula budget by 1994/5, having started with 20 per cent in the first year of LMS, in 1990/91. The base year spend calculation of the school for 1991/92 is derived from the recorded expenditure in the base year 1988/89, adjusted for excepted items, inflation and changes in pupil numbers. It can be seen that the base year spend and formula budget differ by only £47,000, or 3.7 per cent of the formula budget. Indeed, assuming that the number and mix of pupils in future years are similar to those for 1991/92 the Girls County High School will be financially better off as the LEA moves to 100 per cent formula budgeting.

Having received notification of its budget share for the year, the school is then required to allocate that sum over a number of subjective budget headings. A copy of the allocation for 1991/92 is shown in Exhibit 6.1. Although the school is allowed to allocate the budget over the headings as it sees fit, in practice many items of expenditure are both committed and relatively fixed in the short term.

During the financial year the school is required to maintain a complete record of its expenditure and income for comparison with the delegated budget. The Girls County High School uses a computerized accounting package to prepare monthly expenditure reports, an example of which for the financial year 1990/91 is shown in Exhibit 6.2. Each school is expected to balance its budget although no action is taken if the variation for the year does not exceed 2.5 per cent of the budget share. If a school overspends by more than 2.5 per cent interest is charged at the current market rate on the average of the opening and closing balances for the year. Any deficit is carried forward to the following financial year and is taken into account when determining the following year's budget share. On the other hand, if a school has underspent during the year it is allowed to retain the surplus and if the amount underspent is more than 2.5 per cent of the budget share interest at the current market rate will be credited to the school's budget.

QUESTIONS

1. To what extent might the introduction of LMS contribute to the educational objectives of the 1988 Education Reform Act?
2. The budget share for each school in Essex is currently derived from both a formula budget and historic expenditure. What are the arguments for the use of a simple formula budget rather than historic expenditure in LMS schemes?
3. (a) Critically evaluate the Account Summary report used by the headteacher of the Girls County High School for monitoring and evaluating the expenditure of the school against its budget allocation.
   (b) Suggest how the Account Summary report might be improved and what additional information should be included.

FURTHER READING

Burgess, T. (1986) Cambridgeshire's Financial Management Initiative for Schools, *Public Money*, June, pp. 21–4.

Caldwell, B. and Spinks, J. (1988) *The Self-Managing School*, Falmer Press, Basingstoke.

Coopers & Lybrand (1988) *Local Management of Schools: A Report to the Department of Education and Science*, HMSO, London.

DES (1988) *Education Reform Act: Local Management of Schools*, Circular 7/88, DES, London.

Edwards, P. (1989) *Local Management of Schools*, NFER, Slough.

Fisher, P. (1989) Learning your LMS Norfolk style, *Public Finance and Accountancy*, 10 February, pp. 10–12.

Hill, D., Oakley Smith, B. and Spinks, J. (1990) *Local Management of Schools*, Paul Chapman Publishing, London.

HMSO (1988) Education Reform Act 1988, HMSO, London.

Exhibit 6.1 Extracts from the 1991/92 Budget Statement and Allocation Summary for the Girls County High School, Colchester, Essex

SECTION 42 BUDGET STATEMENT
Part 4 : Final Budget Share – Financial Year 1991/92

1) **FORMULA BUDGET**

SCHOOL: *COLCHESTER GIRLS COUNTY HIGH*   *COLCHESTER*
PUPIL NOS.   *655* (January 1991)

ALLOCATION:

i) A sum of money for each pupil

AGE	AMOUNT PER PUPIL	NUMBER OF PUPILS	ALLOCATION £	£
11+	1,253.44	96	120,330	
12+	1,253.72	97	121,611	
13+	1,266.91	96	121,623	
14+	1,492.95	98	146,309	
15+	1,614.80	97	156,636	
16+	2,191.28	89	195,024	
17+	2,197.74	82	180,215	1,041,748

PLUS
ii) Fixed amount (see supporting notes) 158,414

PLUS
iii) Other allowances (see supporting notes)

		£	£
a) Floor area		23,218	
b) Nursery		0	
c) Rent & Rates		37,435	
d) Off Site Sports Facilities		0	
e) Split Site		0	
f) Swimming Pool		0	
g) Fuel Mix	Contract Gas (Med)	787	
h) Teaching Cost Adjustment		0	
i) Social Factor		0	
j) Voluntary Aided		0	
k) London Weighting		0	
l) Administration Support		7,839	
m) Schools Serving MOD Establishments		0	69,279
n) Boarding		0	

FORMULA ALLOCATION   **1,269,441**

2) **BASE YEAR SPEND**

Net expenditure from 1988/89 statement 941,465

Adjusted for inflation and volume changes 1,186,517

Rent & rates	37,435	
Administrative support for LMS	7,839	
Changes in pupil numbers (see enclosed statement)	(9,509)	
Floor Area Adjustment	0	35,765

BASE YEAR SPEND   **1,222,282**

3) **RESOURCE ALLOCATION 1991–92**

Formula Allocation x 40% 507,776

Base Year Spend x 60% 733,369

ALLOCATION AT 1991–92 ESTIMATED OUTTURN PRICES   **1,241,145**

Education Finance   March 1991   Cost Code   5870

SECTION 42 BUDGET STATEMENT
Part 4: Final Budget Share - Financial Year 1991/92

Supporting Notes

1. **Fixed Amount**

   The fixed amounts are:

	£
Primary Schools	42,047
11-16 Secondary Schools	137,045
11-18 Secondary Schools	158,414
Sixth Form Colleges	131,839

2. **Other Allowances**

   (a) **Floor Area**

   £5.44 per square metre. Schools can determine the floor area used by dividing this sum into the figure shown on the statement.

   (b) **Nursery**

   A total allowance of £1258.99 (£823.83 + £435.16) per pupil in a designated nursery class.

   (c) **Rent and Rates**

   Rent and Rates have been included on a "best estimate" basis and adjustments in accordance with the approved Scheme will be made when the situation becomes clear.

   (d) **Off-Site Playing Fields**

   Where the LEA has agreed that on-site facilities are inadequate and a school satisfies agreed criteria, a sum of £4.87 per pupil is allowed. Schools can determine the number of pupils by dividing this sum into the figure shown on the statement.

   (e) **Split Site**

   The allowances are:

Secondary Schools	£
- Over 1 Km but less than 4 Km	65,943
- Over 4 Km)	
- those with at least three sites,)	117,610
two of which are over 1 Km apart)	
Primary Schools	
- Over 1 Km but less than 4 Km	2,934
- Over 4 Km	4,141

   (f) **Swimming Pool**

   £61.93 per square metre of water surface area. Schools can determine the area used by dividing this sum into the figure shown on the statement.

(g) Fuel Mix

The allowance regognises the relative heating costs of oil, contract and tariff gas and electricity. Each school is categorised according to its main fuel. Contract gas (high use) is now the cheapest fuel and the following fuel mix factors have been applied to the basic energy allocation of each school:

Contract gas	- high use	1.00	Oil	1.26
	- medium use	1.05	Tariff gas	1.28
	- low use	1.13	Electricity	1.86

(h) Teaching Cost

An adjustment is made in the case of smaller primary schools with fewer than 10 teachers (excluding the Head and Deputy) where actual costs of standard scale teachers (excluding incentive allowances) are greater or less than the LEA primary average and/or schools have to meet the additional costs of safeguarded Heads and Deputies. The basis of the adjustment is shown in para. 5.2.16(h) of the LMS Scheme, the "set date" being January 1991 payroll.

(i) Social Factor

An allowance taking account of the entitlement to free school meals (primary and secondary age pupils) and, in the case of pupils entering secondary schools, reading scores on entry; further details are given in para. 5.2.16(i) of the LMS Scheme. Entitlement to Income Support has been calculated using January 1991 pupil numbers.

(j) Voluntary Aided

Basic maintenance allocation (including that for swimming pools) is multiplied by 108%.

(k) London Weighting

A percentage addition to a school's age-weighted pupil allocation:

Inner Fringe	3.2%
Outer Fringe	2.9%

(l) Administration Support

Primary	fixed sum	£3,105
	per capita allowance	£7.60
Secondary	fixed sum	£6,038
	per capita allowance	£2.75

(m) Schools Serving MOD Establishments

Where pupil turnover in each of the two previous academic years exceeds 10% of such pupils, an allocation of £129.70 per primary pupil and £64.85 per secondary pupil.

(n) Boarding

For day schools with limited boarding provision a fixed sum of £73,464 plus £1,626 per weighted pupil (weightings are: 1.00 for 11 and 12 year olds; 1.29 for 13 and 14 year olds and 1.43 for 15 year olds and above). For boarding schools a per pupil rate of £2,880 with no fixed sum.

County Education Officer
Essex LEA
March 1991

EFFECT OF CHANGES IN PUPIL NUMBERS 1988/89 TO 1991/9₂

Colchester Co High for Girls

		Full Year No.of posts excl. Head	Part Academic Year	Total Part Academic Years
1987/88	Academic year staffing	41	17.08	
1988/89	Academic year staffing	41	23.92	
1988/89	Financial year staffing (see note 1)			41.00
1990/91	Academic year staffing	39.2	16.33	
1991/92	Academic year staffing	41.5	24.21	
1991/92	Financial year staffing (see note 2)			40.54
Variation				(0.46)
Variation @ £20,747 per post (see note 3)				(9,509)

Notes

1) 1988/89 financial year staffing is calculated by adding 5/12 of 1987/88 and 7/12 of 1988/89 academic year staffing. This represents the periods 1/4/88 to 31/8/88 and 1/9/88 to 31/3/89 respectively.

2) 1991/92 financial year staffing is calculated by adding 5/12 of 1990/91 and 7/12 of 1991/92 academic year staffing. This represents the periods 1/4/91 to 31/8/91 and 1/9/91 to 31/3/92 respectively.

3) £20,747 represents the average M.P.G. salary plus average incentive allowances for Essex plus national insurance and superannuation.

Education Finance   March 1991

COLCHESTER GIRLS COUNTY HIGH, COLCHESTER

SCHOOL OUTTURN AND BASE YEAR SPEND STATEMENT 1988/89

(1)	(2)	(3)	(4)	(5)	(6)
	RECORDED SPEND £	ASB DEFINITION ADJUSTMENT £	ADJUSTED OUTTURN £	BASE YEAR ADJUSTMENT £	BASE YEAR SPEND £
ITEMS NOT YET DELEGATED					
Teaching Staff	721753	31234	752987		752987
Other Staff	85758		85758		85758
Other Employee Expenses	6700	1571	8271		8271
Upkeep of Buildings	114497	-96081	18416		18416
Energy and Water	24266		24266		24266
Joint Use Payments	0		0		0
Rent and Rates	28448		28448	-28448	0
Other Premises Costs	3082		3082		3082
Examination Fees	18754		18754	-1332	17422
Other Supplies and Services	899	3682	4581		4581
Other Expenditure	2961	1418	4379		4379
Gross Expenditure	1007118	-58175	948943	-29780	919163
Rents and Lettings	*2939*	*12131*	*15070*		*15070*
Joint Use Receipts	*0*		*0*		*0*
Other Income	*719*		*719*		*719*
Gross Income	*3658*	*12131*	*15789*		*15789*
NET COST OF ITEMS NOT YET DELEGATED	1003460	-70307	933153	-29780	903373
NET COST OF DELEGATED ITEMS	35213	-1701	33512	4580	38092
NET REVENUE EXPENDITURE	1038673	-72008	966665	-25201	941465
CAPITAL	29954		29954		
PRIVATE FUND CONTRIBUTIONS (memorandum entry only)	143		143		

SCHOOL BUDGET SHARE FOR THE FINANCIAL YEAR 1991/92

NOTES OF GUIDANCE

1. **INTERPRETATION**

    i   "School Budget Share" means - a school's share of the Aggregated Schools Budget determined according to the County Council's resource allocation formula after taking into account the transitional funding arrangements embodied in the Authority's approved Scheme of Delegation. Budget shares do not include any funding associated with earmarked items e.g. TVEI and Special Needs.

    ii "Delegated Budget" means - a school's budget share for the financial year, together with any carry-forward (whether a balance in hand or a deficit) from the previous financial year and any earmarked or other allocations from the central contingency or other excepted items made during the year.

2. **GENERAL**

    School budget shares reflect :

    i   Variations to the Scheme of Delegation as a result of the LMS Review (see LMS Newsletter, Issue 3) ;

    ii The use of the actual 1990/91 and notional 1991/92 academic year teaching staff entitlements, which would have occurred under previous policies, when calculating the effect of changes in pupil numbers between the 1988/89 and 1991/92 financial years ;

    iii The inclusion in the staffing entitlements referred to at ii above of any additional staff associated with the introduction in September 1989 of financial support for those small schools whose numbers on roll are less than 136 ;

    iv The inclusion in the Base Year Spend of Social Priority Allowances for schools in the South East and South West Areas ;

    v   The use of the total Joint Use area (instead of 50% applied last year) when applying the Floor Area Factor to schools with Joint Use facilities ; and

    vi The use of a factor of 26% in order to adjust the 1988/89 Base Year Spend to reflect 1991/92 estimated outturn prices and levels of service.

3. **PRICE BASE**

    School Budget Shares have been prepared on the basis of estimated 1991/92 outturn prices, i.e. including the estimated effects of inflation to 31 March 1992. The latest advice on price movements over the next twelve months is set out in F106.

4. **RENT AND RATES**

    Rent and Rates have been INCLUDED in the Formula Budget and the adjusted Base Year Spend on a "best estimate" basis. It is not envisaged that this will cause schools a problem since the Authority will fund schools on the basis of the actual expenditure incurred and adjustments will be made when the situation becomes clear.

5 **ADMINISTRATIVE SUPPORT FOR LMS**

Introduced with effect from October 1989, for each primary and secondary school with a full delegated budget, in order to assist schools with the increased administrative load arising from the introduction of Local Management. The allowance recognises that the smallest school will have less additional work than the largest schools and consists of a fixed sum and a per capita amount. Half of the allocated sum is available in the financial year preceding that in which a school receives full delegation.

The Formula Budget reflects the additional resources associated with this "new" initiative which was introduced after the end of the 1988/89 financial year. It has, therefore, been necessary to adjust the Base Year Spend Statements in order to ensure the equitable application of the transitional funding arrangements.

6 **CHANGES IN PUPIL NUMBERS AND FLOOR AREA**

The Formula Budget reflects actual January 1991 pupil numbers and floor areas. It has, therefore, been necessary to adjust the Base Year Spend Statements for any change in these factors since 1988/89 in order to ensure the equitable application of the transitional funding arrangements - see also para. 2ii.

7 **FORWARD PLANNING**

When preparing Delegated Budgets for 1991/92, schools may wish to consider likely resource allocations for future years. A broad indication can be obtained, using 1991/92 prices and pupil numbers etc. as the base, by applying the transitional funding arrangements embodied in the Authority's Scheme of Delegation to the main components of the 1991/92 Budget Share, e.g.

£

1992/93
Adjusted Base Year Spend Statement x 40%
Formula Budget for 1991/92 x 60%   _____
                                           _____

1993/94
Adjusted Base Year Spend Statement x 20%
Formula Budget for 1991/92 x 80%   _____
                                           _____

A Budget Planning Pro-Forma which is intended to enhance and inform the planning process in schools for the 1992/93 financial year will be sent to school in cohorts 1, 2 and 3 during the Autumn Term 1991.

County Education Officer
Support Services Division
March 1991

Account Summary for Financial Year 91/92

School: COLCHESTER COUNTY HIGH SCHOOL

Delegated Budget		Allocation
Heading: **Employees**		
Teachers (Contract)		992,673.00
Ancillary		72,600.00
Teachers (Supply)		17,000.00
Weekly Paid		18,496.00
Other Employees Expenses		2,980.00
	Sub-totals	1,103,749.00
Heading: **Capitation**		
Capitation		30,000.00
	Sub-totals	30,000.00
Heading: **Premises**		
Upkeep		10,000.00
Cleaning		15,200.00
Fuel		20,000.00
Water		4,200.00
Rent and Rates		37,435.00
	Sub-totals	86,835.00
Heading: **Transport**		
Staff Transport		900.00
Pupils Transport		600.00
	Sub-totals	1,500.00
Heading: **Administration**		
Furniture and Office Expenses		4,000.00
Postages		850.00
Telephones		7,000.00
	Sub-totals	11,850.00
Heading: **Other Costs**		
Pupil Support		5,580.00
Fees Expenditure		22,500.00
Miscellaneous Expenditure		8,000.00
	Sub-totals	36,080.00
Heading: **Earmarked Items**		
TVEI		0.00
GEST		1,895.00
	Sub-totals	1,895.00

Account Summary for Financial Year 91/92

School: COLCHESTER COUNTY HIGH SCHOOL

		Sub-totals	1.895.00
Heading:	**Contingencies**		
	Contingencies		7,000.00
		Sub-totals	7.000.00
Heading:	**Income**		
	Rent and lettings		(1,650.00)
	Other Income		0.00
		Sub totals	(1.650.00)
			==========
		FUND TOTALS	1,277,259.00
			==========

Fund Audit Trail	Amount
Delegates Budget 91/92 AB/PS/VJH 11.04.91	1,241,145.00
Credit for new telephone installation 15.04.90	4,500.00
TVEI Allocation - Teaching	25,719.00
GEST Allocation at 9.00 per pupil (Teacher Training)	5,895.00
	1,277,259.00
	==========

[Extract re-typed from the original]

Exhibit 6.2 Interim Account Summary for eleven months ending 28 February 1991

Interim Account Summary for 11 months ended 28 February 1991

School: COLCHESTER COUNTY HIGH SCHOOL

Delegated Budget		Allocation (a)	Commitment (b)	Expenditure/ (Income) (c)	Variance (a)-(b)-(c)
Heading:	**Employees**				
	Teachers (Contract)	893,589.00	106,487.02	791,449.19	4,347.21
	Ancillary	68,773.00	8,112.58	61,395.63	735.21
	Teachers (Supply)	6,000.00	1,988.80	(1,326.22)	(5,337.42)
	Weekly Paid	21,500.00	149.04	15,839.16	(5,511.80)
	Foreign Assistants	6,352.00	0.00	7,213.20	861.20
	Sessional Mid-day	2,327.00	0.00	1,089.50	(1,237.50)
	Other Employees	1,790.00	0.00	729.63	(1,060.37)
	Sub-totals	1,000,331.00	116,737.44	876,390.09	(7,203.47)
Heading:	**Capitation**				
	Capitation	40,383.21	1,642.13	28,907.42	(9,833.66)
	Sub-totals	40,383.21	1,642.13	28,907.42	(9,833.66)
Heading:	**Premises**				
	Upkeep	14,644.00	6,913.61	5,159.23	(2,571.16)
	Cleaning	14,711.00	516.55	8,065.78	(6,128.67)
	Electricity	10,072.00	0.00	10,339.20	267.20
	Gas, Oil and Other Fuel	13,152.00	0.00	3,851.38	(9,300.62)
	Water	3,844.00	0.00	2,138.36	(1,705.64)
	Rent and Rates	34,256.00	499.29	33,756.00	(0.71)
	Sub-totals	90,679.00	7,929.45	63,309.95	(19,439.60)
Heading:	**Transport**				
	Staff Transport	750.00	0.00	508.55	(241.45)
	Pupils Transport	200.00	0.00	48.30	(151.70)
	Sub-totals	950.00	0.00	556.85	(393.15)
Heading:	**Other Equipment**				
	Furniture and Admin Equipment	5,032.00	0.00	2,535.16	(2,496.84)
	Capital Expenditure	0.00	0.00	0.00	0.00
	Sub-totals	5,032.00	0.00	2,535.16	(2,496.84)

Interim Account Summary for 11 months ended 28 February 1991

School: COLCHESTER COUNTY HIGH SCHOOL

Heading: **Other Costs**

Postages	850.00	0.00	800.08	(49.92)
Telephones	3,500.00	0.00	3,210.99	(289.01)
Pupil Support	4,000.00	0.00	1,723.07	(2,276.93)
Fees Expenditure	20,100.00	0.00	19,090.50	(1,009.50)
Miscellaneous Expenditure	18,202.79	1,693.12	12,993.28	(3,516.39)
Sub-totals	46,652.79	1,693.12	37,817.92	(7,141.75)

Heading: **Income**

Rent and lettings	(17,302.00)	(40.00)	(4,134.75)	13,127.25
Other Income	(6,150.00)	(2,202.69)	(7,119.75)	(3,172.44)
Sub totals	(23,452.00)	(2,242.69)	(11,254.50)	9,954.81

Heading: **Contingencies**

Contingencies	16,335.00	0.00	0.00	(16,335)
Sub-totals	16,335.00	0.00	0.00	(16,335)

FUND TOTALS	1,176,911.00	125,759.45	998,262.89	(52,888.66)

[Extract re-typed from the original]

Exhibit 6.3 Extracts from the Essex Scheme for Local Management of Schools, February 1990

SECTION C – ITEMS OF EXPENDITURE TO BE DELEGATED AND EXCEPTED ITEMS

C.1 **Introduction – The General Schools Budget and its main divisions**

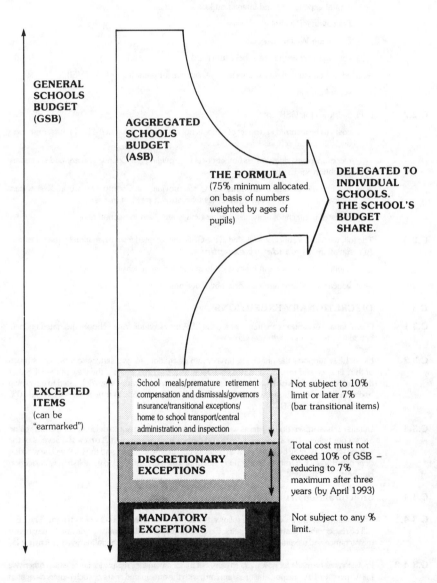

C.2   **Items included in The General Schools Budget (GSB)**

C.2.1   The GSB represents the total expenditure incurred on primary and secondary schools in any one year. It covers all direct costs (e.g. teachers' salaries) and indirect costs (e.g. home-to-school transport). It also includes their share of other support services and costs such as:

- central administration
- inspectors/advisers
- capital expenditure and interest on loans
- Educational Psychology Service
- Education Welfare Service
- education other than at school (EOTAS)
- education expenditure supported by Government grant (e.g. ESG, TVEI)
- school catering

C.2.2   Excluded from the GSB are:

- costs to be incurred in respect of schools not covered by the scheme i.e. (i) nursery schools and (ii) special schools
- recoupment expenditure and other costs of providing out-County primary and secondary education for Essex pupils
- recoupment income from other LEAs for providing in-County primary and secondary education for pupils from other LEAs who are not resident in Essex
- costs of non-school activities (further details are given in Section C.8)

C.2.3   The following items although included in the GSB are excepted from delegation by the Education Act regulations as ***mandatory exceptions***:

- capital expenditure and interest on loans, including all leasing charges
- education expenditure supported by Government grants

C.3   **DISCRETIONARY EXCEPTIONS**

C.3.1   Discretionary exceptions are items which the LEA may exclude from schools' delegated budgets in addition to the mandatory exceptions.

C.3.2   Essex LEA supports the principle of maximum delegation, to give schools control of as much of their finance and resources as possible. However, the LEA accepts the view of the DES that there are some items which may be better retained by the LEA rather than delegated to governing bodies at this stage. These are called discretionary exceptions and in total must not exceed 10% of the value of the GSB.

C.3.3   Details of those discretionary items which the LEA is proposing not to delegate for the time being are set out below. The associated costs and percentages are given in **Annex 2.** Several of the services in the list may be capable of later delegation in whole or part and the LEA will be working during the three-year transitional period to identify which they are and to establish how delegation can best be achieved.

C.3.4   **Structural Repairs and Maintenance – General**

C.3.4.1   The landlord/tenant model is to be followed i.e. LEA as landlord and school as tenant. The LEA will be responsible for structural repairs. Governors' responsibilities will include day-to-day minor maintenance and repairs (e.g. glazing) and internal decoration. The schedule is given in **Annex 3.**

C.3.4.2   Provision will be made for governors to carry out minor emergency repairs for items which otherwise fall within the LEA's responsibility as landlord, with the anticipated costs of such repairs delegated to schools through the formula.

C.3.5 **Structural Repairs and Maintenance: Voluntary Aided Schools**

For voluntary aided schools the Department of Education and Science has advised that *all* costs of maintenance should be delegated through the formula to the Governing Body. The LEA intends to offer such a scheme to voluntary aided schools and to provide a supplementary allocation (see **Annex 5**) in respect of their additional maintenance responsibilities. As an alternative to this scheme the LEA will also offer a pooling arrangement to enable aided schools to make a voluntary contribution (100 per cent of their supplementary allocation) which the LEA will administer in consultation with the Diocesan authorities to ensure that the most urgent repairs are carried out within each financial year. The alternative scheme would operate on a priority needs basis and funding could not be guaranteed to any individual school participating.

C.3.6 **Special Educational Needs (including non-special education units)**

The cost of funding the following will be retained centrally so that expenditure can be clearly earmarked for the benefit of individual pupils who are assessed by the LEA as having particular needs.

a) For pupils about whom a statement is maintained in accordance with Section 7 of the Education Act 1981, expenditure may be incurred in respect of:

– additional teaching staff

– welfare hours

– additional equipment

b) Premises and other costs for pupils in school and non-school based units meeting special needs. The units are scheduled in **Annex 4.**

C.3.7 **Special Staff Costs (safeguarding)**

The additional costs to a school of appointing a teacher with a safeguarded allowance (including a head or deputy) arising from redeployment will be met centrally for up to four years. This will only relate to the extra cost of the safeguarded allowance and not the full cost of the teacher and will come into effect on 1 April 1990. Additional costs associated with staff who are redeployed as a result of a school closure or reorganisation, implemented on 1 September 1989, will also be included under the same conditions as above.

C.3.8 **Pupil Support**

The cost of clothing, footwear and other maintenance grants will be retained centrally since the need for such provision varies considerably from school to school.

C.3.9 **Education Welfare Service**

The services of education welfare officers will be retained centrally so that the LEA can fulfil its statutory duty to ensure that children regularly attend school.

C.3.10 **School Library Service**

In order to sustain the present level of support and to avoid the loss of economies of scale, this service will be retained centrally at least in the first instance to enable some restructuring to take place prior to delegation.

C.3.11 **Education Resources Centre**

In order to sustain the present level of support and to avoid the loss of economies of scale these services will be retained centrally. Some restructuring may be necessary to enable those purchasing and maintenance functions currently operational at the Centre to be delegated to schools by no later than 1 April 1993. Consideration will be given to the possibility of retaining other key functions (e.g. advice to schools) at the Centre beyond April 1993 but it is intended that schools will 'buy in' whatever services are needed either externally or from a restructured Education Resources Centre or from both.

C.3.12   Equipment and Piano Maintenance Units

These services will be delegated to schools at the earliest possible date and in any event no later than 1 April 1993. Schools will 'buy in' whatever services (including advisory services) are required at the time of delegation and thereafter.

C.3.13   Advisory/Peripatetic Teachers

C.3.13.1 Some advisory teachers are funded by Government grant and therefore the costs are treated as a mandatory exception. The remainder will initially be funded centrally in order to make full and efficient use of these resources.

C.3.13.2 This item also includes those teachers supervising the LEA's probationer teachers, the team of peripatetic teachers who serve small primary schools, the team of peripatetic music teachers and the team of peripatetic teachers serving special needs. These will be funded centrally in order to make full and efficient use of these resources.

C.3.14   In-Service Training

Most In-Service Training (INSET) is covered by Government grant and is therefore treated as a mandatory exception. The LEA is to consider delegating the remainder to schools as soon as possible and steps have already been taken in this direction.

C.3.15   Educational Psychology Service

A substantial part of the work of this Service which relates to schools is the provision of advice to enable the LEA to carry out its statutory duty of assessment of pupils under the Education Act 1981. This falls very unevenly between schools and therefore the service is to be retained centrally to meet this statutory duty.

C.3.16   Home Tuition

This service is to be retained centrally to meet the needs of individual children on school rolls who are unable to attend school e.g. long term illness.

C.3.17   Essex Record Office

The Record Office provides valuable service and advice to schools. The LEA's contribution will be retained centrally. Delegation is not considered practical because of the uneven usage by schools even though most or all schools may use the service from time to time. However during the transitional period possible alternative arrangements are to be considered.

C.3.18   LEA Initiatives

Funding is being retained centrally for:

a)   *Opening a new school (not subject to reorganisation under C below)*

A supplement is necessary in view of the high unit costs of operating a newly-opened school (e.g. the initial costs of computer hardware). Additional funding will be provided for a minimum of two and a maximum of three financial years. In the first full financial year the supplement would not exceed a sum equal to the aggregated age-weighted formula allowance to which the school was entitled. Half this supplement would be payable after the first year but the LEA would consider paying double the respective supplementary allowance during any one or more financial years when the pupil roll was below 200. Any supplementary allowance would be delegated to schools without reference to earmarking.

b)   *Closing a school (not subject to reorganisation under C below)*

A supplement is necessary in view of the relatively high unit costs which are likely to result from a reduced number of pupils or pupil groups and hence the uneconomic use of premises, facilities and equipment. Additional funding will be provided for a minimum of two financial years once closure has been formally announced. In the last full financial year before closure the supplement would not exceed a sum equal to the aggregated age-weighted formula allowance to which the school was entitled. Half this supplement would be payable during the penultimate financial year but the LEA would consider paying double the respective supplementary allowance during any one or more financial years when the pupil roll was below 200. Any supplementary allowance would be delegated to schools without reference to earmarking.

c) *School Reorganisation*

A supplement is necessary in view of the additional work required, particularly that relating to liaison with pupils and parents and to managing the larger of two or more schools. The LEA will consider funding the additional costs involved in these circumstances. All such funds would be delegated to schools without reference to earmarking and would apply only during the period of reorganisation and in no event beyond a period of four years.

Additionally special staff costs (see Para C.3.7) may be generated as a result of a school closure or reorganisation; however the number of such staff will not normally exceed two per cent of the total LEA teaching force at any one time.

d) *Special Recruitment Incentives*

The need for such provision varies considerably between schools and subject areas. Resources will be allocated where they are most needed. The incentives available include mortgage subsidy, incentive allowances and early appointment costs.

e) *Curriculum Development and Strategic Support*

The LEA has some flexibility as part of its strategic role to initiate new developments from sources other than specific government grant. There are limited funds available under this category and priority will be afforded to Countywide curriculum developments which benefit all schools.

C.3.19 Performing Rights and Copyright Protection

These costs will be retained centrally in view of the practical difficulties of every school having to negotiate separately if delegated. For a relatively small cost the LEA is able to provide County-wide cover for all schools.

C.3.20 Curriculum Centres

Most curriculum centre costs are covered by Government grant. The remaining costs will be retained centrally.

C.3.21 Sailing, Field and Residential Youth Centres

The costs associated with schools' use of these centres will be retained centrally in order to ensure continued provision of these facilities.

C.3.22 Insurance

The cost of insurance, largely for premises, third party and employers' liability will be met centrally in view of the LEA's responsibilities as owners of premises and employers of staff, and the practical difficulties of every school negotiating separately if delegated. A selection of optional packages (e.g. to cover the risk of theft) may be offered to governing bodies.

C.3.23 School Crossing Patrols

This service will be retained centrally.

C.3.24 Cover for public duties

Within the policies of the County Council the costs of cover for school staff on public duties (e.g. magistrates and teacher representatives) will be met centrally since the need for such provision varies considerably between schools.

C.3.25 **Arts and Sports Grants/Support**

The LEA will continue to provide grants and support for a number of arts and sports groups and museums for the benefit of pupils generally.

C.3.26 **Dismissals and Premature Retirements**

The costs of dismissal and premature retirement compensation (PRC), including current commitments, will normally be met from central provision, except where there is good reason for charging the whole or part of these costs to an individual school's budget share.

C.3.27 **School Meals**

This service will be retained centrally and the situation reviewed after the initial contracts (entered into as a result of the Local Government Act 1988) have expired.

C.4 **TRANSITIONAL EXCEPTED ITEMS**

C.4.1 Detailed specifications for grounds maintenance will have been published before schools receive delegation. Schools will be bound by existing contracts. This service will therefore be retained centrally until initial contracts expire and will then be delegated. The provision of the service at that stage will be governed by the arrangements in **Annex 11.**

C.4.2 Cleaning contracts will have been let before schools receive delegated powers. The costs of cleaning will be delegated and will not therefore be a transitional exception. After the initial contracts expire the arrangements will be as set out in **Annex 11.**

C.5 **HOME TO SCHOOL TRANSPORT**

This service will be retained centrally in accordance with paragraph 62 of Circular 7/88 – "home to school transport necessarily varies significantly between schools and is most cost effectively organised on a central basis".

C.6 **USE OF EARMARKED FUNDING**

C.6.1 The LEA will provide for individual schools to manage some resources which have been excluded from the delegated budget because they are mandatory or discretionary exceptions. Thus in addition to the delegated budget a school will receive specific earmarked sums. Funds passed on in this way will not form part of the school's delegated budget, and governing bodies will not be able to redeploy such resources for other purposes.

C.6.2 Earmarked funding may be used for the following categories of expenditure. Other items may be added at a later date by formal variation to the Essex scheme:

– special educational needs/special units

– special staff costs (safeguarding)

– cover for public duties

– LEA initiatives

– in-service training (grant and non-grant aided) including supply cover

– other Government grant-aided items (e.g. TVEI, ESG)

– contingencies allocated for emergencies.

C.7   CONTINGENCIES

C.7.1   A limited contingency provision will be held centrally and currently this represents 0.6% of the GSB. This is to cover both individual school contingencies and LEA-wide contingencies:

- significant increases in pupil numbers

- emergencies

- correction of errors in applying the formula

- other situations.

   The unallocated balance of the contingency will be distributed to schools as soon as possible in the following year.

C.7.2   Significant increase in pupil numbers

That part of the budget share for each school allocated through a formula on the basis of pupil numbers will be on 'actual' pupil numbers rather than 'forecasts'. This is with the exception of new schools. However in certain situations where there is a significant increase in pupil numbers contingency funding based on the formula will be allocated for part of the year. This funding will not be subject to earmarking but will be added to the delegated budget.

This contingency funding will be allocated where increases in the total pupil roll in mid financial year exceed the 'actual' total roll used in the formula calculation by a given percentage. Extra funding based on the formula will be allocated only for the number of pupils above this percentage, for 7/12 of the year and will apply in the following circumstances.

For *secondary schools*

- The (mid year) actual September number on roll for years one to five will be compared with the actual number on roll for years one to five on the preceding January Form 7 i.e. the one prior to the April budget share allocation. If the increase in the total roll for years one to five is higher than 4% then extra funding will be allocated as soon as possible after the beginning of the autumn term. The amount allocated in excess of the 4% threshold for each pupil will be calculated by reference to the average age-weighted pupil allowance for secondary schools (i.e. 11 to 16 years inclusive) multiplied by 7/12.

- The (mid year) actual September number on roll for secondary years six and seven (minus the difference between the previous year's September and January totals to take account of the rate of drop out) will be compared with the actual number on roll for the sixth and seventh years of secondary education on the preceding January Form 7 i.e. the one prior to the April budget share allocation. If the increase in the total roll for years six and seven is higher than 10% for an 11-18 school or 4% for a sixth form college then extra funding will be allocated as soon as possible after the beginning of the autumn term. The amount allocated in excess of the 10% (11-18 school) or 4% (sixth form college) threshold for each pupil will be calculated by reference to the average age-weighted pupil allowance for the sixth and seventh years of secondary education multiplied by 7/12.

For *junior schools*

- The (mid year) actual September total number on roll will be compared with the total number on roll on the preceding January Form 7 i.e. the one prior to the April budget share allocation. If the increase in the total roll is higher than 10% then extra funding will be allocated as soon as possible after the beginning of the autumn term. The amount allocated in excess of the 10% threshold for each pupil will be calculated by reference to the average age-weighted pupil allowance (for the whole primary age group) multiplied by 7/12.

For *infant and primary schools*

- The (mid year) total number on roll will be the sum of the actual number on roll in September plus the preceding April intake of "rising fives" plus 50% of the previous year's April and mid year September intake of "rising fives" (to take account of the January intake still to come).

This total will be compared with the sum of the total number on roll on the January Form 7 i.e. the one prior to the April budget share allocation plus the actual intake of summer born "rising fives" in the previous April (i.e. at the beginning of the Summer term). If the increase in the total roll is higher than 10% then extra funding will be allocated as soon as possible after the beginning of the autumn term. The amount allocated in excess of the 10% threshold for each pupil will be the same as that calculated for junior schools (above).

This contingency provision will also be applied to the formula allocation based on estimated pupil numbers for new schools.

C.7.3 Emergencies

C.7.3.1 The LEA will meet the cost of those emergencies which, arising from a single event, affect a significant number of schools simultaneously. Serious flood damage along the whole of the Essex coast or damage arising from a hurricane are possible examples.

C.7.3.2 Additionally schools will be advised to build up their own contingency provision to cover their own emergencies and other items of unplanned expenditure. If an event arises which could not reasonably have been foreseen by the school (e.g. severe storm or gale damage) the LEA will in normal circumstances reimburse the school for that part of the resultant expenditure in excess of one per cent of the school's budget share, such additional LEA expenditure being delegated on an earmarked basis.

C.7.4 Errors in applying the formula

C.7.4.1 Contingency funding will also be used for errors in applying the formula including errors resulting from application of the transitional arrangements (further details in Section D.5). This will cover school-based errors as well as those incurred centrally by the LEA but will exclude errors which have cost implications of under £500. This funding will be added to a school's delegated budget and will not be earmarked.

C.7.5 Other situations

C.7.5.1 There may be a limited number of other situations where contingency funding will be required, namely where:

– The floor area used in the formula is increased during the year by more than 10% in which case additional funding will be allocated through the formula for the additional area above the 10% threshold for the relevant proportion of the year.

– Costs arise from claims against governors, where they have acted in good faith or against the LEA where the LEA has no external insurance policy.

– Costs of contract penalties not charged to a school's delegated budget.

C.7.6 The budget allocated will contain sums to cover anticipated pay and price increases during the year. Schools will be expected to contain expenditure within the total given. It is only in exceptional circumstances, such as a major unforeseen increase in teachers' salaries or a major emergency affecting a large number of schools, that the County Council may be able to agree to provide additional resources to schools from outside the GSB.

C.8 ITEMS TO BE DELEGATED TO SCHOOLS

C.8.1 The excepted items and use of earmarking needs to be seen in the full context of the extent of delegation in this Scheme. Currently schools in Essex control about 3% of GSB whereas under the Scheme this will rise immediately to over 70% and will increase as further delegation takes place. Additionally some items will be earmarked immediately and others may be added at a later date.

C.8.2   The main areas of funding to be delegated will be as follows:

– teaching staff (full and part-time).

– non-teaching staff (including mid-day assistants and supervisors).

– foreign language assistants.

– cover for teaching and non-teaching staff (there is an optional LEA "insurance" scheme for maternity leave and illness after the first twenty consecutive working days for secondary and ten for primary).

– recruitment costs (removal package on an LEA "insurance" basis excludes incentives excepted as discretionary (paragraph C.3.18)).

– day-to-day maintenance, minor improvements and emergency structural repairs.

– internal decoration.

– energy.

– building maintenance and energy advisory services.

– caretaking and cleaning.

– joint use facilities.

– on-site staff houses.

– domestic services (including water charges).

– furniture and fittings.

– rent and rates.

– ·educational equipment and materials.

– examination fees.

– telephone, postage etc.

– advertising (including interview expenses).

– staff travel and subsistence.

– field studies and educational visits.

– the costs of courses provided under link and consortium arrangements.

– travel to off-site sports facilities (except that a supplement may be payable at LEA discretion **see Annex 5.**).

– clerking of governing bodies.

– free school meals for staff (excluding DSO staff).

– the costs of implementing the LEA's remissions policy.

C.8.3   The LEA 'insurance' for some supply teacher cover. non-teaching cover and the removal package will be on the following basis:

a)   it will be optional;

b)   it will be self-financing;

c)   there will be a minimum two-year contract;

d)   there will be an annual premium payment relating to each financial year;

e)   overspends or underspends of the LEA insurance scheme will be carried forward into the following financial year.

C.9 COSTS OF NON-SCHOOL ACTIVITIES

C.9.1 Schools' delegated budgets will contain no provision for activities which take place on school premises and which do not form part of their delegated responsibilities. Some of these non-school activities will relate to other parts of the Education Service (e.g. Adult Education), and in other cases to external organisations.

C.9.2 Under the Education (No. 2) Act 1986 governors are responsible with certain exceptions, for the use of school premises but the LEA is able to direct reasonable use of these premises for certain non-school use. In most circumstances a maximum of three evenings per week will apply. This provision includes use by the LEA for its own activities such as Adult Education, Youth Service and for in-service training. The Education Reform Act 1988 does not change this position. Where a school is required to provide facilities for certain LEA non-school use the associated costs will be compensated by the LEA.

C.9.3 This will be done by crediting schools with income based on a standard charge per session according to the number of classrooms, halls and other facilities required. The charge will be set to cover the additional energy, caretaking, cleaning, wear and tear and administration costs of an average primary/secondary school.

C.9.4 Where other parts of the Education Service have premises on school sites, such as youth wings and adult education offices, their running costs will in many cases be met initially from schools' delegated budgets because of the impracticality of separating heating systems etc. In such cases the LEA will compensate schools by crediting them with income at a standard rate based on the floor area involved.

C.9.5 The current complex scheme of making charges to external users of school premises has been simplified. The degree of subsidy depends on the nature of the organisation involved and the nature of the activity.

C.9.6 Under the revised system the LEA will continue to determine the charges to be made by governing bodies and the subsidies to be made by the LEA for pre-school play groups, youth and adult education organisations and in-service training by outside organisations which the LEA wishes to promote. Where the LEA has agreed to subsidise the use of school premises for these activities, the cost of the subsidy will be reimbursed to governing bodies.

C.9.7 In the case of other organisations wishing to use school facilities the LEA will advise governors on the appropriate lettings charge required to cover basic costs, but it will be for governing bodies to decide on the level of charge.

C.9.8 The basis of charges to District Councils for their share of the running costs of joint use facilities is generally laid down in a formal agreement. Changes to the agreement could only be made after formal renegotiation of the terms between all the parties involved.

C.9.9 Schools' delegated budgets will not include provision for the energy and related costs of producing meals in school kitchens and these costs will initially be charged to the school. The School Meals Service will then reimburse schools at standard rates per meal produced in the school kitchen, depending on whether they are produced wholly on site or only reheated on site. This will include meals produced for consumption in other schools and by outside organisations.

C.9.10 Some schools may provide particular services or facilities for children on the roll of other schools, for example consortium courses and primary schools' use of secondary schools' joint use facilities. In such cases the "host" school will be able to charge for the service provided. The LEA will offer guidance on the level of charges that would cover costs.

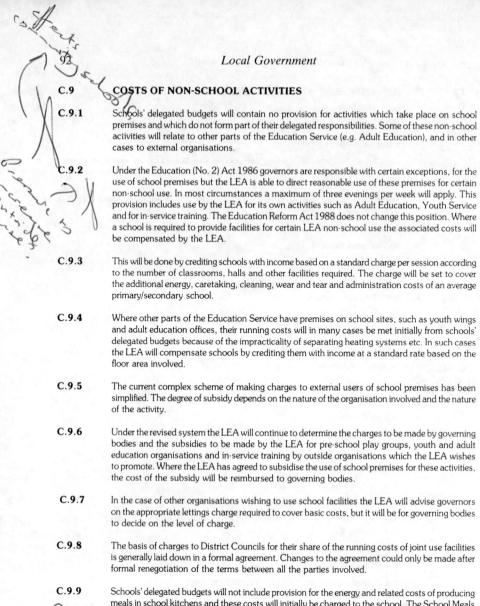

C.10 **SUMMARY: GENERAL SCHOOLS BUDGET, EXCEPTED ITEMS AND AGGREGATED SCHOOLS BUDGET**

C.10.1 **Table**

	£'000	%
GENERAL SCHOOLS BUDGET	355,723	100.00
minus		
DISCRETIONARY EXCEPTED ITEMS (Counting against 10% of GSB limit)	35,257	9.91
minus		
DISCRETIONARY EXCEPTED ITEMS (Not counting against 10% of GSB limit)	28,521	8.02
minus		
MANDATORY EXCEPTED ITEMS	39,496	11.10
leaves		
AGGREGATED SCHOOLS BUDGET to be delegated to schools by a formula – each school receives its budget share.	252,449	70.97

N.B. 1. Cash Figures represent budgeted expenditure for 1988/89 plus the full year cost of new service developments planned for 1989/90 and inflation to March 1989.

2. Percentages are rounded to the nearest 0.01.

This Table is accurate as at 1 December 1989. It will be revised in due course and updated for 1990/91.

SECTION D – THE FORMULA

D.1   **INTRODUCTION**

D.1.1   Each school will receive a budget share for its delegated items. This is the school's share of the Aggregated Schools Budget (ASB) and is determined by a formula.

D.1.2   Under LMS Essex, together with all other LEAs, is required to devise its own formula, having regard to its local needs and circumstances and in accordance with advice and requirements given by the Secretary of State in Circular 7/88.

D.1.3   The formula has been applied to a number of schools to provide examples of their budget shares. **Annex 6** provides some exemplifications.

D.2   **PROPORTION OF AGGREGATED SCHOOLS BUDGET ALLOCATED ON THE BASIS OF PUPILS WEIGHTED BY AGES**

D.2.1   The proportion of the ASB allocated on the basis of age weighted pupil numbers is currently in excess of 76%. However, during phasing in of delegation more schools will be allocated the allowance, "support for school administration" (further details are given in **Annex 5**). As a consequence the percentage of ASB allocated on the basis of pupils weighted by ages is expected to decrease marginally by 1993.

D.3   **BASIS FOR CHARGING COSTS TO SCHOOLS**

D.3.1   Actual costs will be charged to individual schools for each area of spending.

D.3.2   The only variations to the charging of actual costs to individual schools concern:
(i)   optional insurance schemes – see Section C.8.3; and
(ii)   salary cost adjustments for small schools – see Section 4.2.16(h)

D.4   **METHOD USED TO TAKE ACCOUNT OF A) SPECIAL NEEDS B) ADDITIONAL COSTS OF SMALL SCHOOLS AND C) PREMISES COSTS**

D.4.1   **Special needs**

D.4.1.1   Since all schools are considered to have some requirement to cater for children with special needs, the formula includes a basic level of provision for the incidence of such pupils in those schools covered by the scheme. This includes both statemented and non-statemented pupils with learning difficulties as defined in the Education Act 1981. The formula provision for every school therefore provides a sum of money per pupil specifically for special needs.

D.4.1.2   However it is not possible for the formula to meet the total costs of special needs. A significant level of funding is to be retained within the discretionary exceptions so that expenditure can be targeted on the individual pupils who are assessed by the LEA as having exceptional needs. Further details are given in Section C.3.6.

D.4.1.3   Some schools will receive an extra allowance for special needs based on a separate formula determined by social factors. This will be based specifically on the entitlement to free school meals and, in addition for secondary schools, reading scores on entry. Further details are given in **Annex 5.**

D.4.1.4   In addition other discretionary items will be used in part to meet special needs. These include the Educational Psychology Service, home tuition and LEA Initiatives.

D.4.2   **Additional costs of small schools**

D.4.2.1   The formula takes account of the additional costs of small schools in two ways:

a)   Each school will receive a lump sum dependent on the age range of the school. This provides a degree of protection, particularly of the curriculum, for small primary and small secondary schools, and those with small sixth forms.

b) For primary schools an adjustment will be made to schools with fewer than 10 teachers (excluding the head and deputy) where actual teaching staff costs of main professional grade teachers (excluding incentive allowances) are greater or less than the LEA primary school average and/or the school has to meet the additional allowances of safeguarded heads and deputies. The adjustment will be tapered such that the smallest schools are most affected by the degree of protection or limitation of gain.

Further details of these two formula elements are given in **Annex 5.**

D.4.2.2   The transitional arrangements outlined in D.5 will also assist small schools in moving from historic to formula funding.

D.4.3   **Premises**

D.4.3.1   The formula takes account of premises costs in the following ways:

a) The sum of money for every pupil includes part of the costs of minor maintenance, internal decoration, energy, water, cleaning and caretaking.

b) All schools will receive a small fixed allocation to cover part of the costs of caretaking and cleaning.

c) All schools will receive as an extra allowance a floor area based amount covering part of the costs of minor maintenance, internal decoration, energy, caretaking and cleaning.

d) Some schools will receive extra allowances for:

– "Designated" swimming pools, to cover the additional costs of fuel, maintenance and pool chemicals. A "designated" swimming pool is an indoor pool which the Authority has accepted as part of the teaching area of the school (i.e. as distinct from a pool provided by public subscription and which forms a useful but not essential teaching facility).

– Fuel mix, recognising the relative heating costs of tariff and contract gas and electricity above those of oil.

– Social factor, recognising that part of the additional allowance is intended to assist towards the higher maintenance and repair costs of school premises.

e) Rent and rates formula allocations are to be based on estimated costs with an adjustment for previous year costs.

f) Voluntary Aided Schools will receive an extra percentage allowance for their additional maintenance responsibilities.

Split site schools will receive a small additional allocation for caretaking and cleaning costs.

Further details of the premises elements of the formula are given in **Annex 5.**

D.5   **NATURE AND LENGTH OF TRANSITIONAL ARRANGEMENTS**

D.5.1   The application of formula funding will mean that schools will not receive budgets that are the same as they would have obtained under current methods of allocation.

D.5.2   The introduction of formula based budgets will inevitably result in "gainers" and "losers" reflecting the move away from historic funding. During a four year transitional period (from 1 April 1990 to 31 March 1994) it is intended to limit the speed of adjustment from historic to formula funding.

D.5.3   The transitional funding arrangements will be:

1990/91   All schools receive 20% of their budget share by formula and 80% on an historic basis.

Then by equal annual steps to:

1994/95   All schools receive 100% of their budget share by formula and therefore 0% on an historic basis.

D.5.4   The advantages of this are that differences can be smoothed out so that schools have the opportunity to adjust expenditure where necessary over a number of years.

D.5.5   The "historic" basis element of schools' funding will be calculated as follows. Each school's actual expenditure in 1988/89 will be adjusted so that it includes only those items that will be delegated to schools and excludes abnormal one-off items. This adjusted 1988/89 expenditure will be termed the "base year spend", and it will remain constant through the transitional period subject to repricing to the relevant financial year and adjustments for changes in pupil numbers up to that year.

D.5.6   Transitional arrangements cannot be applied to schools which open in 1989/90 or thereafter. These arrangements will however apply to schools reorganised before 1 September 1989.

D.6   CEILING ON BUDGET CHANGES BETWEEN YEARS

D.6.1   After the initial four-year transitional period it is not intended to provide a ceiling on individual school budget changes between years. Major variations will be met in a number of ways:

a)   The use of "actual" pupil numbers will provide a degree of protection to budget changes at schools where pupil numbers are falling. (Further details are given in **Annex 5**).

b)   In certain situations in schools where there is significant increase in pupil numbers contingency funding will be used. (Further details are given in Section C.7).

c)   Forecast pupil numbers will be used in the case of new schools. (Further details are given in **Annex 5**).

D.7   PRICE BASE

D.7.1   Schools will receive budgets showing the cash available for the school to spend during the financial year, including an allowance for estimated increases in pay and prices.

D.7.2   It is not expected that school budgets will be altered during the year. (see Para. C.7.6 for exceptions).

Case 7
Local Authority Financial Report

OBJECTIVES

1. To examine the annual report of a local authority in the context of recent developments in local authority reporting, with particular reference to reporting on service provision.
2. To assess the information content of local authority annual reports.
3. To consider the general problems in trying to assess local authority performance through their annual reports.

MATERIALS

Extracts from Cheshire County Council Financial Report and Accounts 1988–89, pp. 4, 9, 20–27, 34–36 (Exhibit 7.1).

INTRODUCTION

Local authority external reporting has experienced considerable change during the 1980s and this is, in part, connected with the radical changes in local government financing and organization which have taken place during this period. The introduction of the community charge, or poll tax, highlights these radical changes. In this connection it should be noted that references in official pronouncements to 'ratepayers' can now be taken to include 'community charge payers'.

The annual report and accounts for each local authority cover the financial year ended 31 March and the form and content are derived from a number of sources. The Local Government Finance Act 1982 gives the Secretary of State for the Environment powers to control the form and content of local authority accounts. This can be effected by statutory instrument (SI) and the Accounts and Audit Regulations 1983 (SI No. 1761) require (*inter alia*) that a Statement of Accounts should be prepared and should include:

1. summarized statements of income and expenditure of the main funds;
2. summarized statement of capital expenditure;
3. consolidated balance sheet;
4. statement of source and application of funds;
5. statement of accounting principles.

In addition to these statutory regulations, local authority financial statements are drawn up in accordance with a government code of practice published by the Department of the Environment, *Local Authority Annual Reports* (DOE, 1981). This code of practice is particularly relevant to performance measurement, and its objectives are:

1. to give ratepayers clear information about local government's activities;
2. to make it easier for electors, ratepayers and other interested parties to make comparisons of and judgements on the performance of their authorities;
3. to help councillors form judgements about the performance of their own authority.

The code of practice sets out the following minimum contents:

1. an indication of how in overall terms the financial outturn compared with the budget, and an explanation of major variances;
2. a service analysis of gross revenue expenditure and income;
3. net expenditure by service for the year compared with:

    (a) the original estimates plus inflation (or where these are not available, the revised estimate), and
    (b) the actuals for the previous year;

4. comments on any changing pattern of expenditure between services within the authority and any corporate strategy underlying this.

Additional information referred to by the 1981 code of practice includes statistics on the scale and usage of services, measures of cost, comparisons with previous years and a manpower statement at the year-end. Key service indicators should also be published, together with comparisons of actual and average data for other authorities. Although it is only feasible to publish comparative actual data based on previous year information, local authorities are encouraged to publish more recent comparative data based on estimates.

Care needs to be exercised in making comparisons with other authorities. Harrington (CIPFA, 1989, p. 33) refers to the distortions that may arise if authorities use different methods of cost allocation. An example is provided of a borough council which warns in its annual report that its own statistics may be dissimilar to other authorities because it allocates fully the costs of computer services to those services receiving computer facilities. This particular accounting treatment may not always be adopted by other authorities.

Although this case focuses on the reporting of service provision rather than financial statements, it should be noted that the Chartered Institute of Public Finance and Accountancy (CIPFA) makes recommendations on the extent to which statements of standard accounting practice are applicable to local authorities. Some standards are clearly not applicable to local authorities, for instance SSAP 3, *Earnings per Share* and SSAP 8, *The Treatment of Taxation Under the Imputation System*. One particular standard which it has not been possible to apply to local authority annual accounts is SSAP 12, *Accounting for Depreciation*, due largely to the particular nature of capital accounting by local authorities. For further analysis of this issue refer to Case 8, Local Authority Capital Accounting.

In 1987 CIPFA published *Code of Practice on Local Authority*

Accounting (CIPFA, 1987). This code of practice sets out the statements to be included in local authority financial statements. One of the objectives of the code is to narrow areas of difference in accounting treatment and consequently promote the usefulness of published accounts. The code also emphasizes interpretation and explanation of the accounting data.

ANALYSIS

Making comparisons is a central feature of all performance measurement. In making comparisons, it is important to note the different circumstances in which local authorities find themselves. For instance, a local authority with a higher than average proportion of the community over the age of sixty-five would be obliged to spend more on social services. For this reason local authorities are recommended to provide comparative data for *similar* local authorities.

Much of the data in a set of local authority accounts relates to cost and size of providing a service. This may assist judgements about whether, say, 'economy' or 'efficiency' has been achieved but is likely to be less relevant in helping to judge whether 'effectiveness' (quality of service) has been achieved (see Case 3, Performance Indicators). We can refer to the costs of providing services as 'inputs' and the services provided as 'outputs'. If we are trying to determine local authority performance we need to confront issues such as changes in the quality of service provision and whether the quality of service varies for different sections of the community. As an example, comparison of police costs with budget would give an indication of the local authority's *stewardship* during a period. But this information on its own would be insufficient to arrive at an assessment of police service *performance*. For this latter purpose information such as crime detection rates can give an indication of the quality of service. From the extracts from the 1988–89 Financial Report and Accounts of Cheshire County Council (pp. 24, 25) we are provided with a relatively broad spread of information to enable us to arrive at assessments of both stewardship and performance.

As is so often the case in performance evaluation, however, publication of performance-related information is usually only the beginning of the process and not the final answer. Cheshire County Council provides a comparison with an average for similar shires and police forces, covering costs per head of population, reported crimes and traffic offences. The specific shires and forces making up these comparative averages are not revealed (although some local authorities name the shires with which they are making comparisons). An exceptional shire could possibly distort the average figure. It may be of interest to know what the 'best' result was from the comparative shires in order to see if any lessons could be learned.

The data clearly show an increase from 1987 to 1988 in detected crimes relative to reported crimes. Useful additional information could be a breakdown between serious and less serious crimes. There is no suggestion that this is the case, but a police force which believes it is being judged on the percentage of crimes detected could have an incentive to divert resources from following up serious crimes (with high detection costs) to less serious crimes (with lower detection costs).

The question then is, what is an appropriate balance to strike between overwhelming the reader with too much information and supplying the reader with insufficient information to be able to make a worthwhile assessment? Cheshire County Council has probably struck a reasonable balance. The report is relatively succinct with some useful related comments, but at the same time sufficient information is provided for councillors to be able to take up further questions, possibly on the lines of those suggested above.

QUESTIONS

1. Why might the 'Profile of Cheshire' be useful in judging service provision by Cheshire County Council?
2. With regard to the Education Service, which information would you regard as being related to:

   (a) 'inputs', and
   (b) 'outputs', or of assistance in forming a judgement on outputs?

3. What further information might you require in order to assess more fully the quality of Education Service?
4. What factors outside the control of Cheshire County Council are likely to affect the cost of social services? What implications would this have for making comparisons with other local authorities?
5. Provide a brief summary of Library Service provision.

FURTHER READING

Butterworth, P., Gray, R. H. and Haslam, J. (1989) The local authority annual report in the UK: an exploratory study of accounting communication and democracy, *Financial Accountability and Management*, Summer, pp. 73–87.

Chandler, R. and Cook, P. (1986) Compliance with disclosure standards in published reports and accounts of local authorities, *Financial Accountability and Management*, Summer, pp. 75–88.

CIPFA (1987) *Code of Practice on Local Authority Accounts*, CIPFA, London.

CIPFA (1989) *Local Authority Accounts: Survey of Current Practice 1989*, CIPFA, London.

Henley, D., Holtham, C., Likierman, A. and Perrin, J. (1989) *Public Sector Accounting and Financial Control*, 3rd edition, Van Nostrand Reinhold, chapter 6.

Department of the Environment (1981) *Local Authority Annual Reports*, HMSO, London.

Glynn, J. (1987) *Public Sector Financial Control and Accounting*, Blackwell, Oxford, chapter 8.

Rutherford, B. A. (1983) *Financial Reporting in the Public Sector*, Butterworths, London, chapter 10.

Rutherford, B. A. (1990) Towards a conceptual framework for public sector financial reporting, *Public Money and Management*, Summer, pp. 11–15.

PROFILE OF CHESHIRE

THE COUNTY AREA

Cheshire is strategically located in the North West of England. Its extensive motorway system, excellent rail links and an international airport on the doorstep at Manchester provide rapid and efficient communications with the rest of the country and beyond.

In many ways, Cheshire is a county of contrasts from rugged Pennine foothills in the east to the Cheshire plains in the West; from urban areas to rural communities; and from heavy industry to agriculture and tourism. All combine to give the County its unique character.

THE ECONOMY

Cheshire's mixed economy has a good balance of established industries and new concerns. It includes over 250 companies from outside the U.K. Agriculture, chemicals and salt, and vehicle manufacture are all well established. They are complemented by an increasing number of new concerns, particularly in the field of new technology.

With the help of the County Council, Cheshire is becoming an ever more attractive location for business and new technology, offering a quality package equal to any in the U.K. Throughout the County, new employment areas have been set up and derelict land has been reclaimed for industry and housing. Cheshire is now able to offer an extensive range of sites and premises for business and industry. Assistance continues to be given to attract new firms and investment. These and other measures have created several thousand new jobs and guaranteed the safety of many more.

Thanks in part to the County Council's initiatives, unemployment in Cheshire is well below the rest of the North West and continues to decline. The unemployment rate for the County as a whole is now at about the national average. However, the fall in the County-wide rate hides the fact that some parts of the County still have very high unemployment and continue to experience severe economic problems.

TOURISM AND LEISURE

Cheshire has a wide range of tourism and leisure facilities, many provided directly, or supported by the County Council. The Council works to enhance Cheshire's reputation as one of the country's foremost tourist centres, while also ensuring that sport and recreation facilities are provided for the benefit of Cheshire residents. The County's many tourist attractions range from Roman and medieval remains to Jodrell Bank, and from award winning museums to country parks and areas of outstanding natural beauty.

POPULATION

The size of the population and its distribution are significant factors in providing Council services. During recent decades, Cheshire has had one of the fastest growing populations of all English counties. Although the rate of growth has now slowed down, the population, estimated to be 955,800 in mid-1988, is nevertheless expected to exceed one million by the year 2001. An increasing population places increasing demands on Council services.

The County covers an area of 232,846 hectares. This gives a population density of 4.1 persons per hectare, compared with an average for England and Wales of 3.3. The population is very unevenly distributed with rural areas of Cheshire, which cover four fifths of the County, having only one fifth of the population. This means that the problems facing rural areas and the services they require are often very different from those of urban areas.

Different age groups also require different types of Council services. As the size of the age groups change so must the pattern of Council services. Changes in numbers of children most affect Education, while changes in the numbers of of the very elderly mainly affect Social Services. Changes since 1981, the year of the last census, are shown on the diagram.

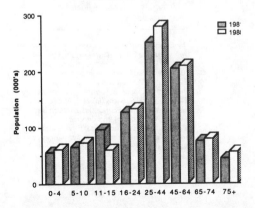

Cheshire's Population-Age Profile

INCOME AND EXPENDITURE

SUMMARY

In 1988-89, the County Council's net expenditure on the provision of services was £527m. The table below shows how these costs were met and how actual expenditure and income compared with the budget set by the Council in February 1988.

	Budget £m	Actual Spending £m
Net service expenditure	528.8	527.1
Financed by:		
Rates	333.6	338.2
Government grants	156.2	168.2
Interest	7.9	5.6
Contribution from Capital Fund	0.1	0.1
Reserves	31.0	15.0
TOTAL	528.8	527.1

The following paragraphs outline the main features of this statement. In addition, they provide a brief explanation of the Council's spending plans for the current year (1989-90) and of the community charge.

SERVICE EXPENDITURE

The difference between the Council's actual spending and the budget approved in February 1988 is explained in the following table:

	£m
Budget	528.8
Pay and price increases greater than provision	1.6
Budget adjustments	−1.2
Revised Budget	529.2
Service Overspendings	0.5
Reduced cost of capital financing	−2.6
Actual spending	527.1

The Council continued to exercise strict control over spending but pressures on services caused overall expenditure to exceed the budget by £0.5m or 0.1%. Overspending on Education (£2.4m) and Waste Disposal (£0.4m) was largely offset by underspending on Police (£0.3m), Social Services (£0.2m), Public Transport (£0.3m), Economic Development (£0.2m), Fire (£0.2m) and Central Services (£1.1m). Details of individual service spending and explanations of significant variances from budget are given in the Outline of Council Services.

In the event the small overspend on service expenditure and higher than anticipated pay and price increases were more than offset by lower than expected capital financing costs and other budgetary adjustments. The level of capital financing costs reflects a reduction in interest rates which also resulted in reduced income from interest on reserves.

OUTLINE OF COUNCIL SERVICES 1988-89

This section contains background information on individual County Council services provided in 1988-89. The order in which services appear has been changed from previous years to reflect the Council's new management structure. This means that the report will be consistent with future County Council publications allowing comparisons to be made. It also provides an opportunity to explain the responsibilities of the new Service Groups. This approach means that the breakdown of net expenditure on the service pages is different from that shown in the formal Statement of Accounts.

In addition to describing their responsibilities and spending this section includes some basic facts about each service and comparisons with other counties. These comparisons are based on statistics published by the Chartered Institute of Public Finance and Accountancy (CIPFA). "Similar counties" are individually chosen for each service to provide the best comparison. The factors considered include population, service demand, and type of service. While these comparisons are very useful some care should be exercised in the way they are interpreted. Figures relating to other counties may differ for a large number of reasons which are not always obvious.

Each service outline also includes details of its activities and any significant developments during the year, and concludes with a list of contacts from whom further information about the service can be obtained. More information about the work of services is given in the Annual Report newspaper which is being circulated to homes and businesses throughout Cheshire.

COMPARISONS WITH OTHER COUNTIES

Net Expenditure per Head of Population

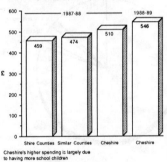

Cheshire's higher spending is largely due to having more school children

Full Time Staff per 1000 Population

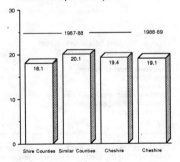

Gross Revenue Spending 1988-89

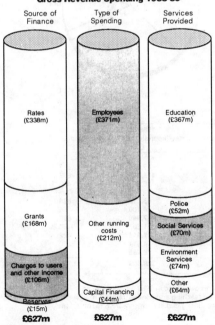

OUTLINE OF COUNCIL SERVICES 1988-89

EDUCATION

The Education Services provide:
— nursery, primary, secondary, special, further,
   adult and agricultural education;
— youth service;
— community education;
— careers service;
— school meals;
— teacher training;
— grounds maintenance.

SOME BASIC FACTS

The County Council meets the education
needs of 220,000 pupils and students, 23%
of the entire population, through 585
establishments throughout the County. It
also provides school meals for 63,500 pupils
and administers grants for over 11,000
students in higher education.

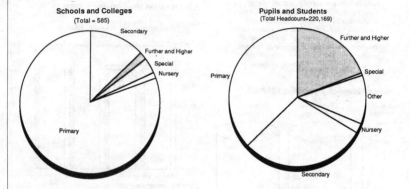

Schools and Colleges
(Total = 585)

Secondary · Further and Higher · Special · Nursery · Primary

Pupils and Students
(Total Headcount=220,169)

Further and Higher · Special · Other · Nursery · Primary · Secondary

SPENDING

	1988-89 Net Expenditure £000	Variance from Budget £000
Nursery	692	31
Primary	89,829	317
Secondary	113,906	633
Special, including Education provided other than at school	16,987	498
Further and Higher	63,732	824
In-Service Teacher Training	4,100	66
School Meals	7,840	−668
Careers	1,107	−90
Administration and Inspection	11,613	422
National Pooling arrangements	14,914	296
Other Education	3,289	32
TOTAL	328,009	2,361

There were two major elements to the Education Services overspend in 1988-89, demand-led
spending on supply teachers; and some overspending on teaching and administrative staff against
a reducing manpower budget. Remedial action has been instigated in necessary areas to control the
budget in future years.

OUTLINE OF COUNCIL SERVICES 1988-89

Pupil Numbers

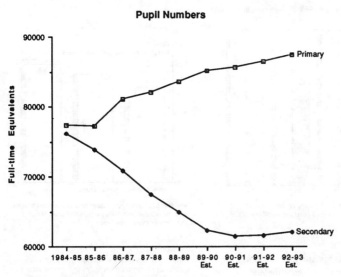

Pupil numbers reflect changes in the birth rate.

COMPARISONS WITH OTHER COUNTIES

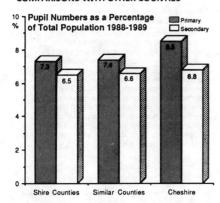

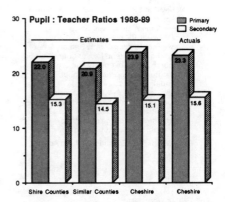

Cheshire County Council has a more generous policy on classroom assistants.

OUTLINE OF COUNCIL SERVICES 1988-89

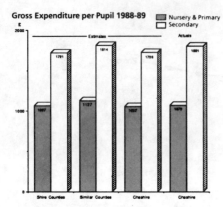

The figures quoted above are for nursery, primary and secondary expenditure. Cheshire's costs per pupil are in the middle of the range.

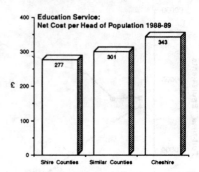

The higher than average number of pupils means that the cost of the education service per head of population is slightly higher than elsewhere.

SIGNIFICANT ACTIVITIES AND DEVELOPMENTS

Capital schemes completed during the year included:

— Crewe Mablins Lane County Primary School, a new 140 place school;
— Alsager Highfields County Primary School, a replacement 245 place school;
— Norley C of E Primary School, a replacement 105 place school;
— Crewe Springfield Special School, a replacement 100 place school;
— Crewe Pebblebrook County Primary School, adaptations to extend former County Junior School to 385 place County Primary School;
— Haslington County Primary School, extending school to 245 places;
— Helsby County High School, extension and adaptations to provide 150 additional places and 105 sixth form places;
— South Cheshire College of Further Education, new sports hall and refectory.

The passing of the Education Reform Act in 1988 has had a major effect on the education service in Cheshire. It includes the introduction of local management of schools and colleges, provision for grant maintained schools, establishment of a national curriculum, the removal of colleges of higher education from local authority control and open enrolment to schools. Much of the Council's efforts have been directed to preparation for implementation of the Act.

The Authority also continued to respond to demographic changes within the County; continuing reductions in secondary school running costs as pupil numbers decline and increases in primary education reflecting the growth in the birth rate. Removal of surplus places in all sectors continues to be an essential part of overall plans to effect economies, and the major rationalisation of the school meals service continues. Implementation of a major review of special education commenced in 1988-89, with an emphasis on more effective methods of operation.

OUTLINE OF COUNCIL SERVICES 1988-89

POLICE

The Police Committee is jointly responsible
with the Home Office for providing the Police
service. The duties of the Police are to:

— protect life and property;
— prevent and detect crime;
— keep the peace;
— facilitate the free passage of traffic;
— initiate the prosecution of offenders.

SOME BASIC FACTS

— During 1988, the Police answered 67,140
  "999" calls and 46,015 crimes were
  recorded of which 50% were detected. In
  addition, there were 42,360 non-
  indictable offences and 52,200 fixed
  penalties were issued.
— There were 1,860 regular Police officers,
  241 special constables, 43 traffic wardens
  and 562 other civilians.
— There are 28 Police stations each serving
  an average population of 34,000.
— 428 Police vehicles covered a total of 8.7
  million miles on duty.

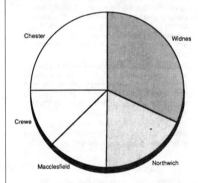

Crime Distribution by Divisions 1988

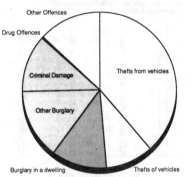

Crime Distribution of Offences 1988

SPENDING

	1988-89 Net Expenditure £000	Variance from Budget £000
Operational	47,255	− 181
Pensions	2,909	− 103
TOTAL	50,164	− 284

After adjustment for the financial effects of the Prison Officers' dispute, the net underspend against
the approved operational budget was £13,000 (− 0.03%).

OUTLINE OF COUNCIL SERVICES 1988-89

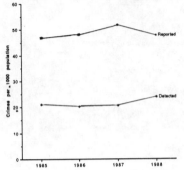

Reported and Detected Crimes per 1000 Population

Detections remained fairly constant between 1985 and 1987 despite a rising crime case load. There was a welcome fall in reported crime in 1988 with a correspondingly higher detection rate.

ACCOUNTABILITY

Home Office Circular 114/73 requires each Chief Constable to prepare objectives and priorities for the force for the forthcoming year.

Each Chief Constable is required to prepare an annual report in accordance with section 30(2) of the Police Act 1964. Copies of the report are on public display.

Additional publications are also issued when necessary to help ensure that the Cheshire Constabulary succeeds in its objectives of maintaining law and order, protecting people and property, and preventing and detecting crime.

The Home Office requires each Chief Constable to prepare detailed inspection notes to facilitate a full, annual inspection by the H.M. Inspector of Constabulary. The HMI is required to make a judgment on the efficiency and effectiveness of the force.

The Chief Constable is also required to demonstrate effective financial management in relation to his annual budget.

COMPARISONS WITH OTHER COUNTIES

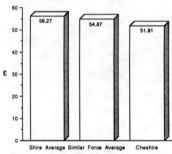

Police Net Cost per Head of Population (1988-1989 Estimates)

Cheshire's lower costs are primarily due to a low civilian administrative and clerical establishment, and a lower Police Officer establishment per 1000 population.

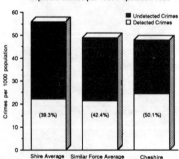

Reported Crimes per 1000 Population 1988

Figures in brackets show detection rates.

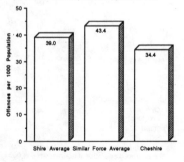

Traffic Offences per 1000 Population 1988

OUTLINE OF COUNCIL SERVICES 1988-89

SOCIAL SERVICES

The Social Services Committee is responsible for providing protection, care, support and advice for people who are at risk in the community. They include:

— children and young people in trouble, and their families;
— elderly people;
— people with physical handicap;
— people with severe learning difficulties;
— people with mental health problems.

SOME BASIC FACTS

Each year over 60,000 requests for help are dealt with. To meet these needs, Cheshire provides a wide variety of services:

— over 2,200 places in elderly persons' homes
— over 200 places in homes for people with severe learning difficulties
— over 250 places for children in care
— over 1.6 million hours of home care each year
— over 9,000 personal aids to disabled people.

SPENDING

	1988-89 Net Expenditure £000	Variance from Budget £000
Children and families	11,285	83
Elderly people	17,961	−543
People with physical handicap	2,469	45
People with severe learning difficulties	4,681	299
People with mental health problems	546	−39
Support services:		
Fieldwork	8,793	41
Administration (incl. management of services)	10,613	−62
Other	556	3
TOTAL	56,904	−173

The underspending on the Elderly was largely due to action taken during the year on the Home Care Service, and also delaying the opening of two establishments. The overspending on people with severe learning difficulties was mainly due to a major restructuring of the residential network, together with day centres, resulting in a significant staffing overspend in the short term.

COMPARISONS WITH OTHER COUNTIES

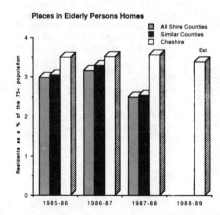

Places in Elderly Persons Homes

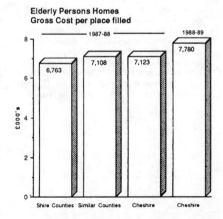

Elderly Persons Homes
Gross Cost per place filled

OUTLINE OF COUNCIL SERVICES 1988-89

Home Help Contact Hours

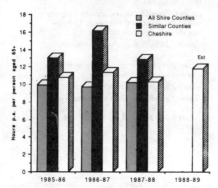

The increase has been principally in services for the elderly.

Social Services Net Cost per Head of Population

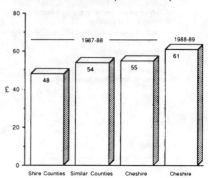

SIGNIFICANT ACTIVITIES AND DEVELOPMENTS

The greatest challenge facing Social Services is the rapid increase in the number of older people. There will be a 20% increase in the number of people aged 85 or more in Cheshire in the next four years and many will need some form of care. Almost one third of the Social Services budget — nearly £20 million — is spent on providing services for the elderly and it is important to ensure that these resources are used in the best way to help as many older people as possible to continue to live in dignity in their own homes. The County Council will continue to work closely with District Councils, Health Authorities and many other organisations in Cheshire to this end.

A number of new services have begun to play their part in providing care for the people of Cheshire:

— In Macclesfield District, Hollins View elderly persons centre has been opened and in Crewe, Lincoln Street elderly persons centre has also become operational. As well as providing permanent homes for some people who can no longer live in their own homes, these centres will provide day time care and short term residential care. This can be invaluable in helping people to recover

from illness, or to learn new ways of looking after themselves and can also provide relief or respite to support relatives.

— The "Home Base" project in Macclesfield is a new approach to helping people at home who would otherwise need to come into a residential centre. It is being carefully evaluated, taking into account the views of the elderly people themselves, relatives, health visitors, community nurses and general practitioners.

— For adults with severe learning difficulties, the "Care in the Community" initiative, in co-operation with the district health authorities, continues to provide new services. Residential units have opened in Knutsford and Handforth and smaller centres are being developed in Warrington. To support these, day centres were opened in 1988 in Knutsford, Wilmslow, Winsford and Nantwich, complementing existing centres in most other Cheshire towns.

OUTLINE OF COUNCIL SERVICES 1988-89

INFORMATION AND LEISURE SERVICES

The Information and Leisure Services Group comprises the following services in addition to Tourism:

— Libraries, Arts and Archives;
— Heritage and Recreation;
— Fair Trading and Advice.

The Group is responsible for:
— public and school library services;
— promotion of the arts;
— archives and information services;
— provision and support of museums and other recreational facilities;
— improvement of the countryside;
— trading standards and consumer advice;
— Registrars, Coroners and Rent Officers;
— tourism.

SOME BASIC FACTS

— library centres	5
— branch libraries	56
— mobile libraries	8
— museums	2
— Country parks, picnic sites	39
— miles of footpath and bridleways	500
— sports centres	2
— Trading Standards Officers	24
— Registry Offices	20

SPENDING

	1988-89 Net Expenditure £000	Variance from Budget £000
Libraries	7,155	25
Arts	323	− 1
Record Office	309	− 2
Countryside	1,871	− 42
Museums	442	− 7
Trading Standards	1,401	− 10
Registrars	381	− 15
Coroners	350	28
Rent Officers (after DoE reimbursement)	2	− 2
Tourism	147	− 3
TOTAL	**12,381**	− 29

The small overspending by Libraries was largely due to redundancy and compensation payments relating to the reduction in Library hours. Savings in Countryside were largely the result of delays in staff appointments. The underspend on Trading Standards was mainly due to high staff turnover and resultant vacancies, while for Registrars the underspend was spread over employee and running costs. The overspend on the Cheshire Coroner's Office related to charges for pathologists' fees and mortuary facilities.

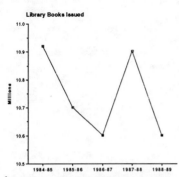

Falling library book issues mirror the cumulative impact of declining book funds. The recent reductions in library opening hours may exacerbate this trend.

OUTLINE OF COUNCIL SERVICES 1988-89

Visitors to Tatton Park

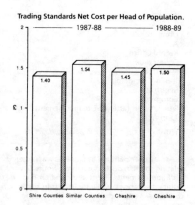

Trading Standards Complaints and Enquiries

A change in emphasis, from enforcement to an advisory role has increased publicity. This has heightened public awareness and increased demand.

COMPARISONS WITH OTHER COUNTIES

Libraries Net Cost per Head of Population.

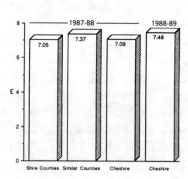

Trading Standards Net Cost per Head of Population.

OUTLINE OF COUNCIL SERVICES 1988-89

SIGNIFICANT ACTIVITIES AND DEVELOPMENTS

In 1988-89, over 10 million library books were issued. The outdated computerised book issue system was replaced and the refurbishment of Hoole, Lymm and Ditton libraries was completed. The hours of opening at 27 libraries were reduced and three library centres were closed and replaced by a mobile library.

Special interest videos were introduced in major libraries.

Additional staffing was provided for the Educational Library Service in order to respond to the increased demands of GCSE students.

The first Cheshire Arts Conference brought both County and District Councillors together with Cheshire's Arts Producers to consider the present condition and future possibilities for the Arts in Cheshire. Subsequently a County Arts Plan was produced. During the year, support was given to 585 artistic performances.

Grants and professional advice were given to a wide range of organisations carrying out landscape and ecological improvements in rural areas. Support for the work of the Bollin and Mersey Valley partnerships continued and the Ranger Service was extended and now, for the first time, covers all eight Cheshire districts.

In collaboration with the Sports Aid Foundation, awards were made to 87 outstanding sportsmen and sportswomen living in Cheshire. The Cheshire Sports Trust was launched to improve the provision of facilities for physical and athletic recreation.

Trading Standards Officers dealt with some 29,000 complaints and enquiries and conducted 1,700 farm and market visits.

Cheshire Coroners handle about 3,555 cases each year. Registrars record over 28,432 births, marriages and deaths.

Case 8
Local Authority Capital Accounting

OBJECTIVES

1. To compare and contrast funding- and usage-based methods of capital accounting.
2. To examine existing and proposed methods of capital accounting in the local authority sector.
3. To explore the nature of accruals accounting in a not-for-profit context.

MATERIALS

Worked example of the revised system of capital accounting proposed in *Capital Accounting in Local Authorities: The Way Forward* (extracted from the consultative implementation manual issued by the Association of County Councils, the Association of District Councils and the Association of Metropolitan Authorities and published by the Chartered Institute of Public Finance and Accountancy, 1989) (Exhibit 8.1).

INTRODUCTION

Local authorities have traditionally accounted for fixed assets in a way that reflects the financing required to meet their cost rather than their pattern of use. This has made local authority capital accounting very different from that employed in the profit-seeking sector. In the latter, all fixed assets acquired are included in the balance sheet and written down progressively over their useful lives by means of charges in the operating statement for depreciation which reflect the cost of using up the asset: this method is adopted regardless of the method used to finance a particular asset.

A number of criticisms of local authority capital accounting have been made over the years and these are explored in the next section. In an attempt to overcome these criticisms a new system has been devised which reflects in local authority operating statements the cost of using fixed assets to provide services. This case considers a worked example of the new system, demonstrating the differences between the new and old systems and the impact the new system will have on the measurement of the cost of providing local government services.

ANALYSIS

The traditional method of capital accounting in local authorities focuses on the method used to finance the relevant fixed assets. Substantial capital projects are characteristically financed by borrowing and the operating statement is then charged with the interest on the loan together with the repayment of principal during the period in question. The balance sheet shows the asset at cost less 'capital discharged', that is, the amount of the loan repaid. No depreciation is charged in the operating statement and the net amount included in the balance sheet for the fixed asset falls as the loan is repaid and reaches zero when the loan is fully paid off and not when the asset reaches the end of its useful life.

Where a fixed asset is paid for out of revenue finance the cost of the asset is charged in the operating statement in the year of acquisition – the capital is 'discharged' immediately by a 'revenue contribution to capital outlay' – so that the net amount included in the balance sheet for the asset is nil.

The advantage of this system is that it promotes accountability for the *financing* of local government activity, the traditional concern of the financial reporting regime. The 'cost' of a service in a given period is the amount the authority must find to finance it: if fixed assets are to be paid for from revenue the finance must be raised (or reserves run down) in the year; if an instalment of a loan repayment is due, again the payment must be financed from revenue and this is included in the operating statement.

Under the system, however, the operating statement will not necessarily reflect, as it would in the profit-seeking sector, the cost of providing services in terms of the resources absorbed (including the using up of fixed assets) in their provision. For fixed assets financed from revenue the figures will clearly be substantially out of line but such financing is rare for material levels of capital expenditure. Where expenditure is financed from borrowing, the term of the loan must not exceed the expected life of the asset but may be shorter: if the life of the loan and the asset are not substantially different the amount charged and the depreciation that would be required under accruals accounting may not differ to a material extent. However, it is optimistic to think that for a large authority these two amounts will substantially coincide. Hence the cost of providing services is obscured and the authority's accountability for that cost is undermined.

A second consideration is that the amount of interest charged in operating statements will depend, among other things, on the pattern of financing of capital expenditure through time. In this respect local authority accounting resembles that in the profit-seeking sector. However, in the profit-seeking sector this is generally considered to be appropriate since the 'bottom line' surplus (profit) after charging interest shows what is available to shareholders as a return for their investment of capital and willingness to bear risk: hence the division of the total cost of providing long-term finance between interest and profit makes economic sense. In the public sector, what is of interest is the total cost of providing services, including the total cost of financing capital assets, whether it is borne explicitly as interest on debt or as 'forgone' interest on monies put up in advance of receiving services by community charge payers or others contributing tax revenue to the local authority sector. Failure to reflect this total cost again undermines, it is argued, the accountability of local authorities for that cost and also impedes comparisons between local authorities, an important method of evaluating 'value for money'.

Finally, the historical cost basis of accounting fails to revise asset values for the effect of changes in price since their acquisition. The historical cost basis is almost universally employed in the profit-seeking sector, earlier experimentation with a system to reflect current prices having been abandoned when inflation fell to a level at which it was felt that it was no longer necessary to require systematic revisions for changing prices. However, the pressure to use a system reflecting current prices has been kept up in the public sector and probably improves the economic interpretation of operating statements and comparability between authorities.

In an attempt to meet the criticisms outlined above a Capital Accounting Steering Group was established in 1988 jointly by the Chartered Institute of Public Finance and Accountancy and the various associations which represent local authorities. The system devised by that group is illustrated in the worked example in Exhibit 8.1, which is drawn from the consultative implementation manual published by the group's sponsors.

Under the proposed new system an authority's revenue (operating) account will be charged with depreciation on fixed assets (based on replacement cost) so that it will be on a full accruals basis. In addition, a 'capital charge' will be made which can be thought of as the equivalent of interest on the full amount of capital invested in fixed assets regardless of how those assets were in fact financed. Again the amount of the investment in fixed assets will be determined on a replacement cost basis.

The proposal to employ replacement cost accounting means that local authority accounting will, at least in this respect, 'leap-frog' over accounting for the profit-seeking sector.

Having established the 'economic costs of operating services' by charging depreciation and quasi-interest, these are then reversed out and the 'traditional' charges for capital, actual interest and provision for the repayment of loans are introduced, so that the 'bottom line' in the statement shows, as in present practice, the financing requirement of the authority:

	£'000
Reversal of:	
Depreciation	(2,800)
Capital charge	(2,794)
	(5,594)
Actual interest	1,900
Provision for repayment of loans	2,400
Net adjustment	(1,294)

In this way the revenue statement gives the best of both worlds: it shows resource costs *and* financing requirements.

QUESTIONS

1. Explain how the proposed new system of capital accounting for local authorities would work, contrasting it with the existing system.
2. Why might it be useful to have a measure of the cost of operating a local authority service and how is the measure provided under the new system better than that provided at the moment? Give specific examples of how information published on the traditional basis might be misleading.
3. What disadvantages might the new system have?

FURTHER READING

Association of County Councils, Association of District Councils and Association of Metropolitan Authorities (1989) *Capital Accounting in Local Authorities: The Way Forward* (consultative implementation manual), CIPFA, London.

Jones, R. and Pendlebury, M. (1988) *Public Sector Accounting*, 2nd edition, Pitman, London, chapter 9.

Rutherford, B. A. (1983) *Financial Reporting in the Public Sector*, Butterworths, London, chapters 6, 10 and 13.

Exhibit 8.1 Worked example of the revised system of capital accounting proposed in *Capital Accounting in Local Authorities: The Way Forward*

Statement of Accounting Policies

General

The accounts have been prepared in accordance with the Code of Practice on Local Authority Accounting, issued in July 1987 by the Chartered Institute of Public Finance and Accountancy (CIPFA), and also with guidance notes issued by CIPFA on the application of accounting standards (SSAPs), as amended in respect of the accounting treatment of fixed assets referred to below.

Fixed assets

Fixed assets are stated in the balance sheet at replacement cost less depreciation in accordance with the CIPFA statement 'Capital Accounting: The Way Forward'. This represents a change in the basis of accounting for fixed assets, which were previously stated in the balance sheet mainly at historical cost after deducting 'capital discharged', being amounts previously charged to revenue by way of loan repayments, revenue contributions or financed from reserves or capital receipts. The comparative figures in these accounts have been restated to reflect the accounting policy now adopted.

The surplus on revaluation of the fixed assets has been transferred to a revaluation reserve in the consolidated balance sheet and is summarized in note 3 thereto.

Leased assets

Assets acquired under finance leases which effectively transfer the risks and rewards of ownership to the authority are included as fixed assets in the balance sheet at replacement cost. The aggregate amounts of the related obligations for future rentals payable are included as liabilities in the balance sheet.

For assets acquired under other (operating) leases the leasing rentals payable are charged to revenue by equal annual instalments over the period of the leases. No account is taken of the obligations for future rentals payable.

Deferred charges

Deferred charges comprise principally improvement and smoke control grants made, which are charged to revenue in annual instalments as the related outstanding loan debt is repaid and are largely offset by revenue grants receivable.

Previously deferred charges also included the amounts of undischarged loan debt in respect of fixed assets which have been disposed of. Following the introduction of the new system of accounting for fixed assets referred to above the amounts outstanding at 31 March 1990 have been written off against the capital reserve.

Revenue charges for use of assets

These charges comprise depreciation and a capital charge relating to the use of assets.

Depreciation is provided in respect of all assets, other than land, at varying rates in order to charge their replacement cost to revenue in equal annual instalments over their expected useful lives as follows:

Council dwellings	−25 to	50 years
Other buildings	−	50 years
Infrastructure	−	40 years
Vehicles	−	4 years
Plant and equipment−		10 years
Furniture	−	15 years

The capital charges represent charges in respect of capital tied up in the provision of fixed assets at an annual rate of 5 per cent based on their closing net (depreciated) replacement cost. These charges are made in the service revenue accounts in order to determine the economic costs of operating services and are reversed out as financing adjustments in the general rate fund summary revenue account and housing revenue account.

Previously, charges for the use of assets were based on annual debt charges in respect of interest and principal repayments of advances made from the consolidated loans fund administered by the authority to manage its borrowings. After taking account of the financial adjustments and contribution to capital, referred to below, there is no overall effect on the revenue account of this change in accounting policy for fixed assets.

Contributions to capital

These represent the aggregate amounts required to be set aside annually for the repayment of the amounts of principal of loans outstanding, from which are deducted amounts provided in the revenue accounts in respect of depreciation and other revenue contributions to capital expenditure.

Disposals of fixed assets

Surpluses arising on the disposal of fixed assets, representing the excess of net sale proceeds over their book amounts, are transferred to a capital reserve account included in the consolidated balance sheet. Deficits arising on such disposals are deducted from the capital reserve.

Previously, capital receipts from the disposal of fixed assets were included in a capital receipts unapplied account until utilized to finance capital expenditure or to repay loan debt. The balance of capital receipts at the beginning of the year has been transferred to the capital reserve account following the implementation of the new capital accounting system.

Explanatory notes

1. Expenditure on fixed assets should be accounted for on an accruals basis, so that provisions should be made for work done or expenditure arising before the year-end but not paid for until after the year-end − if material. Such provisions have been ignored for the purpose of this example.
2. Capital grants receivable in respect of fixed assets should be taken to a deferred credit account and released to the service revenue accounts over the estimated lives of the assets concerned. No account has been taken of such grants for the purpose of this example. The accounting treatment of grants and contributions in respect of fixed assets is discussed in Section 5.06 of this manual.
3. Certain additional accounting policies shown in the example included with the Guidance Notes to the Accounts Code have not been repeated here, since they will not change as a result of the implementation of the new system for capital accounting.

General Rate Fund Summary Revenue Account

	1990/91 Present practices	1990/91 New system		1991/92 New system
	£'000	£'000		£'000
Operating costs	6,772	6,772		8,085
Charges for use of assets:				
depreciation		2,800		3,150
capital		2,794		3,127
Financing charges (note 1)	4,300			
	11,072			
Economic costs of operating services		12,366		14,362
Financing:				
External interest (note 2)		1,900	2,005	
Contribution to capital (note 3)		(400)	(612)	
		1,500	1,393	
Reversal of capital charge		(2,794) (1,294)	(3,127)	(1,734)
	11,072	11,072		12,628
Surplus on market undertaking	(57)	(57)		(52)
	11,015	11,015		12,576
Exceptional item	1,287	1,287		1,547
	12,302	12,302		14,123
Block grant	(5,489)	(5,489)		(6,315)
Rates	(6,535)	(6,535)		(7,156)
Deficit for the year deducted from general rate fund balance	278	278		652

Explanatory notes

1. The comparative figures for 1990/91 have been restated to comply with the accounting policy adopted in 1991/92.
2. No contribution to the housing revenue account has been disclosed in view of the government's proposals to 'ring-fence' the HRA.
3. The first column above (1990/91 present practices) is shown for illustration purposes only and need not be disclosed in the accounts.
4. It is assumed for illustration that the financing charges were £4.3 million for 1990/91 and £4.543 million for 1991/92 made up as shown in notes 1 and 2 to the GRF account.

Notes to General Rate Fund Summary Revenue Account

	1990/91 Present practices	1990/91 New system	1991/92 New system
	£'000	£'000	£'000
1. Financing charges			
Provision for repayments of principal of loans	2,400	2,400	2,538
External interest (note 2 below)	1,900	1,900	2,005
	4,300	4,300	4,543
2. External interest			
Interest charged by the Consolidated Loans Fund to GRF services	3,129	3,129	3,744
Interest due to the GRF in respect of its balances of revenue and capital reserves	(1,229)	(1,229)	(1,739)
	1,900	1,900	2,005
3. Contribution to capital			
Provision for repayments of principal of loans (note 1 above)	Not applicable	2,400	2,538
Depreciation (see note 1) to the Consolidated Balance Sheet		(2,800)	(3,150)
	–	(400)	(612)

Explanatory note

The capital charges are calculated as follows:	1990/91		1991/92
	£'000		£'000
Net replacement cost of fixed assets at end of year	135,161		146,250
5% thereof	6,758		7,313
Allocated to revenue accounts:			
GRF	2,794		3,127
HRA	3,964		4,186
	6,758		7,313

Consolidated Balance Sheet at 31 March 1992

	31 March 1991 Present practices	31 March 1991 New system	31 March 1992 New system
	£'000	£'000	£'000
Fixed assets (note 1)			
Council dwellings	69,281	79,281	83,711
Other land and buildings	7,985	27,985	32,997
Infrastructure	1,952	23,952	25,599
Vehicles, plant, furniture and equipment	1,943	3,943	3,943
	81,161	135,161	146,250
Deferred charges (note 2)	2,936	1,666	2,194
Investments	5,048	5,048	5,051
Long-term debtors	25,632	25,632	22,339
Total long-term assets	114,777	167,507	175,834
Current assets	6,664	6,664	9,476
Current liabilities	(10,426)	(10,426)	(12,349)
Net current liabilities	(3,762)	(3,762)	(2,873)
	111,015	163,745	172,961
Long-term borrowing	52,054	52,054	56,392
Provisions	3,169	3,169	3,406
Revaluation reserve (note 3)		54,000	60,006
Capital reserve (note 4)		41,683	40,393
Deferred capital receipts	21,439		
Capital receipts unapplied	21,514		
Other reserves	10,111	10,111	11,208
Revenue account balances	2,728	2,728	1,556
	111,015	163,745	172,961

Notes to the Consolidated Balance Sheet

1 Fixed assets

	Council dwellings	Other land and buildings	Infrastructure	Vehicles, plant furniture and equipment	Total
	£'000	£'000	£'000	£'000	£'000
Cost or valuation					
Balance at 31 March 1991 as originally reported	69,281	7,985	1,952	1,943	81,161
Revaluation to replacement cost	20,719	42,015	33,048	3,057	98,839
Balance at 31 March 1991 as restated	90,000	50,000	35,000	5,000	180,000
Additions 1991/92 at cost	16,590	1,657	176	618	19,041
Disposals 1991/92	(11,879)	(160)	(227)	(28)	(12,294)
Revaluation adjustment for 1991/92	5,000	7,500	3,750	250	16,500
Balance at 31 March 1992	99,711	58,997	38,699	5,840	203,247
Depreciation					
Balance at 31 March 1991 as originally reported	–	–	–	–	–
Adjustment on revaluation to replacement cost	10,719	22,015	11,048	1,057	44,839
Balance at 31 March 1991 as restated	10,719	22,015	11,048	1,057	44,839
Depreciation for 1991/92	2,850	1,150	969	1,031	6,000
Depreciation on disposals 1991/92	(3,524)	(467)	(101)	(244)	(4,336)
Depreciation backlog adjustment on revaluation 1991/92	5,955	3,302	1,184	53	10,494
Balance at 31 March 1992	16,000	26,000	13,100	1,897	56,997
Net book amount 31 March 1992 (net replacement cost)	83,711	32,997	25,599	3,943	146,250

Explanatory notes to note 1

1. It is assumed for the purpose of the example that the gross replacement costs of the fixed assets amounted in aggregate to £180 million as at 31 March 1991, with accumulated depreciation of £44,839 million in respect of the proportions expired of the lives of the assets and their state and condition.

   The revaluation of the assets will reflect the gross replacement cost of all of the assets owned by the authority, based on a complete inventory of assets, including assets which are 'debt free' or otherwise not previously included in the accounts.

   The gross replacement costs may be determined as outlined in this manual. For example, the GRC of council dwellings may be grouped into similar categories, i.e. flats, bungalows, three-bedroomed houses etc. and by geographical areas if land values are likely to differ significantly. Estimates of land values and current building costs may be provided by professional valuers or the authority's property department for each category of dwellings to give reasonable estimates of gross replacement costs.

   The net replacement costs will be determined by making deductions from the GRC to allow for the estimated proportions of the asset lives which have expired. The determination of asset lives and proportions expired will necessarily involve subjective judgements and should be carried out by experienced property and engineering staff or with the assistance of professional valuers.

2. It is assumed that the gross replacement costs of the assets increased in aggregate during 1991/92 by £16.5 million, arising from specific price changes, and that the aggregate depreciation adjustment arising from this revaluation (depreciation backlog) amounted to £10.494 million. These revaluation adjustments are applied to the restated book amounts at 31 March 1991 less disposals in 1991/92.

3. Asset disposals in 1991/92 will be deleted at amounts at which they were included in the opening balance sheet (as restated) at 31 March 1991.

4. It is assumed that the depreciation for 1991/92 amounted in aggregate to £6 million, allocated as shown in note 1 to the consolidated balance sheet.

5. It is assumed that no depreciation will have been provided in the balance sheet at 31 March 1991 as originally reported.

6. Of the accumulated depreciation of £44.839 million at 31 March 1991 in respect of the proportion of asset lives expired, it is assumed for the purpose of the example that £5.45 million relates to depreciation for the year 1990/91, charged to the revenue account for that year in the restated comparative figures.

7. The depreciation charges have been charged to the revenue accounts as follows:

	1990/91	*1991/92*
	£'000	*£'000*
GRF	2,800	3,150
HRA	2,650	2,850
	5.450	6,000

8. The following matters should also be disclosed by way of notes to the accounts:
   (a) The basis of calculation of the current cost valuation of each principal class of asset should be briefly described, particularly any abatement factors used and the treatment of grants receivable.
   (b) Indices used to calculate the revaluation surplus arising in intervening years between full valuations of assets should be briefly explained.
   (c) The asset lives used for the purpose of calculation of the depreciation charges should be disclosed.
   (d) Consideration should be given to disclosing the opening and closing net amounts of assets employed by each of the committees/services.

2 Deferred charges

	Improvement grants	Other grants	Outstanding loan on council houses sold	Total
	£'000	£'000	£'000	£'000
Balance 31 March 1991 as originally reported	1,560	106	1,270	2,936
Amount written off to capital reserves on implementation of new capital accounting system (note 4)			(1,270)	(1,270)
Balance 31 March 1991 as restated	1,560	106	–	1,666
Expenditure in 1991/92	720			720
Amounts written off to revenue in 1991/92	(180)	(12)		(192)
Balance 31 March 1992	2,100	94	–	2,194

3 Revaluation reserve

The revaluation reserve arising on the implementation of the new capital accounting system comprises:

	£'000
Surplus on revaluation of fixed assets to gross replacement cost (note 1)	98,839
Less: Accumulated depreciation in respect of proportion of asset lives expired (note 1)	(44,839)
Balance as at 31 March 1991	54,000
Revaluation adjustments in 1991/92 (note 1):	
to gross replacement cost	16,500
backlog depreciation	(10,494)
Balance 31 March 1992	60,006

Explanatory note

1. The revaluation adjustment to GRC in 1991/92 is assumed for this example to have arisen from the application of indices reflecting specific price changes during the year. The adjustment in respect of depreciation relates to the additional cumulative depreciation (backlog) arising from the revaluation in the year.

4   Capital reserves

		£'000
Transfer of balances at 31 March 1991 previously reported in respect of:		
deferred capital receipts		21,439
capital receipts unapplied		21,514
		42,953
Less: deferred charges as at 31 March 1991 in respect of outstanding loans on council houses sold – written off (note 2)		(1,270)
Balance of capital reserve at 31 March 1991 as restated		41,683
Loss on disposal of fixed assets during 1991/92 (see explanatory working note attached)		(759)
		40,924
Contribution to capital for 1991/92:		
General rate fund	(612)	
Housing revenue account	81	(531)
Balance of capital reserve at 31 March 1992		40,393

Explanatory note

1. The balances of deferred capital receipts and capital receipts unapplied at 31 March 1991 have been combined as capital reserves for this example, on the implementation of the new capital accounting system. In practice it may be necessary to continue to maintain memoranda records of such balances to enable the authority to identify amounts available for capital finance and loan debt repayments.

   The profit on disposal of assets during 1991/92 comprises:

			£'000
Cost/valuation of assets disposed of during 1991/92 (see note below)			14,107
Less: Accumulated depreciation thereon (note 1)			(4,336)
			9,771
Proceeds of disposal:			
Amount of capital receipts (per note 10 to the consolidated balance sheet in Accounts Code example)		11,940	
Less: Mortgage repayments in the year included therein:			
Deferred capital receipts balances			
31 March 1991	21,439		
31 March 1992	18,511	(2,928)	9,012
Loss on disposal			(759)

Note: The cost/valuation of assets disposed of during 1991/92 comprises:

	£'000
Disposals as shown in note 1 to the consolidated balance sheet in the Accounts Code example	12,294
Amount included in deferred charges in note 3 to Accounts Code example in respect of outstanding loan on disposals of assets	1,813
	14,107

NATIONAL
HEALTH SERVICE

Case 9
Health Authority Financial Report and Accounts

OBJECTIVES

1. To examine the statutory and voluntary annual reports and accounts of a district health authority.
2. To compare the usefulness of the information in these reports for making health authorities accountable to their stakeholders.
3. To discuss the general problems of evaluating the operational performance of health authorities through their annual reports and accounts.

MATERIALS

1. North East Essex Health Authority Statutory Annual Accounts 1990–91, RP2 pp. 1–2 and Accounts pp. 3–6, 9–11, 14–17 (Exhibit 9.1).
2. North East Essex Health Authority Annual Report and Accounts 1987/88, pp. 7–12, 15, 17, 25–28 (Exhibit 9.2).

INTRODUCTION

As shown in Figure 9.1, district health authorities (DHAs) are formally accountable to the Secretary of State for Health via the regional health authorities (RHAs), the NHS Management Board and the Health Services Supervisory Board. England is divided into fourteen RHAs, whose primary roles include capital planning, the allocation of financial resources between districts and the monitoring of the operational performance of districts. The NHS Management Board is responsible for promoting the implementation of broad policy decisions and the improvement of management performance and cost effectiveness within the NHS. The Supervisory Board provides the conduit between the political and managerial levels of hierarchy in the NHS.

There are some 190 DHAs in England, each responsible for the health of between 100,000 and one million people. An average DHA will have a budget in excess of £50 million and some 4,000 employees. All DHAs are managed by a board of members who, since 1990, are appointed by the DHA chairman and are supported by a full-time management structure, as illustrated in Figure 9.2.

Arising from the recommendations of the Griffiths Report (1983) all management levels within the NHS are headed by general managers.

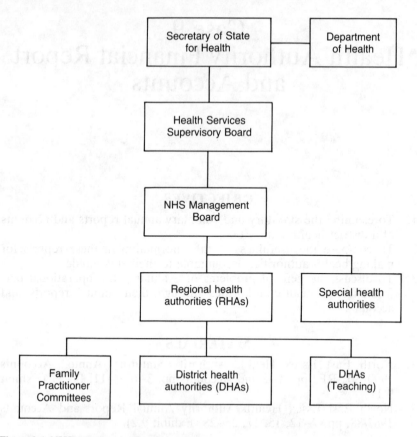

Figure 9.1 NHS structure in England

Within a DHA there are also unit general managers, for example in charge of specific hospitals or community services, who are accountable to the district general manager (DGM). DGMs are responsible for the overall planning, control, allocation of resources and performance of the district while unit general managers (UGMs) are responsible for the efficient management of the human and financial resources allocated to their units.

Revenue is allocated to the RHAs by means of the Resource Allocation Working Party (RAWP) formulae, which are based on population adjusted for age, sex, standard mortality ratios and the cross-boundary flows of patients. The objective of the RAWP allocations is to ensure that funds are allocated to the regions of England on the basis of equitable, objective criteria of need. Capital is also allocated according to RAWP formulae with the aim of having an equitable distribution of capital stock based on relative need over the next ten to twenty years. Inevitably, because of the differences in age and quality of existing hospitals between regions there has been even slower progress towards an equitable distribution of capital funds than of revenue funds.

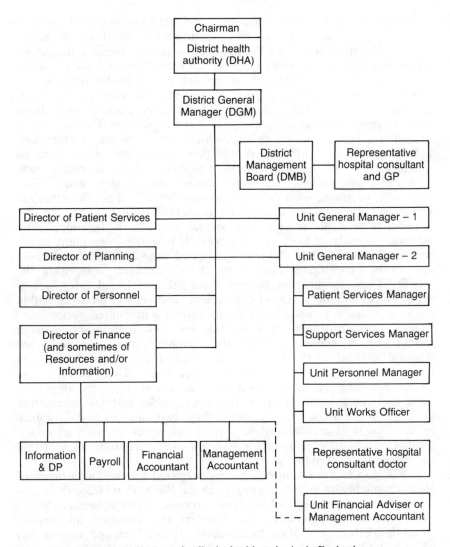

Figure 9.2 Management structure of a district health authority in England

ANALYSIS

Because DHAs must keep only a minimum cash balance in their bank the amount of funds available to spend is determined almost entirely by the amount of funds received under the RAWP distribution. Consequently, it is very important that accurate records of cash flow are maintained. The DHA is required to send to the Department of Health an annual receipts and payments return, an example of which is included in Exhibit 9.1 (RP2). Because the receipts and payments return does not reflect movements in other types of working capital, for example debtors, creditors and stocks, there is also a requirement for DHAs to prepare their main annual accounts on an income and expenditure basis. This is the equivalent to the full accruals-based profit and loss account found in the private sector, but with one notable exception. No recognition is made of the use of fixed assets or capital stock in the delivery of health services, and hence no depreciation is charged in the accounts. Moreover, the summary income and expenditure account adds together both revenue items (current year's revenue and expenditure) and capital items to arrive at an overall net excess income or expenditure figure as the 'bottom line' indicator. It is now widely accepted that the absence of a system for measuring the use and consumption of capital stock has inhibited health authorities from making the most efficient use of their assets. Consequently, beginning with the financial year 1991/92 all health authorities will incur both interest and depreciation on their capital stock.

The structure of the statutory annual accounts is functional with expenditure analysed by service, for example hospitals, community health and headquarters. Behind these aggregated amounts lies the detailed analysis of expenditure incurred by the departments comprising the service. Thus, for hospital services there are two broad categories of expenditure: patient treatment departments and general services. Within the former almost two-thirds of the expenditure is accounted by one item, 'Wards' (see illustration on page 141) but this item is not analysed further into specialties. Instead, the accounts provide an additional separate analysis of the total revenue expenditure of the North East Essex Health Authority by type of expenditure. Thus, there is one amount for the total cost of consultants, one amount for each category of nurse and one amount for drugs. It is not possible, with the information disclosed in the accounts, to combine these two analyses of expenditure so that the total expenditure of a particular specialty, such as orthopaedics, can be identified, although such analyses are to be found within the detailed cost accounts.

In addition to the statutory accounts prepared for the Department of Health some health authorities began, in the 1980s, to produce their own voluntary annual report and financial accounts. These voluntary reports were intended to summarize the financial and statistical information about the performance of the health authority in a form and manner that could be understood by groups who have an interest in health care in the local community, for example patients, employees, local authorities and voluntary agencies. Accordingly, these annual reports often presented information in the form of graphs, bar charts and pie charts and provided explanatory text. Exhibit 9.2 shows extracts from the North East Essex Health Authority Annual Report and Accounts for 1987/88.

The emphasis in the voluntary report and accounts is on describing how the financial resources were used to fund the various health activities of the DHA and on explaining how efficiently the DHA has managed those resources in the face of cash limits, inflation and increased demand for health care. The report itself is not audited but the figures in the accounts are derived from the statutory returns which are subject to audit by the Audit Commission.

The report provides an overview of the total expenditure of the DHA and a detailed analysis or 'profile' of all the units. For example, the acute unit profile, which comprises the main hospitals in the DHA, describes graphically the increases in the number of patients treated over the previous five years and also compares the unit costs of the North East Essex Health Authority with the average for the region and the country as a whole.

The 1987/88 Report and Accounts was in fact the last voluntary report produced by the North East Essex Health Authority and there are, at the time of writing, no plans to publish any voluntary reports in the future. The main reason given for ceasing to produce these more comprehensible reports was cost; in the words of the Director of Finance of the North East Essex Health Authority, 'many people thought that money spent on publishing glossy reports could be better spent on patient care'.

QUESTIONS

1. What role do the formal statutory accounts have in making the North East Essex Health Authority accountable for the use of its resources? How successfully do the accounts fulfil this role?
2. Discuss the usefulness of the information in the 1987/88 Annual Report and Accounts of the North East Essex Health Authority for evaluating the performance of a district health authority.
3. Discuss the arguments for and against charging interest and depreciation on capital stock in the accounts of health authorities.

FURTHER READING

Department of Health (1989) *Working for Patients: The Health Service: Caring for the 1990s*, HMSO, London.

Jones, T. and Prowle, M. (1987) *Health Service Finance: An Introduction*, 3rd edition, Certified Accountants Educational Trust, London.

Henley, D., Holtham, C., Likierman, A. and Perrin, J. (1989) *Public Sector Accounting and Financial Control*, 3rd edition, Van Nostrand Reinhold (International), chapter 8. London.

Mellett, H. (1990) Capital accounting and charges in the National Health Service after 1991, *Financial Accountability and Management*, Vol. 6, no. 4., Winter, pp. 263–84.

NHS Management Inquiry Report (1983) (Chairman, R. Griffiths), DHSS, London.

NHS/DHSS Steering Group on Health Services Information (Chair, Mrs E. Körner) (1984) *Sixth Report* (on the collection and use of financial information in the National Health Service), HMSO, London.

Pollitt, C., Harrison, S., Hunter, D. J. and Marnoch, G. (1991) General management in the NHS: the initial impact 1983–88, *Public Administration*, Vol. 69, Spring, pp. 61–83.

Exhibit 9.1   North East Essex Health Authority Statutory Annual Accounts 1990–91, RP2, pp. 1–2 and Accounts, pp. 3–6, 9–11, 14–17

RECEIPTS AND PAYMENTS RETURN

YEAR ENDED 31 MARCH 19..91.

NORTH EAST ESSEX .... **HEALTH AUTHORITY**   **AUTHORITY CODE** | F | 0 | 3 |

INCOME RECEIPTS

	SUB CODE	REVENUE MAINCODE 03	
		£	p
HEALTH SERVICES REVENUE INCOME RECEIPTS			
From patients - supply of drugs and supply and repair of appliances:			
for appliances more expensive than prescribed	100	5109	85
for repair and replacement of appliances necessitated by lack of care	110	950	74
for dental and optical appliances	120	29603	35
for prescriptions dispensed by hospitals etc. - (including wigs, fabric supports)	130	28832	34
for prescriptions on form FP(10)HP	140	7738	90
From patients - accommodation in single rooms or small wards (Section 63 NHS Act 1977)	150	(20	87)
Private in-patients (Section 65)	160	94026	59
Private non-resident patients (Section 66)	170	140611	02
Overseas visitors (Section 121)	180	740	00
Accommodation and services provided under Section 58 of the NHS Act 1977	190		
Under the Road Traffic Act 1972	200	22942	89
Blood Handling Charges - under Section 25 of the NHS Act 1977	210		
Registration fees for Nursing Homes - under the Registered Homes Act 1984	220	4634	18
Miscellaneous:			
Rents (Land and Premises)	225	52851	34
Sale of inventory items and equipment	230	1767	57
Maintenance charges, working patients	235		–
Other income (major items to be specified) N. E. ESSEX COMMUNITY CARE .... £ 173345.00 TRUST – REIMBURSEMENT (NEECCT) £ .... £	250	186930	51
TOTAL HEALTH SERVICES REVENUE INCOME RECEIPTS (To agree with Return RP1 subcode 190 Revenue)	260	576718	41

RP2A

RETURN RP2   (Page 2 of 2)

RECEIPTS AND PAYMENTS RETURN

YEAR ENDED 31 MARCH 19.91..

NORTH..EAST..ESSEX............... HEALTH AUTHORITY   AUTHORITY CODE | F | 0 | 3 |

INCOME RECEIPTS

	SUB CODE	CAPITAL MAINCODE 03	
		£	p
CAPITAL INCOME RECEIPTS			
a. Sale of vehicles	300	30354	54
b. Sale of surplus land	310		
c. Sale of staff accommodation	320		
d. Sale of other buildings	330		
e. All other capital income receipts	340	18423	66
TOTAL CAPITAL INCOME RECEIPTS (To agree with Return RP1 subcode 190 Capital)	400	48778	20

	SUB CODE	REVENUE & CAPITAL MAINCODE 03	
TOTAL INCOME RECEIPTS (Total of subcodes 260 and 400)	410	625496	61

	SUB CODE	REVENUE MAINCODE 03	
		£	p
TOTAL RECEIPTS - DIRECT CREDITS (To agree with Return RP1 subcode 195 Revenue)	420	1768188	31

RP2B

NORTH EAST ESSEX .... HEALTH AUTHORITY   AUTHORITY CODE | F | 0 | 3 |

REVENUE AND CAPITAL INCOME AND EXPENDITURE
FOR THE YEAR ENDED 31 MARCH 19.9.1...

19..89/90		SUB CODE	MAINCODE 06
£			£
	INCOME		
	Cash Advances and other resources made available by the Department on account of:		
71880673	Revenue	100	78660712
5423610	Capital	110	2362217
	Other income		
383828	Revenue (see note 10)	120	631425
19159	Capital (see note 11)	130	48778
77707270	**Total Revenue and Capital Income**	140	81703132
	EXPENDITURE		
	Revenue		
2190836	Headquarters (see note 2)	150	2554750
65212712	Hospital Services (see note 3)	160	66163465
10099650	Community Health Services (see note 4)	170	11513126
–	Patient Transport Services (see note 5)	180	–
–	Blood Transfusion Services (see note 6)	190	–
–2869046	Other Services (see note 7)	200	–1090433
39052	Community Health Councils (see note 8)	210	41423
74673204	Total Expenditure on Revenue Account	220	79182331
	Capital		
5675003	Capital Expenditure (see note 9)	230	1908216
80348207	**Total Revenue and Capital Expenditure**	240	81090547
(2640937)	(Excess of Expenditure over Income) Excess of Income over Expenditure	250	612585

AA1

ACCOUNTS 19 90/91   (Page 4 of 40)

NORTH EAST ESSEX .... **HEALTH AUTHORITY**   **AUTHORITY CODE** | F | 0 | 3 |

STATEMENT OF WORKING BALANCES
AT 31 MARCH 19..9.1..

	SUB CODE	BALANCES AS AT 31 MARCH 19.9.0.	BALANCES AS AT 31 MARCH 19..9.1.	INCREASE (DECREASE) IN BALANCES
CURRENT ASSETS		MAINCODE 07	MAINCODE 08	MAINCODE 09
STOCK:		£	£	£
Revenue	100	851,031	915,737	64,706
Capital	110			
TOTAL	120	851,031	915,737	64,706
DEBTORS:				
Income: Revenue	130	83,188	137,894	54,706
Capital	140	–		
Other: Revenue				
Car loans	160	24,681	10,150	(14,531)
Assistance with house purchase	170	56,780	61,211	4,431
Other	180	2,236,970	1,977,096	(259,874)
Capital	190	310,000	–	(310,000)
TOTAL	200	2,711,619	2,186,351	(525,268)
CASH AT BANK AND IN HAND	210	23,359	105,967	82,608
TOTAL ASSETS	220	3,586,009	3,208,055	(377,954)
CURRENT LIABILITIES				
CREDITORS:				
Revenue: Wage awards	230			
Salaries & wages	240	149,460	132,870	(16,590)
Patients money	250	1,266,957	1,331,993	65,036
Other	260	5,418,076	5,191,870	(226,206)
TOTAL	270	6,834,493	6,656,733	(177,760)
Capital	280	972,460	159,681	(812,779)
TOTAL CREDITORS	290	7,806,953	6,816,414	(990,539)
RECEIPTS IN ADVANCE:				
Revenue	300	–		
Capital	310	–		
TOTAL	320	–		
TOTAL LIABILITIES	330	7,806,953	6,816,414	(990,539)
BALANCE DUE TO / (FROM) DEPARTMENT	340	(4,220,944)	(3,608,359)	612,585

NOTE: *Average cleared exchequer bank balances during the financial year £* ....34878..............................   AA2

........................./.:/.................................. Director of Finance

NORTH EAST ESSEX............... HEALTH AUTHORITY   AUTHORITY CODE | F | 0 | 3 |

SOURCE AND APPLICATION OF FUNDS STATEMENT
FOR THE YEAR ENDED 31 MARCH 19.91..

19...89/90		SUB CODE	MAINCODE 10
£	SOURCE OF FUNDS		£
	Resources made available from the Department:		
	Cash Advances allocated to:		
5517390	(a) Revenue	100	18077783
5423610	(b) Capital	110	2362217
10941000	TOTAL CASH ADVANCES	120	20440000
6723	Agency Receipts on behalf of the Department	130	7202
−86051	Less Agency Payments on behalf of the Department	140	− 103322
	Retention of sums paid / adjusted centrally by the Department on behalf of authority:		
4224200	Superannuation	150	4642046
6749674	National Insurance	160	7263542
8682461	Income Tax	170	10022759
	Provided by the Department without cash payment:		
−	Supplies (a) Revenue	180	−
−	(b) Capital	190	−
−	Advisory Service	200	−
	Agreed non cash settlements for value received from other authorities:		
58099844	(a) Revenue	210	50557101
−	(b) Capital	220	
88617851	Total Resources from the Department	230	92829328
383828	Local Income: (a) Revenue (see note 10)	240	631425
19159	(b) Capital (see note 11)	250	48778
89020838	TOTAL SOURCE OF FUNDS	260	93509531

AA3A

| NORTH EAST ESSEX .... HEALTH AUTHORITY | AUTHORITY CODE | F | O | 3 |

SOURCE AND APPLICATION OF FUNDS STATEMENT (Contd.)
FOR THE YEAR ENDED 31 MARCH 19.91..

19.89/90		SUB CODE	MAINCODE 10
£			£
	APPLICATION OF FUNDS		
	Revenue Expenditure:		
2190836	Headquarters (see note 2)	280	2554750
65212712	Hospital Services (see note 3)	290	66163465
10099650	Community Health Service (see note 4)	300	11513126
–	Patient Transport Services (see note 5)	310	–
–	Blood Transfusion Services (see note 6)	320	–
–2869046	Other Services (see note 7)	330	–1090433
39052	Community Health Councils (see note 8)	340	41423
5675003	Capital Expenditure (see note 9)	350	1908216
	Agreed non cash settlements for value given to other authorities:		
11313568	(a) Revenue	360	11806399
–	(b) Capital	370	–
91661775	**TOTAL APPLICATION OF FUNDS**	380	92896946
(2640937)	**INCREASE / (DECREASE) IN WORKING BALANCES**	390	612585
89020838	**TOTAL (To agree with subcode 260)**	400	93509531

AA3B

NORTH EAST ESSEX .... **HEALTH AUTHORITY**   **AUTHORITY CODE** | F | O | 3 |

NOTES TO THE ACCOUNTS (Contd.)

2. HEADQUARTERS - Departmental Analysis of Revenue Expenditure

19.89./90		SUB CODE	MAINCODE 11
£			£
	EXPENDITURE ON DEPARTMENTS:		
50417	General Manager / Associated Expenses	101	66138
115958	Administrative Support	102	136267
181739	Personnel	103	219366
	Supplies - Procurement	104	
	Legal	105	
	Public Relations	106	
116002	Planning and Information	107	61340
985161	Finance	108	1235470
	Monitoring	109	
112546	Medical Management	110	275053
	Dental Management	111	
	Patient Transport Services Management	112	
	Scientific Management	113	
	Pharmaceutical Management	114	
62361	Nursing Management	115	92340
335034	Estate Management	116	364333
	Other Management	117	
	Management Services:		
125221	(i) Work Study including O & M	118	19267
	(ii) Operational Research	119	
	(iii) Computers	120	
28560	Training and Education	121	8835
	EXPENDITURE ON GENERAL SERVICES:		
52230	Office Services and Expenses	150	57050
1190	Catering	151	–
	Domestic / Cleaning	152	
	Portering	153	
	Transport	154	
7411	Estate Maintenance	155	9256
4038	Energy	156	9565
461	Water and Sewerage	157	470
	Grounds and Gardens	158	
12448	General Estate Expenses	159	
59	Miscellaneous Services and Expenses	160	
2190836	**TOTAL : HEADQUARTERS**	200	2554750

AA4

......NORTH EAST ESSEX............ **HEALTH AUTHORITY** **AUTHORITY CODE** | F | 0 | 3 |

NOTES TO THE ACCOUNTS (Contd.)

3. HOSPITAL SERVICES - Departmental Analysis of Revenue Expenditure

19..89./90		SUB CODE	MAINCODE 12
£	**PATIENT TREATMENT DEPARTMENTS**		£
30,180,762	Wards	101	30,999,371
3,964,490	Outpatients clinics	102	3,734,264
1,338,209	Day care facilities	103	1,359,949
706,328	A and E departments	104	937,701
468,473	Radiotherapy departments	105	435,533
174,117	Audiology	106	225,904
26,002	Chiropody	107	35,653
		108	
126,458	Dietetics	109	131,618
41,861	Electrocardiography	110	42,931
47,244	Electroencephalography	111	76,618
16,207	Industrial therapy	112	65,020
51,010	Medical illustration and photography	113	72,747
23,970	Medical physics	114	51,682
123,482	Nuclear medicine	115	189,878
933,995	Occupational therapy	116	927,389
3,211,885	Operating theatres	117	3,698,892
164,196	Optical services	118	222,435
337,118	Pathology: (i) Chemical pathology	119	312,891
19,147	(ii) Cytogenetics	120	23,397
431,318	(iii) Haematology	121	319,209
89,681	(iv) Histopathology	122	166,269
-	(v) Immunology	123	-
176,921	(vi) Microbiology	124	189,773
		125	
		126	
717,634	Pharmacy	127	597,622
704,489	Physiotherapy	128	771,379
146,227	Psychology	129	211,345
1,009,227	Radiology	130	1,025,083
77,839	Speech therapy	131	73,911
77,462	Miscellaneous patient treatment services	132	51,014
45,385,752	**TOTAL : PATIENT TREATMENT DEPARTMENTS**	140	46,949,528
	GENERAL SERVICES		
154,776	General Managers	150	188,029
2,975,108	Catering	151	2,773,755
657,641	Laundry	152	718,735
557,666	Linen	153	436,678
1,707,970	Administrative office	154	2,321,909
888,923	Medical records	155	1,040,780
2,511,743	Training and education	156	3,125,995
2,636,199	Domestic / cleaning	157	2,465,699
856,297	Portering	158	905,881
395,186	Transport	159	493,155
1,671,803	Estate management: (i) Engineering maintenance	160	1,606,219
1,957,925	(ii) Building maintenance	161	1,097,761
1,256,263	(iii) Energy	162	1,350,985
319,215	(iv) Water and Sewerage	163	336,733
214,117	(v) Grounds and gardens	164	169,945
853,593	(vi) General estate expenses	165	29,322
223,059	Miscellaneous services and expenses	166	152,356
- 10,524	General Services direct credits	167	-
19,826,960	**TOTAL : GENERAL SERVICES**	200	19,213,937
65,212,712	**TOTAL : HOSPITAL SERVICES**	300	66,163,465

AA5

NORTH EAST ESSEX .... **HEALTH AUTHORITY**   **AUTHORITY CODE** | F | 0 | 3 |

NOTES TO THE ACCOUNTS (Contd.)

4. COMMUNITY HEALTH SERVICES - Departmental Analysis of Revenue Expenditure

19..89./90		SUB CODE	MAINCODE 13
£			£
312,460	**PATIENT TREATMENT SERVICES :** Medical services	101	540,587
205,954	Dental services	102	226,068
2,563,184	Nursing services: (i) District nursing	103	2,386,006
1,105,755	(ii) Health visiting	104	1,217,169
891,766	(iii) Psychiatric nursing	105	1,074,108
685,269	(iv) Mental handicap nursing	106	823,057
530,713	(v) Midwifery	107	778,645
204,920	(vi) Other nursing	108	271,487
17,077	Audiology	109	–
202,145	Chiropody	110	284,175
130,611	Health programme support: (i) Health education	111	183,686
31,399	(ii) Immunisation	112	38,448
35,899	(iii) Family planning	113	12,023
–	(iv) All other	114	–
253,227	Occupational therapy	115	318,024
–	Optical services	116	–
921,927	Pathology	117	1,286,458
37,931	Pharmacy	118	27,661
79,937	Physiotherapy and remedial gymnastics	119	99,246
270,631	Psychology	120	205,890
248,403	Radiology	121	420,066
145,775	Speech Therapy	122	167,893
37,815	Other patient treatment services and direct support services	123	53,377
8,912,798	**TOTAL : PATIENT TREATMENT SERVICES**	140	10,414,074
	GENERAL SERVICES: General manager	150	
18,246		150	33,020
40,828	Catering	151	5,114
1,293	Laundry	152	1,797
126,149	Linen	153	132,357
696,131	Administrative office	154	801,529
11,741	Medical records	155	–
159,050	Training and education	156	109,688
49,603	Domestic / cleaning	157	55,995
4,716	Portering	158	8,435
30,674	Transport	159	4,893
41,434	Estate management: (i) Engineering maintenance	160	53,795
95,275	(ii) Building maintenance	161	74,251
36,475	(iii) Energy	162	48,295
9,672	(iv) Water and sewerage	163	10,378
7,851	(v) Grounds and gardens	164	9,316
90,846	(vi) General estate expenses	165	10,168
(25,111)	Miscellaneous services and expenses	166	63,847
(208,021)	General services direct credits	167	– 323,826
1,186,852	**TOTAL : GENERAL SERVICES**	200	1,099,052
10,099,650	**TOTAL : COMMUNITY HEALTH SERVICES**	300	11,513,126

NORTH EAST ESSEX .... **HEALTH AUTHORITY** **AUTHORITY CODE** | F | 0 | 3 |

NOTES TO THE ACCOUNTS (Contd.)

7. OTHER SERVICES - Revenue Expenditure

19...89/90		SUB CODE	MAINCODE 16
£			£
–	Emergency bed service	001	–
659475	Contractual hospitals and homes	002	1946461
–	Grants to voluntary bodies	003	5000
205542	Occupational health services	004	209014
735870	Projects jointly financed with Local Authorities	005	800955
	Care in the Community:		
190520	(i) Health and personal social services	006	244585
–	(ii) Housing	007	–
–	(iii) Education	008	–
27055	Registration and inspection of nursing homes	009	29711
–	Inner cities partnership and programme projects	010	–
–	Postgraduate medical and dental education	011	–
–	Trainees on nationally or regionally organised training schemes (excluding trainees in community medicine and youth training scheme)	012	–
8078	Youth Training Scheme : Payments to trainees	013	5182
–	Research and development	014	
–	Home defence planning	015	
417256	Losses not allocated to a specific departmental statement and special payments	016	440724
–370888	Staff accommodation	017	–89757
–	Mass radiography	018	
15891	Radiation protection	019	30780
49503	Social work support	020	34164
–	Commissioning and de-commissioning of health service buildings (including the maintenance and security of those not in current use)	021	–
–	Services to non NHS bodies	022	–
–	Receipts from non NHS bodies	023	–
–4807347	Other services (details to be specified below) *	024	–4747252
–2869045	**TOTAL : OTHER SERVICES**	100	–1090433

AA9

* *includes the following major items:*

(a) £ – 4,912,094 Revenue Adjustments

(b) £

(c) £

(d) £

......NORTH..EAST..ESSEX............ **HEALTH AUTHORITY**   **AUTHORI**ı**Y CODE** | F | O | 3 |

NOTES TO THE ACCOUNTS (Contd.)

8. COMMUNITY HEALTH COUNCILS - Revenue Expenditure

19.89/90		SUB CODE	MAINCODE 17
£			£
26640	Secretariat	100	32535
7449	Office services and expenses	110	5299
1080	Accommodation, overheads and other services	120	1096
2873	Members expenses	130	1731
1010	Other services	140	762
39052	**TOTAL : COMMUNITY HEALTH COUNCILS**	150	41423

AA10

.....NORTH EAST ESSEX.......... **HEALTH AUTHORITY** AUTHORITY CODE | F | 0 | 3 |

NOTES TO THE ACCOUNTS (Contd.)

9. CAPITAL EXPENDITURE

19.89./90 £		SUB CODE	MAINCODE 18 £
	HOSPITALS New and replacement hospitals and existing hospital undergoing virtual reconstruction:		
2511577	Wards	100	451013
–	Day hospital accommodation	110	–
–	Out-patient departments	120	–
–	Accident and emergency departments	130	–
–	Other departments and services: (i) Medical	140	–
68988	(ii) Non-medical	150	9323
651534	Other hospitals: Wards	160	658421
–	Day hospitals accommodation	170	–
–	Out-patient departments	180	–
=	Accident and emergency departments	190	–
207230	Other departments and services: (i) Medical	200	41769
810664	(ii) Non-medical	210	424947
–	Vehicles	220	13639
1103923	Acquisition of land and buildings for: (i) New and replacement hospitals and existing hospitals undergoing virtual reconstruction	230	19942
–	(ii) Other hospitals	240	81464
5353916	**TOTAL : HOSPITALS**	250	1700518
	COMMUNITY HEALTH SERVICES Health centres and clinics: (i) Health centres	260	–
814	(ii) Clinics	270	3000
–	Other schemes	280	–
–	Vehicles: (i) Health centres and clinics:	290	–
–	(ii) Other	300	–
–	Acquisition of land and buildings: (i) Health centres and clinics	310	–
–	(ii) Other	320	–
814	**TOTAL : COMMUNITY HEALTH SERVICES**	330	3000

AA11A

NORTH EAST ESSEX .... HEALTH AUTHORITY   AUTHORITY CODE | F | O | 3 |

NOTES TO THE ACCOUNTS (Contd.)

9. CAPITAL EXPENDITURE (contd.)

19 89/90		SUB CODE	MAINCODE 18
£			£
	PATIENT TRANSPORT SERVICES		
–	Ambulance stations and control centres etc.	340	–
	Vehicles:		
–	(i) Ambulances	350	–
–	(ii) Other	360	–
–	Acquisition of land and buildings	370	–
–	**TOTAL : PATIENT TRANSPORT SERVICES**	380	–
	OTHER SERVICES		
–	Administrative offices of health authorities	390	–
–	Other health authority schemes (specify)*	400	50000
–	Vehicles other than at subcodes 220, 290, 300, 350, 360 above.	410	–
–	Acquisition of land and buildings for purposes other than hospital, community health and patient transport services	420	–
–	Projects financed jointly with local authorities	430	90000
	Care in the community:		
–	(i) Personal social services	440	–
271446	(ii) Housing	450	8520
–	(iii) Education	460	–
271446	**TOTAL : OTHER SERVICES**	470	148520
	STAFF SERVICES		
48827	Salaries and wages expenses etc. of staff of professional and technical departments charged to capital account	480	56178
5675003	**TOTAL : CAPITAL EXPENDITURE**	490	1908216

AA11B

* Subcode 400 specified :-   Installation of Gas Main to Colchester General Hospital £50,000.

Exhibit 9.2 North East Essex Health Authority Annual Report and Accounts 1987/88, pp. 7–12, 15, 17, 25–28

Changes In Resource Position During The Year

	£000	£000
Initial Budgetary Position		**Nil**
Increased Cost Pressures Above Budgeted Levels		
NURSING COSTS TO MEET ENB REQUIREMENTS	180	
PAY INFLATION	280	
NON PAY INFLATION	100	
INCREASED ACTIVITY	375	
INABILITY TO USE EXTERNAL SOURCES OF FINANCE FOR MENTAL HANDICAP SERVICES	150	
INCREASED DRUGS PRESCRIBING	110	1195
Increased Funds Above Budgeted Levels		
INCREASED COST IMPROVEMENTS	100	
REPROVISION OF SERVICES	40	
STAFF VACANCIES	100	
LOWER ENERGY USAGE	100	
NON RECURRING ALLOCATION FROM GOVERNMENT	360	700
Recurring Overspend Level at Year End		495
CHANGES IN ACCOUNTING PRACTICE		215
Gross Overspend at Year End		710
Financed By:		
REVENUE CASH LIMIT OVERSPEND		150
INCREASE IN NET LIABILITIES		560
		710

The increased cost pressures mainly reflect external factors over which the Authority has little control, and which are difficult to forecast. On the other hand, the Authority's cash resources are very much controlled by the level allocated by the Government via the Regional Health Authority. The inability to raise resources to match increased cost pressures meant that action had to be taken to restrict expenditure.

The 1987/8 overspend was alleviated by a one off allocation from the Government. It must be emphasised that this money is not available in 1988/9 onwards, although the cost pressures, highlighted above, will still be evident.

The measures used to fund the overspend are available for 1987/8 only. The final recurring overspend of £495,000 will need to be carried forward into 1988/9 and deducted from relevant budgets, thus reducing the amount available for spend.

Where The Money Went By Expenditure

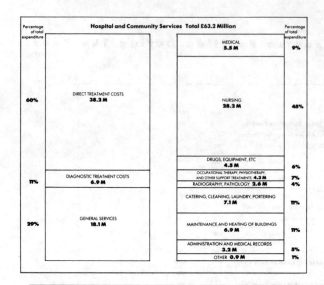

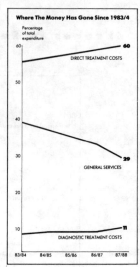

The charts on the left highlight the split of revenue costs between designated general headings within the final accounts for hospital and community services.

The charts show that the highest proportion of expenditure was on costs associated with the direct treatment of patients (doctors, nurses, drugs, equipment).

Just under one third was spent on the day to day running of services, effectively being essential support for service delivery such as maintenance and heating of buildings, catering, portering and cleaning, administration and medical records.

The remainder was spent on general diagnosis and support treatment of patients including radiography, physiotherapy, occupational therapy, speech therapy and other miscellaneous paramedical services.

The split between direct treatment and general service costs is somewhat arbitary. Nevertheless, in general terms, policy should be to transfer as many resources as possible to the direct treatment heading. The chart on the right shows the extent to which this has been achieved over the last five years. The change in proportions of spend mean the £3.7 million has been transferred from general service to direct patient treatment provision.

Where The Money Went By Unit

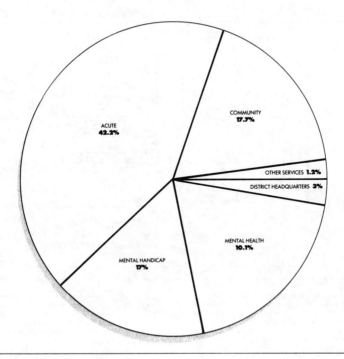

The chart above highlights the split of revenue costs between the relevant units of management, along with District Headquarters and Other Services.

The significant feature of the figures is the extent to which resources are spread over a range of services. This District is one of the few in the country which has a significant presence of both mental health and mental handicap hospital provision. Expenditure levels in the mental handicap and mental health sectors include the cost of providing a service for residents from other Districts.

Where The Money Went By Workload

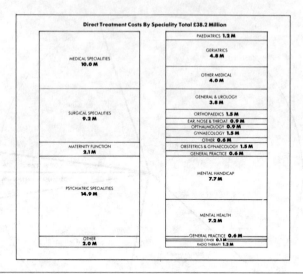

Direct Treatment Costs By Speciality Total £38.2 Million

MEDICAL SPECIALITIES **10.0 M**	PAEDIATRICS **1.2 M**
	GERIATRICS **4.8 M**
	OTHER MEDICAL **4.0 M**
SURGICAL SPECIALITIES **9.2 M**	GENERAL & UROLOGY **3.8 M**
	ORTHOPAEDICS **1.5 M**
	EAR, NOSE & THROAT **0.9 M**
	OPTHALMOLOGY **0.9 M**
	GYNAECOLOGY **1.5 M**
	OTHER **0.6 M**
MATERNITY FUNCTION **2.1 M**	OBSTETRICS & GYNAECOLOGY **1.5 M**
	GENERAL PRACTICE **0.6 M**
PSYCHIATRIC SPECIALITIES **14.9 M**	MENTAL HANDICAP **7.7 M**
	MENTAL HEALTH **7.2 M**
	GENERAL PRACTICE **0.6 M**
	OTHER **0.1 M**
OTHER **2.0 M**	RADIO THERAPY **1.3 M**

For years, costed activity data within the N.H.S. has been restricted to an analysis of unit costs over inpatient days and cases, and outpatient and accident and emergency attendances. Whilst useful, the value of such information is restricted.

Changes in the accounts for 1987/8 show, for the first time, costs by workload type. As this costing system develops, a different, and a more sophisticated system of cost review can emerge. This will relate more closely to specific types of activity, and to the component parts of the overall costs of that activity.

Costs are summarised in the chart above. Development of the costing system will allow the provision of more information, together with comparatives, in future reports.

Changing Financial Pressures Over Time

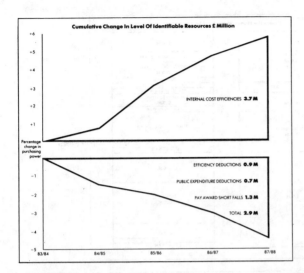

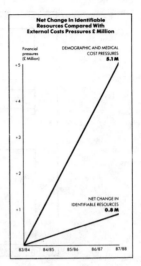

There has been a lot of discussion in the media over the level of funding within the N.H.S. and the effect of changes in the level of funding in recent years.

Unfortunately, most of this discussion has concentrated upon movements in cash levels. However, the latter are not necessarily meaningful, and it is more relevant to examine changes in purchasing power over time by relating, for example, cash changes to inflation changes.

The chart on the left shows the effect of changes in the level of purchasing power of this District's base 1983/4 allocation. The three main reductions relate to efficiency reductions (mainly Regional policy), a public expenditure reduction imposed in 1984/5 and inflation shortfalls (both national policies). The total effect of these is a reduction in purchasing power of £2.9 million.

Offsetting this reduction is the increase in purchasing power through the identification of cost efficiencies within the District. These have amounted to £3.7 million.

Therefore, internal efforts have compensated the reduction in purchasing power caused by external policies.

It is recognised that the N.H.S. has faced, and will face, particular cost pressure as a result of demographic change, and medical advancement. The impact of the former on this District is shown on page 26. The extent to which internal efforts have funded external purchasing power reductions and the cost effects of demographic and medical change is shown by the chart on the right. A deficit of £4.3 million is indicated.

The above figures relate to changes in the District's base 1983/4 allocation. Allocations have been received from Region in this period for specific purposes, in particular, for the revenue consequences associated with the District General Hospital, and for specific Mental Health developments.

Capital

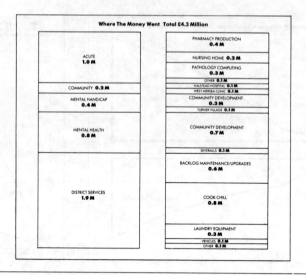

Where The Money Went Total £4.3 Million

ACUTE **1.0 M**	PHARMACY PRODUCTION **0.4 M**
	NURSING HOME **0.2 M**
	PATHOLOGY COMPUTING **0.3 M**
COMMUNITY **0.2 M**	OTHER **0.1 M**
	HALSTEAD HOSPITAL **0.1 M**
	WEST MERSEA CLINIC **0.1 M**
MENTAL HANDICAP **0.4 M**	COMMUNITY DEVELOPMENT **0.3 M**
	TURNER VILLAGE **0.1 M**
MENTAL HEALTH **0.8 M**	COMMUNITY DEVELOPMENT **0.7 M**
	SEVERALLS **0.1 M**
	BACKLOG MAINTENANCE/UPGRADES **0.6 M**
DISTRICT SERVICES **1.9 M**	COOK CHILL **0.8 M**
	LAUNDRY EQUIPMENT **0.3 M**
	VEHICLES **0.1 M**
	OTHER **0.1 M**

The District was able to fulfil a larger than average capital programme in 1987/8. This was made possible through the use of funds realised from the sale of surplus land and property. The ability to maintain a progressive capital programme will be dependent largely upon realisation of further sales.

These are shown in the chart above with spend representing improvements in infrastructure, capital developments in community care settings within the mental health and mental handicap sectors and capital schemes which will result in future revenue savings. Expenditure in this table reflects costs of commitments and work done in 1987/8, although some payments were actually made in 1988/9.

Acute Unit Profile

Review

Introduction   Any annual review of the acute unit must be viewed in the context of the significant change in style and pattern of service provision which is a natural consequence of the opening of the District General Hospital, and the planned reprovision of services from the other existing hospitals into the expanded development.

Physical Changes   The main ward changes during the year were the closure of Beard Ward at Myland Hospital, the transfer of E.N.T. (Ear, Nose and Throat) and Plastic Surgery inpatient services to Colchester General and the closure of 24 surgical beds on Langham Ward.

Problems   It was stated in last year's Report that the acute unit has faced financial difficulties in 1986/7. The Authority's budget deliberations for 1987/8 took these into account, and extra resources were injected into the unit. However increases in activity during 1987/8, together with the cost effect of unfunded inflationary pressures caused severe financial problems yet again. These meant that bed capacity, especially at Colchester General, had to be reduced.

Achievements   Despite the reduction in beds, activity increased compared with 1986/7. This was achieved largely by the greater efficiency in use of beds. Another achievement was the retention of the English National Board training status which required the funding and recruitment of increased numbers of nurses, and an improvement in skill mix.

Medium and Long Term Review   Exciting developments are planned, culminating in the centralisation of acute services at an expanded Colchester District General Hospital site. Immediate plans to help fulfil this include the expected closure of Myland Hospital in 1988/9, with the reprovision of services in a more suitable environment. It is hoped that patient activity levels and throughput efficiency can be improved. The intention will be to achieve this through a targeted 5% increase in day case activity which will include the impact of the opening of a dedicated day theatre in 1988/9.

National Health Service

Acute Unit Profile

Activity And Efficiency Changes

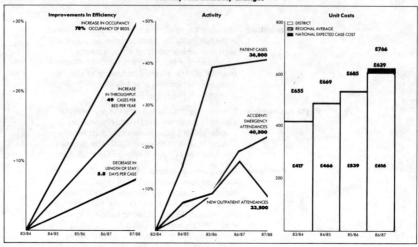

The increase in the number of patients treated is illustrated by the middle chart.

This increase in activity has been achieved during a period of financial constraints, as indicated by the comments and figures on page 11. In order to help fund the increase in activity, therefore, working practices have changed. These are indicated by the trends included in the left hand chart. Increased efficiency in use, and management, of beds has allowed activity to expand at low extra cost.

The chart on the right shows changes in unit cost, together with comparisons with Regional averages. The figures indicate case costs far below Regional averages; a comparison with national expected case costs (i.e. after taking into account actual cost of case mix) shows that actual unit costs are marginally lower than national unit costs.

Elderly Services Profile

Review

Introduction Last year's report focused on services for children;, this year the other end of life's span is examined.

Expected Changes in Numbers There will be a large increase in the elderly population in this District in the next ten years. Figures are shown on page 26. The elderly represent a high user of health care services. The financial effect of the increase is also shown in the chart on page 26.

Health Status The health status of the elderly is influenced by life style led before the advent of old age. The graph·on page 27 shows the rate of mortality within different age groups in this District.

A major reason for the higher death rates in men within the older age groups is the effect of smoking, which, in the past, has been more common in men than women.

Causes of Hospital Admission The most common causes for hospital admissions are heart diseases, stroke and chest diseases. Greater adherence to health promotion issues, especially stopping smoking, moderate drinking, sensible eating, and exercise, would have reduced the level of hospital admissions; these issues must be pursued vigorously in the future.

Other major causes of hospital admissions for the elderly are cataract, prostrate and hip fracture conditions.

Implications of Treatments Treatment of medical conditions associated with the elderly require lengthy rehabilitation and follow up treatment. As emphasised in the community unit profile, it will be essential to ensure that contact is maintained between the Health Authority and the people with a demand for health care.

Other Hospital Demands Approximately 5% of the age group over 65 suffer from dementia, with the percentage increasing to 20% for those aged over 85. These figures, when applied to the growth in population over the next ten years, mean that there could be an increase in the number of people suffering from dementia in this District of over 700 by 1997.

Elderly Services Profile

Projected Changes in Numbers, and Possible Financial Consequences

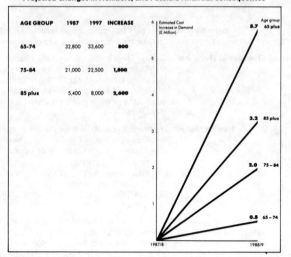

AGE GROUP	1987	1997	INCREASE
65-74	32,800	33,600	800
75-84	21,000	22,500	1,500
85 plus	5,400	8,000	2,600

The above table highlights the significant increase in the numbers of elderly which is expected to occur within the next ten years.

The possible financial implications of this growth is reflected in the graph on the right. Absorption of this cost pressure will require co-ordination with non NHS agencies and reviews of utilisation and sources of finance.

Elderly Services Profile

District Death Rates Per Thousand Over Age

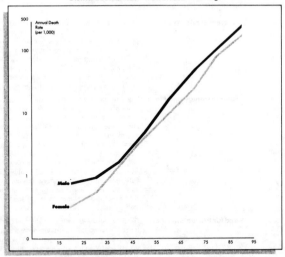

One of the reasons for the high costs of treating the elderly is the high rates of hospitalisation. This is reflected in the above graph. The rate of hospitalisation can be reduced if health promotion advice is acted upon. An active health promotion policy followed now will help reduce cost pressures in the future.

Elderly Services Profile

Services For The Elderly

Current Service Provision

Services for the elderly are currently provided by a number of agencies including voluntary bodies, the private sector, Social Services as well as the Health Authority. In-patient services within the Health Authority are concentrated within hospital wards at Heath, St. Mary's, Myland and Black Notley Hospitals. Non hospital services are provided through the work of community nurses.

Future Strategy and Plans

The main thrust of the future plans for hospital based services is the replacement of ward provision, with nursing home provision. This will involve improvements in quality of care provision but will also mean that bed numbers may reduce. The ability to increase throughput in line with any reduction in bed numbers will need to be reviewed closely.

Complementary to the plans for hospital based services is the need to improve the quality of care outside the hospital environment. This improvement encompasses the need to increase the input which can be provided by therapists, nurses and medical staff.

Need for Preventative Care

The potential drastic increase in demand caused by the rise in numbers can be dampened if preventative health care for the elderly is planned. This could involve pre-retirement courses, well patient clinics and educational support for carers.

Impact on Psychogeriatric Services

Another issue arising from the increased numbers of elderly is the consequential increase in demand for psychogeriatric services. Future strategy will need to address how this service provision is to be cared for in terms of location and style, and how suitable staff can be recruited and funded to support the increase in demand.

Need for Co-ordination

Successful implementation of the strategy will require a co-ordinating role to oversee the various agencies providing health care for the elderly, and to ensure that the varied service demands which will be a natural consequence of the increased numbers are taken into account within an overall District health care plan.

Case 10
District Hospital Management Budget

OBJECTIVES

1. To examine the West Suffolk Hospital Management Budgeting Report for the year ending 31 March 1989.
2. To evaluate the usefulness of management budgeting for improving hospital efficiency and effectiveness.
3. To consider the benefits and difficulties of giving clinicians responsibility for their own budgets.

MATERIALS

Extracts from the West Suffolk Hospital Management Budgeting Report for the year ending 31 March 1989: pp. 8–11, 17–20, 35–36, 53–54, 70, 80 (Exhibit 10.1).

INTRODUCTION

Until the 1980s the traditional type of budgeting in the National Health Service was functional. The term derives from the functional form of organization adopted by the NHS in 1974 which emphasized the management of the service by functions, or disciplines of professional specialization, for example clinicians, nursing and administration. Thus, the district nursing officer was accountable for the use of all nursing resources, salaries, training and other expenses across the whole district, although parts of the budget could be delegated to senior nursing managers within the district. Under the functional system of budgeting it was possible to identify both the cost of each function per patient and the total cost per patient. However, these simple average measures of cost camouflaged great variations in the cost of treatment for different specialties, for example general surgery against paediatrics, and hence were not very useful for either cost control purposes or improving the efficient and effective use of human and physical resources.

A number of health authorities then began to experiment with alternative types of budgeting which aimed to reconstitute the functional costs into specialty costs. One example was clinical budgeting, which was an attempt to allocate budgets to clinical teams (consultants) by negotiated consensual agreement. Under clinical budgeting all consultants in a hospital were given regular reports of their use of all diagnostic and some of the support departments and the related cost, and the number of patients treated by them. A number of studies of clinical budgeting (see, for example, Wickings *et al.*, 1983) indicated that there was very little change in the consultants' pattern of work or expenditure during the period of the experiments. It was clear that clinicians had no commitment to this alternative form of budgeting, perhaps because the cost information reported was primarily of an *ex-post* nature and because the clinicians were not consulted about the kind of information they would find helpful.

Specialty costing was given a boost by the Griffiths Report, which recommended, in addition to the appointment of clinicians as unit and general managers, that each hospital and unit develop management budgets which involve clinicians in taking responsibility for the total cost of the resources they use. The Griffiths Report recognized that it is clinical decisions that determine costs, and hence any management budgeting system which is to be successful must encourage clinicians to accept the management responsibility that goes with clinical freedom. The management budgeting system proposed by the DHSS and introduced on an experimental basis in a number of sites set up four categories of budget holder: support service managers (catering, cleaning and laundry); nurses; diagnostic and treatment service managers; and consultants. The system would operate by recharging costs from budget holders supplying services to budget holders using them, on the basis of an agreed price list. In this way, the clinicians would be given budget statements which included not only the direct costs traceable to their decisions but also an allocation of the fixed costs of the support departments and the general overheads of the hospital or unit.

This form of management budgeting was criticized because its system of recharging was not well understood and was difficult to implement as a result of inadequate information and reporting systems. Management budgeting was also largely a top-down system, creating resentment among health care professionals, who were not accustomed to such close managerial supervision and discipline. The Griffiths Report perhaps overestimated the ability of an essentially technical set of procedures and rules borrowed from the private sector to bring about fundamental changes in the behaviour of health care professionals. In particular, too little recognition was given to the importance of the organizational and professional cultures in the NHS.

On the other hand, the first set of experiments in management budgeting were barely under way when the DHSS announced in 1986 that a new programme, the Resource Management Initiative (RMI), was to be developed. The RMI directly addressed one of the main criticisms of the management budgeting system by establishing a bottom-up approach, involving the identification of the information which would be useful to doctors and nurses and then developing data capture and information analysis systems to provide this information. The RMI is more of a total management system than a budgeting or costing system. It starts by reorganizing the management structure of a hospital or unit so that decision-making and financial responsibility are devolved to clinical directorates, comprising all the consultants in a particular specialty. A part-time director is appointed or elected from among the consultants to lead the directorate. Each director is usually supported by a full-time business manager and between them they would prepare a budget for approval by the board, consisting of all the directors. Under RMI the budget system is simply one part of a fully decentralized management structure which emphasizes the importance of autonomous decision-making and provides incentives for clinicians to take responsibility for the resources they consume.

ANALYSIS

West Suffolk Health Authority provides the case study of management budgeting in the NHS. Exhibit 10.1 contains extracts from the Management Budgeting Report for one of its main units, the West Suffolk Hospital, for the year ended 31 March 1989. Although West Suffolk Health Authority was not one of the original experimental sites for management budgeting, it became a second-generation site following a visit by the Treasurer to the Newcastle DHA in 1984. The management of the West Suffolk Health Authority was enthusiastic about developing its own management budgeting system to provide useful information to clinicians. To this end the authority engaged a firm of management consultants to implement a system using ten pilot hospital consultants, following which the remaining hospital consultants were incorporated into the system by internal financial management.

The main elements of the West Suffolk system are the reporting of costs by service and by specialty. Thus, hospital expenditure is analysed into the five main services – acute, maternity, elderly, mental illness and diagnostic/paramedic – and the budgeted costs, actual costs and variance are reported both for the first six months and the full year. For simplicity, costs which cannot be traced directly to individual services are allocated in proportion to the total of direct costs. Each service is further analysed by ward, including not only total cost information but also some performance indicators, such as occupied bed-days.

The second element within the Management Budgeting Report is the analysis of expenditure and performance measures by specialty, for example paediatrics, obstetrics and general surgery. The Report includes several bar charts and pie diagrams to facilitate comparisons of performance between the specialties. For example, one bar chart identifies the over- or under-spend by specialty based upon detailed supporting analyses of expenditure. Examples of these detailed analyses for obstetrics and ENT surgery are included in Exhibit 10.1. The total cost of a specialty is analysed into four main categories: direct costs, which are primarily the salaries of clinicians in the specialty; other costs, for example physiotherapy; costs from facilities, for example ward nursing; and cross-functional charges such as theatre costs and haematology. Most of these latter costs are attributed to an individual specialty in proportion to the use made of the service by the specialty. However, it is likely that some of the costs, for example hospital overhead charges, are allocated in a fairly arbitrary manner. The specialty reports also include a great deal of statistical information from which both output- and input-based performance measures can be derived.

At the time of writing the future of the West Suffolk Hospital Manage-

ment Budgeting Report was uncertain. First, although there was some
initial enthusiasm from some of the consultants for the project, a more
common response was apathy and even hostility. The consultants may
have perceived the exercise simply as a mask for cost cutting or they may
not have appreciated how useful the information might be to them.
Although the lack of commitment by clinicians may have prevented the
West Suffolk scheme from fulfilling all its potential, it is very probable
that many of the principles and reporting practices of its management
budgeting system will be of much value if the Resource Management
Initiative (RMI) is implemented in all district health authorities.

QUESTIONS

1. Why have there been so many attempts to introduce new budgeting
    systems into the NHS and why have they been relatively unsuccessful
    in achieving their objectives?
2. Consider the information in the West Suffolk Management Budgeting
    Report. To what extent is it more useful than a conventional func-
    tional budget report?
3. Discuss the problems of identifying all the costs incurred by a clinical
    specialty. How useful is it for clinicians to be held responsible for
    overheads over which they have very little control?

FURTHER READING

Abernathy, M. A. and Stoelwinder, J. U. (1990) Physicians and resource
    management in hospitals: an empirical investigation, *Financial
    Accountability & Management*, Vol. 6, no. 1, Spring, pp. 17–32.
Bourn, A. M. and Ezzamel, M. A. (1986) Costing and budgeting in the
    National Health Service, *Financial Accountability & Management*, Vol.
    2, no. 1, Spring, pp. 53–71.
Bourn, A. M. and Ezzamel, M. A. (1986) Organisational culture in
    hospitals in the National Health Service, *Financial Accountability &
    Management*, Vol. 2, no. 3, Autumn, pp. 203–26.
Henley, D., Holtham, C., Likierman, A. and Perrin, J. (1989) *Public
    Sector Accounting and Financial Control*, 3rd edition, Van Nostrand
    Reinhold (International), chapters 3 and 8.
Pendlebury, M. W. (ed.) (1989) *Management Accounting in the Public
    Sector*, Heinemann Professional, London, chapter 7.
Perrin, J. (1988) *Resource Management in the NHS*, Van Nostrand
    Reinhold (International), in association with the Health Service
    Management Centre, Birmingham.
Pollitt, C., Harrison, S., Hunter, D. and Marnoch, G. (1988) The
    reluctant managers: clinicians and budgets in the NHS, *Financial
    Accountability & Management*, Vol. 4, no. 3, Autumn, pp. 213–34.
Wickings, I., Coles, J. M., Flux, R. and Howard, L. (1983) Review of
    clinical budgeting and costing experiments, *British Medical Journal*,
    Vol. 286, 12 February, pp. 575–8.

Exhibit 10.1 Extracts from the West Suffolk Hospital Management Budgeting Report for the year ending 31 March 1989

BUDGET VARIANCE REPORT				FINANCIAL SUMMARY		West Suffolk District Health Authorit	
Period 12 Ending 31/03/89						R066.06.23 Printed 17/05/89 Page	

------- 1st Six Months -------			Expense Codes	--------- Full Year ---------		
Budget	Actual	Variance		Budget	Actual	Variance
			FINANCIAL SUMMARY ==================			
3536900	3561745	24845	ACUTE SERVICES	7671488	7666467	-5021
1059353	1060274	921	MATERNITY SERVICES	2291270	2331091	39821
1080288	1076558	-3730	SERVICES FOR THE ELDERLY	2324731	2318137	-6594
1179192	1125959	-53233	SERVICES FOR THE MENTALLY ILL	2588630	2508363	-80267
1034902	1051742	16840	DIAGNOSTIC & PARAMEDICAL	2164592	2228645	64053
1574822	1493295	-81527	OTHER COSTS	3143665	3244803	101138
------	------	------		------	------	------
9465457	9369573	-95884	WEST SUFFOLK HOSPITAL TOTALS	20184376	20297506	113130
======	======	======		======	======	======

WEST SUFFOLK HOSPITAL 1988/89
Expenditure by Service

ACUTE
MATERNITY
ELDERLY
MENTAL ILLNESS
DIAGNOSTIC/PARAMEDIC

(45%)
(14%)
(14%)
(15%)
(13%)

Assuming Other (Overheads) Spread Proportionately

BUDGET VARIANCE REPORT   ***** FINANCIAL / WORKLOAD *****   West Suffolk District Health Authorit,
Period 12   Ending 31/03/89   R062.02.23 Printed 16/05/89 Page 1

	1st Six Months		Expense Codes	Full Year		
Budget	Actual	Variance		Budget	Actual	Variance

FINANCIAL & STATISTICAL REPORT
==============================

ACUTE SERVICES
==============

Budget	Actual	Variance		Budget	Actual	Variance
			WARD F1 51% AVAILABLE BED DAYS			
205567	170259	-35308	TOTAL COSTS	447164	391474	-55690
2226	2000	-226	OCCUPIED BED DAYS	-4476	-4229	247
42	36	-6	DAY CASES	-84	-92	-8
750	772	22	DISCHARGES & DEATHS	-1500	-1638	-138
			WARD F2 66% AVAILABLE BED DAYS			
147876	166537	18661	TOTAL COSTS	330200	348801	18601
2574	2455	-119	OCCUPIED BED DAYS	-5148	-4480	668
198	158	-40	DAY CASES	-402	-348	54
870	997	127	DISCHARGES & DEATHS	-1740	-1872	-132
			WARD F3 72% AVAILABLE BED DAYS			
192368	193205	837	TOTAL COSTS	422763	422375	-388
4482	4409	-73	OCCUPIED BED DAYS	-8943	-9147	-204
			DISCHARGES & DEATHS		-1	-1
			WARD F4 77% AVAILABLE BED DAYS			
194428	190554	-3874	TOTAL COSTS	422345	408152	-14193
4794	4551	-243	OCCUPIED BED DAYS	-9563	-9532	31
378	411	33	DISCHARGES & DEATHS	-756	-784	-28
			WARD F5 78% AVAILABLE BED DAYS			
205709	201493	-4216	TOTAL COSTS	441524	425410	-16114
4992	4489	-503	OCCUPIED BED DAYS	-9965	-9067	898
-648	-739	-91	DISCHARGES & DEATHS	-1296	-1472	-176
			WARD F6 72% AVAILABLE BED DAYS			
217241	209019	-8222	TOTAL COSTS	467024	466852	-172
4740	4583	-157	OCCUPIED BED DAYS	-9461	-9622	-161
	3	3	DAY CASES		-10	-10
624	736	112	DISCHARGES & DEATHS	-1248	-1464	-216
			WARD F7 84% AVAILABLE BED DAYS			
194036	181047	-12989	TOTAL COSTS	421695	408641	-13054
5532	5220	-312	OCCUPIED BED DAYS	-11041	-10935	106
540	544	4	DISCHARGES & DEATHS	-1080	-1164	-84
			WARD F8 78% AVAILABLE BED DAYS			
183307	185594	2287	TOTAL COSTS	398369	400391	2022
4992	4744	-248	OCCUPIED BED DAYS	-9968	-10416	-448
498	469	29	DISCHARGES & DEATHS	-996	-957	39
			WARD F9 66% AVAILABLE BED DAYS			
152255	160223	7968	TOTAL COSTS	338705	353711	15006
3498	3461	-37	OCCUPIED BED DAYS	-6981	-7035	-54
	4	4	DAY CASES		-7	-7
1032	1105	73	DISCHARGES & DEATHS	-2064	-2226	-162
			WARD F12 56% AVAILABLE BED DAY			
86276	95623	9347	TOTAL COSTS	192359	205072	12713
780	867	87	OCCUPIED BED DAYS	-1560	-1576	-16
6	17	11	DAY CASES	-12	-27	-15
138	146	8	DISCHARGES & DEATHS	-276	-269	7

BUDGET VARIANCE REPORT   ***** FINANCIAL / WORKLOAD *****   West Suffolk District Health Authority
Period 12   Ending 31/03/89   R062.02.23 Printed 16/05/89 Page 2

1st Six Months			Expense Codes	Full Year		
Budget	Actual	Variance		Budget	Actual	Variance
			ITU/CCU 56% AVAILABLE BED DAYS			
298103	321270	23167	TOTAL COSTS	664705	677939	13234
816	808	8	OCCUPIED BED DAYS	-1632	-1603	29
126	53	73	DISCHARGES & DEATHS	-252	-111	141
			WARD G1 70% AVAILABLE BED DAYS			
118875	123082	4207	TOTAL COSTS	264228	268946	4718
1284	1276	8	OCCUPIED BED DAYS	-2568	-2581	-13
	3	-3	DAY CASES		-9	-9
120	97	23	DISCHARGES & DEATHS	-240	-232	8
			CENTRAL TREATMENT ROOM			
76619	78865	2246	TOTAL COSTS	164376	160373	-4003
2850		2850	NUMBER OF PATIENTS TREATED	-5700		5700
	3079	-3079	NUMBER OF PROCEDURES		-6064	-6064
			DAY & EMERGENCY WARD			
101892	105445	3553	TOTAL COSTS	227536	237610	10074
924	964	-40	OCCUPIED BED DAYS	-1848	-1941	-93
966	999	-33	NUMBER OF DAY CASES	-1932	-2040	-108
			DISCHARGES & DEATHS			
			OUT PATIENT DEPARTMENT			
137331	149151	11820	TOTAL COSTS	309180	314009	4829
35472	34944	528	NUMBER OF ATTENDANCES	-70947	-70128	819
10794	10756	38	NUMBER OF NEW PATIENTS	-21597	-21798	-201
			ACCIDENT & EMERGENCY			
335367	341693	6326	TOTAL COSTS	702447	702552	105
10416	12987	2571	NUMBER OF ATTENDANCES	20832	24674	3842
			OPERATING DEPARTMENT			
689650	688685	-965	TOTAL COSTS	1456868	1474159	17291
1224	54304	53080	* NOTIONAL THEATRE SESSIONS	2439	2281	-158
	17727	17727	OVER-RUN HOURS		664	664
3536900	3561745	24845	TOTAL COSTS	7671488	7666467	-5021

* Notional Theatre sessions are booked sessions plus emergency hours
  converted into notional sessions.

x% Available Bed Days states the percentage of available bed days on
which the statistical budget was based.

BUDGET VARIANCE REPORT
Period 12 Ending 31/03/89

***** FINANCIAL / WORKLOAD *****

West Suffolk District Health Authority,
R065.05.23 Printed 16/05/89 Page 1

| ------- 1st Six Months ------- | | | Expense Codes | --------- Full Year --------- | | |
Budget	Actual	Variance		Budget	Actual	Variance
			WEST SUFFOLK HOSPITAL			
			FINANCIAL & STATISTICAL REPORT =============================			
			MATERNITY SERVICES ==================			
			WARD F11A 44% AVAILABLE B/DAYS			
120573	127840	7267	TOTAL COSTS	257952	284890	26938
1776	1833	-57	OCCUPIED BED DAYS	-3552	-3688	-136
264	239	25	DISCHARGES & DEATHS	-528	-476	52
			WARD F11B 60% AVAILABLE B/DAYS			
246183	241070	-5113	TOTAL COSTS	526192	509426	-16766
3948	3618	330	OCCUPIED BED DAYS	-7896	-6869	1027
1068	1094	-26	DISCHARGES & DEATHS	-2136	-2107	29
			CENTRAL DELIVERY SUITE			
290137	281424	-8713	TOTAL COSTS	628619	619391	-9228
1140	1169	-29	TOTAL DELIVERIES	-2303	-2242	61
			SCBU 45% AVAILABLE BED DAYS			
122600	122561	-39	TOTAL COSTS	267263	281385	14122
990	897	93	OCCUPIED BED DAYS	-1980	-2092	-112
96	65	31	DISCHARGES & DEATHS	-192	-135	57
			ANTE NATAL CLINIC			
56488	54496	-1992	TOTAL COSTS	121056	125162	4106
3570	3618	-48	NO. OF ATTENDANCES	-7140	-7920	-780
-------	------	-------		-------	-------	------
835981	827391	-8590	SUB-TOTAL OF COSTS	1801082	1820254	19172
223372	232883	9511	COMMUNITY MIDWIVES	490188	510837	20649
-------	------	-------		-------	-------	------
1059353	1060274	921	TOTAL COSTS	2291270	2331091	39821
======	======	======		======	======	======

WEST SUFFOLK HOSP' MANAGE'T BUDGETING
Occupied Bed Days 1988/89

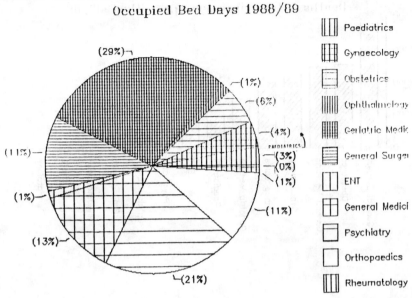

	Paediatrics
	Gynaecology
	Obstetrics
	Ophthalmology
	Geriatric Medic
	General Surgei
	ENT
	General Medici
	Psychiatry
	Orthopaedics
	Rheumatology

WEST SUFFOLK HOSP' MANAGE'T BUDGETING
Deaths & Discharges 1988/89

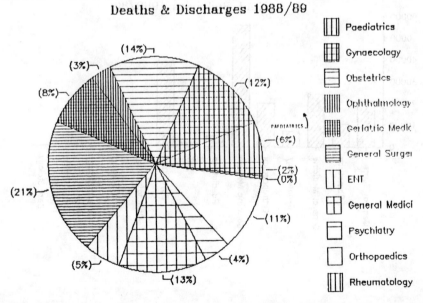

	Paediatrics
	Gynaecology
	Obstetrics
	Ophthalmology
	Geriatric Medic
	General Surgei
	ENT
	General Medici
	Psychiatry
	Orthopaedics
	Rheumatology

WEST SUFFOLK HOSP' MANAGE'T BUDGETING
Deaths & Discharges by Specialtly 1988/89

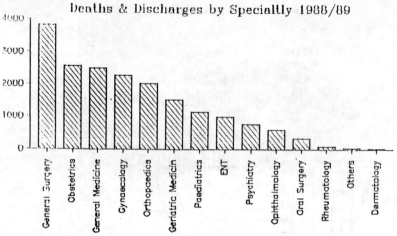

WEST SUFFOLK HOSP' MANAGE'T BUDGETING
In-Patient Bed Days 1988/89

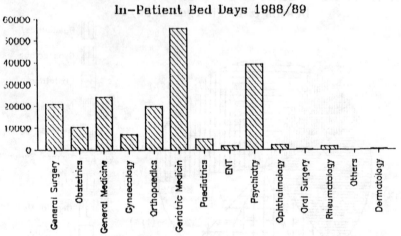

WEST SUFFOLK HOSP' MANAGE'T BUDGETING
Expenditure by Specialty 1988/89

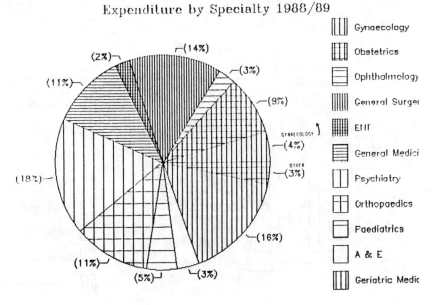

Gynaecology
Obstetrics
Ophthalmology
General Surger
ENT
General Medici
Psychiatry
Orthopaedics
Paediatrics
A & E
Geriatric Medic

WEST SUFFOLK HOSP' MANAGE'T BUDGETING
Notional Over/Underspend by Specialty 1988/89

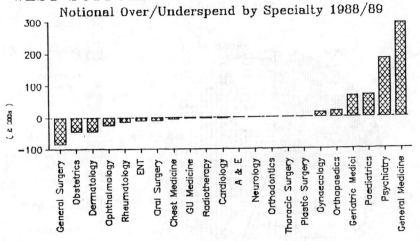

WEST SUFFOLK HOSP' MANAGE'T BUDGETING
Out–Patient Attendances 1988/89

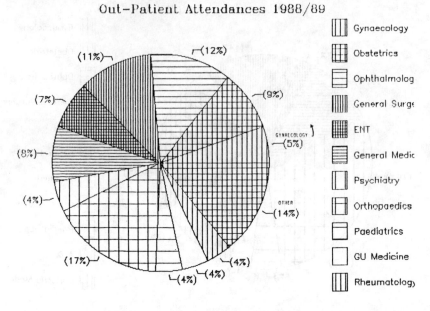

Gynaecology
Obstetrics
Ophthalmolog
General Surge
ENT
General Medic
Psychiatry
Orthopaedics
Paediatrics
GU Medicine
Rheumatolog)

WEST SUFFOLK HOSP' MANAGE'T BUDGETING
New Out–Patients 1988/9

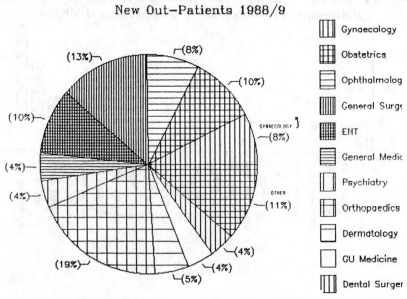

Gynaecology
Obstetrics
Ophthalmolog
General Surge
ENT
General Medic
Psychiatry
Orthopaedics
Dermatology
GU Medicine
Dental Surger

BUDGET VARIANCE REPORT   OBSTETRICS   West Suffolk District Health Authorit

Period 12   Ending 31/03/89   R190.V5.23 Printed 16/05/89 Page 1

1st Six Months			Expense Codes		Full Year		
Budget	Actual	Variance			Budget	Actual	Variance
			DIRECT COSTS				
31704	32966	1262		SENIOR MEDICAL STAFF	63442	63449	7
35239	35651	412		JUNIOR MEDICAL STAFF	66793	75230	8437
12606	8875	-3731		LOCUM MEDICAL STAFF	25258	17233	-8025
4265	4723	458	108	MEDICAL SECRETARIES	8574	8684	110
83814	82215	-1599		TOTAL	164067	164596	529
			OTHER COSTS				
1329	1836	507	723	PHYSIOTHERAPY CHARGES	2626	2268	-358
452	484	32	727	DIETETIC CHARGES	923	961	38
1781	2320	539		TOTAL	3549	3229	-320
			COSTS FROM FACILITIES				
	41	41	617	WARD F9		48	48
120939	117433	-3506	620	F11A	256276	251277	-4999
283743	290597	6854	622	C.D.S.	614190	607394	-6796
56749	54504	-2245	623	ANTE-NATAL CLINIC	120586	125162	4576
244003	224032	-19971	624	F11B	518381	451681	-66700
			631	I.T.U./C.C.U.		404	404
354	4354	4000	810	DAY CASES	765	11755	10990
705788	690961	-14827		TOTAL	1510198	1447721	-62477
			CROSS FUNCTIONAL CHARGES				
29574	25726	-3848		THEATRE CHARGES	59167	59942	775
4368	4660	292	704	MICROBIOLOGY CHARGES	8767	9640	873
42	265	223	705	HISTOLOGY CHARGES	95	364	269
12060	15619	3559	706	HAEMATOLOGY CHARGES	24153	32706	8553
2496	3149	653	707	BIOCHEMISTRY CHARGES	5017	5338	321
1008	1052	44	708	CYTOLOGY CHARGES	2023	2128	105
	17	17	713	RADIOLOGY ON-CALL CHARGES		34	34
1464	1130	-334	714	RADIOLOGY NORMAL HOURS CHARGES	2953	1993	-960
12	9	-3	717	E.C.G. CHARGES	30	15	-15
53850	53235	-615	803	HOSPITAL OVERHEAD CHARGE	109800	116974	7174
104874	104862	-12		TOTAL	212005	229134	17129
896257	880358	-15899		**TOTAL COSTS**	1889819	1844680	-45139

BUDGET VARIANCE REPORT   OBSTETRICS   West Suffolk District Health Authority
Period 12 Ending 31/03/89   R190.V5.23 Printed 16/05/89 Page 2

\-\-\-\-\-\-\- 1st Six Months \-\-\-\-\-\-\-			Expense Codes	\-\-\-\-\-\-\-\- Full Year \-\-\-\-\-\-\-\-		
Budget	Actual	Variance		Budget	Actual	Variance
			STATISTICS			
1770	1823	53	849 WARD F11A OCCUPIED BED DAYS	3540	3677	137
3894	3575	-319	852 WARD F11B OCCUPIED BED DAYS	7788	6802	-986
	1	1	859 WARD F9 OCCUPIED BED DAYS		1	1
			865 I.T.U./C.C.U. OCC BED DAYS		1	1
5664	5399	-265	TOTAL OCCUPIED BED DAYS	11328	10481	-847
	1	1	895 WARD F9 DISCHARGES/DEATHS		1	1
258	236	-22	896 F11A DISCHARGES/DEATHS	516	472	-44
1044	1073	29	897 F11B DISCHARGES/DEATHS	2088	2074	-14
1302	1310	8	TOTAL DISCHARGES & DEATHS	2604	2547	-57
			861 POST NATAL CHECKS			
468	487	19	950 REES NO. OF DELIVERIES	946	971	25
210	205	-5	951 VENN NO. OF DELIVERIES	428	391	-37
438	461	23	952 SPENCER NO. OF DELIVERIES	881	854	-27
144	101	-43	826 DAY CASES	288	254	-34
			NOTIONAL THEATRE SESSIONS	87	79	-8
			THEATRE OVERUN HOURS			
1116	1071	-45	824 TOTAL NEW OUTPATIENTS	2232	2235	3
3570	3618	48	862 ANTE NATAL CLINIC ATTENDANCES	7140	7920	780
24	30	6	981 OUTPATIENTS SEEN ON WARD	48	40	-8
3594	3648	54	TOTAL OUTPATIENT ATTENDANCES	7188	7960	772
168	83	-85	831 RADIOLOGY TESTS - NORMAL HOURS	336	147	-189
	1	1	832 RADIOLOGY TESTS - ON-CALL		2	2
3918	3991	73	833 MICROBIOLOGY TESTS	7836	8173	337
2280	2300	20	843 MICROBIOLOGY REQUESTS	4560	4635	75
870	1065	195	834 BIOCHEMISTRY TESTS	1740	2209	469
666	670	4	844 BIOCHEMISTRY REQUESTS	1332	1439	107
18	29	11	835 HISTOLOGY TESTS	36	40	4
6	17	11	846 HISTOLOGY REQUESTS	12	28	16
270	279	9	836 CYTOLOGY TESTS	540	516	-24
270	279	9	847 CYTOLOGY REQUESTS	540	516	-24
7938	8377	439	837 HAEMATOLOGY TESTS	15876	17616	1740
7044	7004	-40	848 HAEMATOLOGY REQUESTS	14088	14952	864
210	335	125	838 PHYSIOTHERAPY-NEW PATIENTS	432	426	-6
351	484	133	839 PHYSIOTHERAPY-ATTENDANCES	708	597	-111
120	120		841 DIETETIC 20 MIN. UNIT	240	240	
6	4	-2	842 E.C.G. NO. OF PATIENTS	12	7	-5

BUDGET VARIANCE REPORT   E N T SURGERY   West Suffolk District Health Authority
Period 12   Ending 31/03/89   R280.V5.23 Printed 16/05/89 Page 1

| 1st Six Months | | | Expense Codes | | Full Year | | |
Budget	Actual	Variance			Budget	Actual	Variance
			DIRECT COSTS				
20454	20466	12		SENIOR MEDICAL STAFF	40930	40932	2
22922	28951	6029		JUNIOR MEDICAL STAFF	45875	54270	8395
4923	409	-4514		LOCUM MEDICAL STAFF	9869	5099	-4770
3032	3100	68	108	MEDICAL SECRETARIES	6103	6278	175
51331	52926	1595		TOTAL	102777	106579	3802
			OTHER COSTS				
1023	41	-982	723	PHYSIOTHERAPY CHARGES	2026	46	-1980
	50	50	725	OCCUP. THERAPY CHARGES		50	50
116	248	132	727	DIETETIC CHARGES	241	486	245
1139	339	-800		TOTAL	2267	582	-1685
			COSTS FROM FACILITIES				
			601	WARD F1		196	196
53147	54695	1548	603	WARD F2	117987	112703	-5284
			611	WARD F6		147	147
1332	663	-669	629	WARD F12	2969	1722	-1247
2191	1096	-1095	631	I.T.U./C.C.U.	4858	1212	-3646
	26	26	645	CENTRAL TREATMENT ROOM		29	29
11983	12982	999	647	OUTPATIENT DEPARTMENT	24992	26780	1788
4068	3695	-373	810	DAY CASES	8151	9170	1019
72721	73157	436		TOTAL	158957	151959	-6998
			CROSS FUNCTIONAL CHARGES				
52159	50535	-1624		THEATRE CHARGES	110449	103189	-7260
192	189	-3	704	MICROBIOLOGY CHARGES	404	389	-15
522	1100	578	705	HISTOLOGY CHARGES	1052	2398	1346
624	868	244	706	HAEMATOLOGY CHARGES	1279	1598	319
180	159	-21	707	BIOCHEMISTRY CHARGES	366	245	-121
	50	50	713	RADIOLOGY ON-CALL CHARGES		87	87
1848	2314	466	714	RADIOLOGY NORMAL HOURS CHARGES	3725	4403	678
24	12	-12	717	E.C.G. CHARGES	60	30	-30
39270	37506	-1764	733	AUDIOLOGY CHARGES	79988	78090	-1898
9325	9446	121	803	HOSPITAL OVERHEAD CHARGE	19073	20631	1558
104144	102179	-1965		TOTAL	216396	211060	-5336
229335	228601	-734		**TOTAL COSTS**	480397	470180	-10217

BUDGET VARIANCE REPORT   E N T SURGERY   West Suffolk District Health Authority
Period 12 - Ending 31/03/89   R280.V5.23 Printed 16/05/89 Page 2

1st Six Months			Expense Codes	Full Year		
Budget	Actual	Variance		Budget	Actual	Variance
			STATISTICS			
			850 WARD F1 OCCUPIED BED DAYS		2	2
966	1000	34	851 WARD F2 OCCUPIED BED DAYS	1932	1855	-77
			856 WARD F6 OCCUPIED BED DAYS		3	3
12	6	-6	864 WARD F12 OCCUPIED BED DAYS	24	14	-10
6	3	-3	865 I.T.U./C.C.U. OCC BED DAYS	12	3	-9
984	1009	25	TOTAL OCCUPIED BED DAYS	1968	1877	-91
			886 WARD F1 DISCHARGES/DEATHS		2	2
414	525	111	887 WARD F2 DISCHARGES/DEATHS	828	967	139
			891 WARD F6 DISCHARGES/DEATHS		2	2
6	2	-4	898 F12 DISCHARGES/DEATHS	12	7	-5
420	527	107	TOTAL DISCHARGES & DEATHS	840	978	138
114	101	-13	826 DAY CASES	228	225	-3
			NOTIONAL THEATRE SESSIONS	154	141	-13
			THEATRE OVERUN HOURS		17	17
1050	1144	94	824 TOTAL NEW OUTPATIENTS	2100	2222	122
2658	2774	116	827 OUTPATIENT DEPT. ATTENDANCES	5316	5516	200
78	61	-17	981 OUTPATIENTS SEEN ON WARD	156	161	5
192	242	50	986 HEARING AID CLINIC	384	481	97
2928	3077	149	TOTAL OUTPATIENT ATTENDANCES	5856	6158	302
144	177	33	831 RADIOLOGY TESTS - NORMAL HOURS	288	336	48
	4	4	832 RADIOLOGY TESTS - ON-CALL		7	7
108	95	-13	833 MICROBIOLOGY TESTS	216	188	-28
66	49	-17	843 MICROBIOLOGY REQUESTS	132	90	-42
90	60	-30	834 BIOCHEMISTRY TESTS	180	92	-88
48	34	-14	844 BIOCHEMISTRY REQUESTS	96	59	-37
78	121	43	835 HISTOLOGY TESTS	156	262	106
48	50	2	846 HISTOLOGY REQUESTS	96	124	28
372	423	51	837 HAEMATOLOGY TESTS	744	791	47
204	252	48	848 HAEMATOLOGY REQUESTS	408	486	78
	3	3	838 PHYSIOTHERAPY-NEW PATIENTS		4	4
162	10	-152	839 PHYSIOTHERAPY-ATTENDANCES	336	12	-324
	8	8	840 OCCUP.THERAPY 1/2 HOUR SESSION		8	8
30	30		841 DIETETIC 20 MIN. UNIT	60	60	
12	6	-6	842 E.C.G. NO. OF PATIENTS	24	14	-10
1020	1090	70	954 AUDIOLOGY ATTENDANCES	2050	2168	118
4590	4163	-427	956 HEARING AID ATTENDANCES	9180	8814	-366
	1	1	902 CTR - PROCEDURES		1	1

BUDGET VARIANCE REPORT
Period 12   Ending 31/03/89

***** MONTHLY STATISTICAL REPORT *****

West Suffolk District Health Authority
R017.35.23 Printed 16/05/89 Page 1

WEST SUFFOLK HOSPITAL
STATISTICAL REPORT

PHYSIOTHERAPY ATTENDANCES
=========================

------- 1st Six Months -------			Expense Codes	--------- Full Year ---------		
Budget	Actual	Variance		Budget	Actual	Variance
1383	845	-538	PAEDIATRICS	2748	2402	-346
	8	8	CARDIOLOGY		12	12
267	71	-196	DERMATOLOGY	540	240	-300
	5	5	PLASTIC SURGERY		5	5
21	4	-17	RADIOTHERAPY	48	9	-39
3150	2318	-832	RHEUMATOLOGY	6192	4282	-1910
255	245	-10	GYNAECOLOGY	528	528	
351	484	133	OBSTETRICS	708	597	-111
60	25	-35	DENTAL SURGERY	132	85	-47
111	128	17	NEUROLOGY	228	172	-56
33	54	21	CHEST MEDICINE	72	76	4
3	2	-1	OPTHAMOLOGY	12	6	-6
7098	4930	-2168	GERIATRICS	13956	9332	-4624
2178	1632	-546	GENERAL SURGERY	4332	3088	-1244
162	10	-152	E N T SURGERY	336	12	-324
3003	3156	153	GENERAL MEDICINE	5928	7220	1292
1506	4239	2733	PSYCHIATRY	2988	8637	5649
8496	8536	40	ORTHOPAEDICS	16728	15905	-823
15	22	7	ANAESTHESIA	36	25	-11
4503	4089	-414	G.P.s	8844	7932	-912
531	612	81	OTHER	1068	1104	36
------	------	------		------	------	------
33126	31415	-1711	TOTAL	65424	61669	-3755
======	======	======		======	======	======

------- 1st Six Months -------			Expense Codes	--------- Full Year ---------		
Budget	Actual	Variance		Budget	Actual	Variance
			WEST SUFFOLK HOSPITAL			
			STATISTICAL REPORT			

			IN-PATIENT BED DAYS			
			====================			
2376	2082	-294	PAEDIATRICS	4776	4925	149
516	176	-340	DERMATOLOGY	1030	286	-744
1008	973	-35	RHEUMATOLOGY	1996	1568	-428
3618	3584	-34	GYNAECOLOGY	7221	7122	-99
5664	5399	-265	OBSTETRICS	11328	10481	-847
186	172	-14	DENTAL SURGERY	372	335	-37
1440	1314	-126	OPTHAMOLOGY	2880	2301	-579
27432	27755	323	GERIATRICS	54864	55581	717
11460	10545	-915	GENERAL SURGERY	22882	21161	-1721
984	1009	25	E N T SURGERY	1968	1877	-91
10554	10957	403	GENERAL MEDICINE	21079	24274	3195
18726	19638	912	PSYCHIATRY	37452	39098	1646
10422	9807	-615	ORTHOPAEDICS	20810	20055	-755
60	53	-7	GENERAL PRACTIONERS	120	78	-42
	5	5	ANAESTHESIA		5	5
-------	-------	-------		-------	-------	-------
94446	93469	-977	TOTAL	188778	189147	369
======	======	======		======	======	======

OTHER PUBLIC SECTOR
ORGANIZATIONS

Case 11
Nationalized Industry Annual Report and Accounts

OBJECTIVES

1. To examine the published financial statements and performance indicators of a nationalized industry.
2. To consider the problems in trying to assess the performance of a nationalized industry through its annual report and accounts.

MATERIALS

Extracts from British Railways Board Annual Report and Accounts 1988/89:

1. Quality of Service Report (Exhibit 11.1).
2. Network SouthEast (Exhibit 11.2).
3. Direction on Public Service Obligation (Exhibit 11.3).
4. Group profit and loss account and balance sheet and selected notes to the accounts (Exhibit 11.4).
5. Group current cost profit and loss account and balance sheet (Exhibit 11.5).
6. Performance indicators 1984/85 to 1988/89 (Exhibit 11.6).

INTRODUCTION

Compared to private sector companies, the nationalized industries tend to have quite wide-ranging obligations. Likierman, in Henley *et al.* (1989, p. 172), quotes the duties and obligations of British Rail as set out in the 1962 Transport Act: 'It shall be the duty of the Railways Board . . . to provide railway services in Great Britain . . . and to provide other services and facilities as appear to the Board to be expedient and to have due regard . . . to efficiency and economy and safety of operation.' Such guidelines are not particularly helpful to the nationalized industries generally since they do not provide a basis for deciding on priorities. Clearly, 'economy', 'efficiency' and 'safety of operation' can all be conflicting objectives.

One interesting feature of the accounts of British Rail (which is referred to in more detail below) is the Public Service Obligation (PSO) grant. Essentially this is a grant from central government to British Rail, provided so that British Rail will carry out services it would otherwise not carry out if it were acting on a purely commercial basis. In other words, central government is paying British Rail to continue services which it believes are socially desirable. The PSO grant is perhaps not always clearly understood by readers of British Rail accounts and is often mistakenly viewed as a subsidy for inefficient operation. It is interesting that the Secretary of State's direction on Public Service Obligation is expressed in quite vague terms, e.g. 'the British Railways Board shall operate their railway passenger system so as to provide a public service which is comparable generally with that provided by the Board at present' (see Exhibit 11.3). It is not clear that such a direction is helpful to the board of British Rail in trying to determine priorities.

It is perhaps not surprising that in 1976 in a study of UK nationalized industries the National Economic Development Office expressed the view that, 'Annual reports and accounts perform a limited function in their present form and are not an adequate means of assessing the performance of statutory duties' (NEDO, 1976, p. 39).

Following on from the 1976 NEDO Report, the 1978 White Paper, *The Nationalized Industries*, supported the publication of performance indicators, stating that where a monopoly situation exists, financial targets can be met simply by increasing prices or by reducing the level of service. The performance indicators published by British Rail are shown in Exhibit 11.6. It should be noted that the decision on which indicators should be published is taken by the nationalized industry in consultation with its sponsoring department. In addition, British Rail provides a useful report on quality of service (Exhibit 11.1) and separate reports for each division (space constraints dictate that only the report for Network SouthEast is reproduced here, in Exhibit 11.3). The report for Network SouthEast includes narrative, gross income and operating loss data, quality of service objectives and performance data.

ANALYSIS

The financial results of British Rail are conveyed primarily through the statements and notes, from which extracts are reproduced in Exhibits 11.4 and 11.5. The Group profit and loss account prepared on the historic cost basis is reproduced in Exhibit 11.4. There are three factors which need to be understood before an assessment of financial performance can be attempted.

First, we can note the receipt of grant of £606.5 million for the year ended 31 March 1989 (compared with £803.8 million for the previous year). Note 9 to the accounts informs us that this grant is in respect of British Rail's Public Service Obligation. The direction by the Secretary of State for Transport with respect to Public Service Obligation is reproduced in Exhibit 11.3. The report on Network SouthEast refers to operating loss (before government grant) of £137.7 million. This may, unfortunately, reinforce the belief that this grant is paid to finance 'inefficiency'.

Second, we can note that British Rail makes an operating profit before exceptional items (in historic cost terms) of £107 million. The major part of this operating surplus is derived from rail activities and property letting. British Rail has also made substantial sales of property during

1987/88 and 1988/89. It is not clear from the accounts to what extent such sales have been ordered by the sponsoring ministry (i.e. the Department of Transport). It could be argued that asset sales to the private sector are very much a form of privatization in the same way that British Rail was required to sell its hotels to the private sector in the early 1980s.

A third point worth noting is that although British Rail made a historic cost surplus (after exceptional items, before interest) of £49.1 million, it made a current cost loss of £105.6 million. The main reason for this loss is the heavy supplementary depreciation charge of £192.2 million.

QUESTIONS

1. Why is the analysis of the group operating result (see Exhibit 11.4) useful in understanding the present and future performance of British Rail?
2. What implications does the current cost loss of £105.6 million have for future operations?
3. To what extent do the performance indicators (see Exhibit 11.6) report on quality of service?

FURTHER READING

Glynn, J. (1987) *Public Sector Financial Control and Accounting*, Blackwell, Oxford, chapter 10.

Henley, D., Holtham, C., Likierman, A. and Perrin, J. (1989) *Public Sector Accounting and Financial Control*, 3rd edition, Van Nostrand Reinhold, chapter 7.

National Economic Development Office (NEDO) (1976) *A Study of UK Nationalised Industries: Their Role in the Economy and Control in the Future*, HMSO, London.

Rutherford, B. A. (1983) *Financial Reporting in the Public Sector*, Butterworths, London, pp. 223–33.

Rutherford, B. A. (1990) Towards a conceptual framework for public sector financial reporting, *Public Money and Management*, Summer, pp. 11–15.

White Paper (1978) *The Nationalized Industries*, Cmnd 7131, HMSO, London.

Exhibit 11.1 Extract from British Railways Board Annual Report and Accounts 1988/89: Quality of Service Report

QUALITY OF SERVICE

The continuing drive to improve the overall quality of service is a recurring theme in this Report. Investment of £540m in 1988/89 enabled more of the railway to be renewed, with new trains, new track and signalling and modernised stations. The improvement in the physical environment is providing the impetus to change attitudes among management and staff and so extend quality from that offered by new equipment into all areas of service to the customer and to a consistent standard throughout the railway.

Overall punctuality was just below last year, with 89% of passenger trains arriving within five minutes of scheduled time (90% in 1987/88). New systems which measure the impact of train delays are being used to identify the main causes so that immediate action can be taken or, in the longer term, investment priorities changed. Under the new train crew agreement, nearly 2,000 guards have been selected for their suitability to train as drivers. Those who qualify will eventually help to ease the staff shortages which have been the main cause of an increase in train cancellations.

During the year 608 new passenger coaches were delivered and a further 1,009 refurbished, providing extra seats to meet increased demand, and extending the range of facilities for the disabled traveller. Twenty-two new stations were opened and others modernised.

ENGINEERING FOR QUALITY

Civil engineers relaid 198 miles of track with continuous welded rail. Use of 12 dynamic track stabilisers and laser levelling systems allowed trains to run at up to 125mph as soon as lines reopened to traffic, reducing both journey times and operating costs. Major track alterations were completed at Manchester Piccadilly for the link providing through services across Manchester from south to north-west, and as a prelude to electrification, track layouts have been remodelled at York and Edinburgh. Tunnelling to take the new rail link under the runway at Stansted Airport began, following construction of a bridge under the M11, and two new junctions on the Liverpool Street to Cambridge line.

QUALITY OF SERVICE

Mechanical and electrical engineers working on electrification of the east coast main line reached Leeds by July 1988 and are now working north from Doncaster and south from Edinburgh for electric services to begin between Kings Cross and Edinburgh in 1991. The first batch of Class 91 electric locomotives went into revenue-earning service seven months ahead of schedule and revised maintenance schedules enabled Provincial Sprinters to run twice their forecast annual mileage.

Signal and telecommunications engineers are working on new signalling over some 245 track miles and on new signalling centres at Liverpool Street, York and Newcastle. Sixty-three level crossings were modernised, another 14 modified and the prototype of a new train-operated barrier installed at Beccles in Suffolk. A further 37 telephone exchanges were renewed and customer information systems improved at a number of stations. Secure driver to signal box radios are being installed ready for driver only operation of Thameslink and some Victoria and London Bridge suburban trains, followed by trains between Euston, Watford and Northampton and then Waterloo suburban services.

Engineers, architects and designers have combined to improve the total environment for customers at stations. Work on the Network SouthEast programme of station renewal has accelerated with 60 stations modernised to date and 250 refurbished. Queueing time at booking offices has been reduced by putting in some 400 automatic ticket machines and nearly 800 more have been ordered. In the North-west, the Provincial sector is working closely with local authorities in upgrading and rebranding over 200 urban and rural stations.

The Railway Heritage Trust, an independent organisation supported by the Board, made grants of £1m with external funds of £0·3m to support 34 schemes to restore listed buildings and structures, including stations at Great Malvern, Ingatestone, Beverley, Scarborough, Dunbar, Aylesford and Hereford.

QUALITY THROUGH PEOPLE

The Board has launched a major initiative — Quality Through People — aimed at changing attitudes so that all staff give the proper priority to delivering a high quality of service to customers. A Director, Quality Through People, has been appointed to lead a programme related to both people and work processes. The programme is inevitably long term but will foster new attitudes towards the satisfaction of the customer and thus the continuing success of the railway business.

Exhibit 11.2   Extract from British Railways Board Annual Report and Accounts 1988/89: Network SouthEast

NETWORK SOUTHEAST

Network SouthEast almost halved its call on Government support in 1988/89. This was largely achieved through extra income from the continuing boom in demand for its services, which in turn helped fund investment to provide extra capacity. The sector was set an objective to reduce support to £139m (at current price levels) by March 1990. It almost reached the target by March 1989, requiring only £141m support in the year.

Earnings increased by nearly 11% in 1988/89 while costs were contained despite the introduction of new services. The higher income was matched by higher investment to a new record of £272m, a prelude to the sector's five year plan to invest a further £1,400m to improve quality and financial performance.

In May 1988, the new cross-London Thameslink service was opened and has attracted 20,000 passengers a day in its first year. The original fleet of 60 trains is being increased by 24 to meet demand. In the last three years over 500 new coaches have been delivered to Network SouthEast and orders placed for 280 more.

The high performance electric motors for the new generation of Networker trains to be introduced on suburban routes into Charing Cross and Cannon Street from 1991 are already being tested in public service on a prototype. Networker trains will offer major improvements in reliability and comfort and will form the basis of future train fleets.

MORE ELECTRIFICATION

Four new stations were opened and more than two-thirds of the sector's 942 stations have had a facelift over the past three years. Electrification was completed on the Royston/Cambridge, Watford/St Albans, and Bournemouth/Weymouth lines and work has begun on the lines between Southampton, Eastleigh and Portsmouth. Authority was given to extend electrification from Cambridge to King's Lynn.

The number of passengers coming into London on Network SouthEast services during the morning peak increased by a further 4% to 468,000, the highest figure recorded since regular surveys were conducted. Despite this, overcrowding has been reduced in total by adjusting train formations and their timing and calling patterns, to balance out the changes in demand. Off peak traffic also increased and One Day Travelcards are now sold to 1·5m customers every month, an increase of 31% on last year.

Overall punctuality again bettered the objective set, response times at telephone enquiry bureaux improved and ticket office queues were shorter. Slightly more trains were cancelled than last year, due to staff shortages which also affected carriage cleaning performance.

The Central London Rail Study reported on ways of meeting increased demand for peak travel to and through central London. Tunnels carrying trains on an east/west line from Liverpool Street to Paddington, and on a north/south line linking Euston and Kings Cross with Victoria are being examined for technical feasibility along with the options for funding such a major development.

QUALITY OF SERVICE

	Objective	Performance
PUNCTUALITY		1988/9 (87/8)
	90% to arrive on time +/– 5 mins	**92% (92%)**
SERVICE PROVISION		
	At least 99% of services to run	**98·8% (98·8%)**
ENQUIRY BUREAUX		
	95% of calls answered in 30 secs	**90% (85%)**
TICKET OFFICES *Queueing time*		
	5 mins peak: 3 mins off peak	**97·5% (97%)**
CARRIAGE CLEANING		
	100% daily interior/exterior	**89% (94%)**
	100% heavy interior (every 28 days)	**88% (91%)**
LOAD FACTORS		
	Sliding door trains 135% max ⎫	*on average*
	Slam door trains 110% max ⎬	**4% (4·2%)**
	No standing over 20 mins ⎭	*over target*

GROSS INCOME
£892·3m

OPERATING LOSS
before Government grant
£137·7m

Exhibit 11.3 Extract from British Railways Board Annual Report and Accounts 1988/89: Direction on Public Service Obligation

DIRECTION ON PUBLIC SERVICE OBLIGATION

The Secretary of State for Transport hereby gives the following direction to the British Railways Board in exercise of his powers under Section 3(1) and (3) of the Railways Act 1974:

1   This direction is subject to the provisions of Section 3(4) of the said Act of 1974 and shall have effect on and from 1 April 1988.

2   Subject to the provisions of paragraphs 3 and 4 below, the British Railways Board shall operate their railway passenger system so as to provide a public service which is comparable generally with that provided by the Board at present.

3   This direction shall not extend to the operation, after the date on which the consent can be implemented, of any railway passenger service or substitute bus service, for the discontinuance of which the Secretary of State gives, or has given, his consent under Section 56 of the Transport Act 1962 or Section 122 of the Transport Act 1985 as the case may be.

4   This direction shall not apply to the following services:

i)   any railway passenger service which is at present, or may at any time be, provided as part of the Board's InterCity sector;

ii)   any railway passenger service which is, or at any time has been, provided on an experimental basis within the meaning of Section 56A of the Transport Act 1962;

iii)   any railway passenger service which is at present, or may at any time be, provided in pursuance of any agreement made between a Passenger Transport Executive and the Board under Section 20 of the Transport Act 1968.

5   The direction under Section 3(1) of the Railways Act 1974 given by the Secretary of State for the Environment on 19 December 1974 is hereby revoked with effect from 1 April 1988.

Paul Channon
Secretary of State for Transport
30 March 1988

Exhibit 11.4   Extracts from British Railways Board Annual Report and Accounts 1988/89:
Group profit and loss account and balance sheet and selected notes to the accounts

GROUP PROFIT AND LOSS ACCOUNT

Note		Year to 31 March 1989 £m	Year to 31 March 1989 £m	Year to 31 March 1988 £m	Year to 31 March 1988 £m
Note	**TURNOVER**				
	Turnover excluding grant	**2,789·4**		2,580·4	
9(a), 9(b)	Grant	**606·5**		803·8	
			3,395·9		3,384·2
	OPERATING EXPENDITURE				
11(e)	Staff costs	**2,007·3**		2,034·5	
	Materials, supplies and services	**1,273·5**		1,307·6	
	Depreciation and amortisation	**114·2**		108·5	
9(a)	Capital renewal provision	**74·5**		123·4	
	Own work capitalised and work outside the normal course of business	**(180·6)**		(298·3)	
			3,288·9		3,275·7
11	**OPERATING SURPLUS BEFORE EXCEPTIONAL ITEM**		**107·0**		108·5
12	Exceptional item — Grant repayment		**(64·5)**		—
13	**OPERATING SURPLUS AFTER EXCEPTIONAL ITEM**		**42·5**		108·5
13	Other income		**6·6**		4·5
	SURPLUS BEFORE INTEREST		**49·1**		113·0
14	Interest payable and similar charges		**30·6**		65·7
15	Taxation		**0·3**		—
1	**SURPLUS ON ORDINARY ACTIVITIES** . . .		**18·2**		47·3
16	**EXTRAORDINARY ITEMS**				
	Surplus on sale of assets	**268·4**		185·0	
9(a)	Grant for restructuring costs.	**7·0**		67·6	
	Loss on sale of subsidiaries	**(2·2)**		(7·6)	
	Other.	**12·9**		(1·4)	
	EXTRAORDINARY SURPLUS		**286·1**		243·6
	GROUP SURPLUS FOR THE YEAR		**304·3**		290·9
27	**APPROPRIATION OF SURPLUS FOR THE YEAR**				
	Transfer to General Reserve .·		**196·2**		177·7
	Surplus after transfer to General Reserve		**108·1**		113·2
			304·3		290·9

GROUP BALANCE SHEET

Note		31 March 1989		31 March 1988	
		£m	£m	£m	£m
	FIXED ASSETS				
	Tangible assets				
18(a)	Buildings, way and structures	912·9		815·8	
18(b)	Rolling stock, plant and equipment	1,068·5		971·1	
19(b)	Investments	0·7		0·9	
			1,982·1		1,787·8
	CURRENT ASSETS				
20	Stocks	165·4		188·0	
21	Debtors	398·2		375·2	
22	Interest in Non-operational Property.	250·3		236·5	
4	Investment in BREL (1988) Ltd.	13·6		—	
	Cash at bank and in hand.	209·4		44·2	
		1,036·9		843·9	
	Less creditors:				
23(a)	amounts falling due within one year	821·7		724·8	
	NET CURRENT ASSETS		215·2		119·1
	TOTAL ASSETS LESS CURRENT LIABILITIES		2,197·3		1,906·9
	Less creditors:				
23(b)	amounts falling due after more than one year		89·3		57·8
			2,108·0		1,849·1
	PROVISIONS FOR RESTRUCTURING				
24	**COSTS**		28·2		127·0
	CAPITAL AND RESERVES				
25	Capital liabilities to Secretary of State	233·0		254·5	
26	Loans and leasing liabilities	275·5		277·4	
27(a)	Revaluation reserve	209·0		206·7	
27(b)	Other reserves.	1,997·8		1,727·1	
27(c)	Profit and Loss Account	(635·5)		(743·6)	
			2,079·8		1,722·1
			2,108·0		1,849·1

Signed on behalf of the Board   8 June 1989

Sir Robert Reid
Chairman

Derek Fowler
Vice Chairman

D. P. Hornby
Board Member

NOTES TO THE ACCOUNTS

1 ANALYSIS OF GROUP OPERATING RESULT

Year to 31 March 1989

	Rail	InterCity On Board Services	Operational Property letting	Non-operational Property letting	BREL (1988) Ltd (Note 4)	BRML	Freightliners Ltd (Note 6)	Travellers Fare Ltd (Note 7)	Transmark	Other minor companies	Corporate Body (Note 8)	Intra-group items	Total
	£m	£m	£m	£m	£m	£m	£m	£m	£m	£m	£m	£m	£m
Gross income	3,145·4	41·8	89·2	11·4	135·6	211·9	50·9	55·7	5·9	2·5	19·7	(374·1)	3,395·9
Expenditure													
Staff costs	1,800·3	23·8	6·3	1·5	55·6	48·7	11·5	17·3	1·1	—	41·2	—	2,007·3
Materials, supplies and services	967·6	28·9	10·9	3·9	60·1	107·7	21·9	28·2	2·8	2·9	38·6	—	1,273·5
Depreciation and amortisation	102·9	0·7	0·2	—	2·4	2·2	1·7	1·4	—	0·4	2·3	—	114·2
Capital renewal provision	74·5	—	—	—	—	—	—	—	—	—	—	—	74·5
Own work capitalised and work outside normal course of business	(178·8)	(0·4)	—	—	—	(1·4)	—	—	—	—	—	—	(180·6)
Intra-group charges (net)	325·0	1·6	5·3	0·6	12·5	38·7	21·0	9·3	1·5	(0·2)	(41·2)	(374·1)	—
Total operating expenditure	3,091·5	54·6	22·7	6·0	130·6	195·9	56·1	56·2	5·4	3·1	40·9	(374·1)	3,288·9
Operating surplus/(loss)	53·9	(12·8)	66·5	5·4	5·0	16·0	(5·2)	(0·5)	0·5	(0·6)	(21·2)	—	107·0
Exceptional item	(64·5)	—	—	—	—	—	—	—	—	—	—	—	(64·5)
Other income	6·5	—	—	—	—	—	—	—	—	—	0·1	—	6·6
Interest (payable)/receivable	(60·8)	0·5	—	—	(2·9)	(7·8)	(1·1)	0·4	(0·1)	0·3	40·9	—	(30·6)
Taxation	—	—	—	—	—	—	—	—	—	(0·1)	(0·2)	—	(0·3)
Surplus/(loss) after interest and other income	(64·9)	(12·3)	66·5	5·4	2·1	8·2	(6·3)	(0·1)	0·4	(0·4)	19·6	—	18·2

NOTES TO THE ACCOUNTS

4 BREL (1988) LIMITED

On 1 April 1988, a new company, BREL (1988) Ltd, was formed into which all the assets and liabilities (other than land and buildings) of British Rail Engineering Ltd which were to be sold were transferred. The Board's interest in BREL (1988) Ltd was sold on 18 April 1989 (after the balance sheet date) to a consortium which included the management of BREL (1988) Ltd. As part of the arrangements for the sale, the accounting year of BREL (1988) Ltd was shortened to 8 October 1988. The results to that date, which was the effective date of sale, have been consolidated into the Board's results in Note 1. At 31 March 1989, the Board's investment in BREL (1988) Ltd was written down to the agreed sale price and has been included in the balance sheet as a current investment. The book loss arising has been treated as an extraordinary item in Note 16. As a result of the sale, that part of the restructuring provision raised in previous years' accounts which remained unused (other than a small amount required to cover on-going liabilities such as Alternative Employment Schemes) was written back as an extraordinary item (Note 16).

British Rail Engineering Ltd retained certain obligations, including aspects of rationalisation of the company's previous activities, and the loss arising in this company has been included in Note 1 under minor companies.

9 TRANSPORT GRANT

	Year to 31 March 1989	Year to 31 March 1988
	£m	£m
(a) Public Service Obligation grant		
EEC Regulation 1191/69 and Railways Act 1974 Section 3		
Included in turnover	530·6	726·2
Included as an exceptional item	(64·5)	—
Included in extraordinary items	7·0	67·6
Total Public Service Obligation grant	473·1	793·8

An amount of £74·5m (1987/88 £123·4m) has been included as a Capital Renewal Provision. An equivalent amount has been charged to Profit and Loss Account towards the cost of the replacement of passenger assets in the supported sectors and this has been credited to Capital Reserve.

The claim for Public Service Obligation grant has not yet been finally agreed.

	Year to 31 March 1989	Year to 31 March 1988
	£m	£m
(b) Passenger Transport Executive grant		
Transport Act 1968 Section 20(4)		
Included in turnover	75·9	77·6
(c) Grant included as a reduction in expenditure		
EEC Regulations 1192/69		
Operation and maintenance of level crossings	20·9	22·0
(d) The grants reflect adjustments in respect of previous years of:		
Public Service Obligation		
Included in turnover	1·1	(5·7)
Included as an exceptional item	(64·5)	—
Passenger Transport Executives	(3·6)	1·1
Level crossings	(0·6)	0·4
	(67·6)	(4·2)

(e) Actual cash received in respect of grants in the year to 31 March 1989	Cash received for current year	In respect of previous years
	£m	£m
Public Service Obligation	564·0	(31·9)
Passenger Transport Executives	71·5	(1·6)
Level crossings	21·1	(2·1)

(f) The limit on Central Government compensation payable to the Board for its Public Service Obligation, as laid down in the Railways Act 1974, as amended by the Transport (Finance) Act 1982, was increased by the provisions of the British Railways Board (Increase of Compensation Limit) Order 1986, whereby the aggregate amount which may be paid in respect of periods after 1978 is limited to £10,000m. At 31 March 1989 the Board has received £7,342m in respect of periods since 1 January 1979 under EEC Regulation 1191/69.

12 EXCEPTIONAL ITEM

During the year, a change in the method of calculating the PSO grant was made by the Secretary of State for Transport. This has had the effect of reducing the grant received in respect of 1988/89 by £33·0m. The changed procedures have been retrospectively applied to 1986/87 resulting in a repayment of grant of £64·5m. This amount is being recovered by the Government by deduction from current grant payments. In order not to distort the trading position of the current year, this prior year recovery has been shown separately in the Profit and Loss Account as an exceptional item.

16 EXTRAORDINARY ITEMS

	Year to 31 March 1989		Year to 31 March 1988	
	£m	£m	£m	£m
Surplus on sale of assets				
Non-operational Property	263·5		181·4	
Scrap assets	4·9		2·8	
Minor investments	—		0·8	
		268·4		185·0
Grant for restructuring costs		7·0		67·6
Disposal of subsidiaries				
BREL (1988) Ltd — loss on sale	(75·2)		—	
— write-back of provisions	70·0		—	
Travellers Fare Ltd	9·2		—	
Horwich Foundry Ltd	(6·2)		—	
Doncaster Wagon Works Ltd	—		(7·2)	
British Transport Advertising Ltd	—		(0·4)	
		(2·2)		(7·6)
Other				
BRML restructuring provision write-back	12·1		—	
Other	0·8		(1·4)	
		12·9		(1·4)
Net extraordinary surplus		286·1		243·6

Exhibit 11.5 Extracts from British Railways Board Annual Report and Accounts 1988/89: Group current cost profit and loss account and balance sheet

GROUP CURRENT COST PROFIT AND LOSS ACCOUNT

	Year to 31 March 1989	Year to 31 March 1988
	£m	£m
Turnover	3,395·9	3,384·2
Historical cost surplus before interest	49·1	113·0
Current cost operating adjustments	(154·7)	(93·9)
Current cost surplus/(loss)	(105·6)	19·1
Interest payable and similar charges	30·6	65·7
Taxation	0·3	—
Current cost loss on ordinary activities	(136·5)	(46·6)
Extraordinary surplus	264·2	239·2
Group current cost surplus for the year	127·7	192·6
Appropriation of surplus for the year:		
Transfer to Reserves	196·2	177·7
Surplus/(deficit) after transfer to Reserves	(68·5)	14·9
	127·7	192·6

SUMMARISED GROUP CURRENT COST BALANCE SHEET

	31 March 1989	31 March 1988
	£m	£m
Fixed assets		
Tangible assets	3,945·3	3,686·8
Investments	0·7	0·9
	3,946·0	3,687·7
Net current assets		
Stocks	166·9	189·6
Interest in Non-operational Property	250·3	236·5
Investment in BREL (1988) Ltd	13·6	—
Monetary working capital	(487·8)	(409·2)
Other working capital	184·4	46·1
	4,073·4	3,750·7
Provision for liabilities and charges	28·2	127·0
Capital and reserves		
Capital liabilities to Secretary of State	233·0	254·5
Loans and leasing liabilities	275·5	277·4
Reserves		
Current cost	3,141·3	2,900·8
Other	395·4	191·0
	4,073·4	3,750·7

NOTES TO THE CURRENT COST ACCOUNTS

1 ADJUSTMENTS TO OPERATING RESULTS

	Year to 31 March 1989	Year to 31 March 1988
	£m	£m
Depreciation	192·2	184·1
Capital renewal provision	(74·5)	(123·4)
Amortisation	37·0	33·2
Cost of sales	9·8	8·9
Monetary working capital	(9·8)	(8·9)
	154·7	93·9

Exhibit 11.6 Extract from British Railways Board Annual Report and Accounts 1988/89: Performance Indicators 1984/85 to 1988/89

PERFORMANCE INDICATORS

1984/85 — 1988/89

PASSENGER BUSINESS	1984/85*	1985/86	1986/87	1987/88	1988/89
Total supported businesses					
1 PSO grant per supported passenger mile . . . . pence	6·61	5·39	4·39	4·35	**4·58**
2 PSO grant as a percentage of other receipts . . . . %	71·0	61·4	49·5	49·0	**50·2**
InterCity					
3 Profit/(loss) as a percentage of receipts . . . . %	(3·0)	(21·1)	(16·0)	(12·4)	**0·7**
4 Receipts per train mile . . . . £	11·53	12·73	13·50	14·31	**14·60**
5 Receipts per passenger mile . . . . pence	7·73	8·15	8·43	8·44	**8·72**
6 Passenger miles per loaded train mile (average train load) . . . . passengers	155	161	165	175	**174**
7 Total operating expenses per train mile . . . . £	16·47	15·64	15·89	16·28	**13·61**
8 Percentages of trains arriving within 10 minutes of booked time . . . . %	n/a	n/a	85	87	**87**
9 Percentage of trains cancelled . . . . %	n/a	n/a	0·8	0·5	**1·0**
Network SouthEast					
10 PSO grant per passenger mile . . . . pence	4·16	3·72	2·66	2·78	**1·44**
11 PSO grant as a percentage of other receipts . . . . %	45·8	43·0	30·5	31·5	**16·3**
12 Receipts per train mile . . . . £	8·14	8·38	8·88	9·23	**9·41**
13 Receipts per passenger mile . . . . pence	9·10	8·66	8·73	8·84	**8·86**
14 Passenger miles per loaded train mile (average train load) . . . . passengers	95	103	107	111	**113**
15 Total operating expenses per train mile . . . . £	11·76	11·72	11·30	11·61	**11·26**
16 Percentages of trains arriving within 5 minutes of booked time . . . . %	90	91	91	92	**92**
17 Percentage of trains cancelled . . . . %	1·9	1·9	1·6	1·2	**1·4**
Provincial					
18 PSO grant per PSO supported passenger mile . . . . pence	27·46	28·47	23·48	21·17	**16·61**
19 PTE grant per PTE supported passenger mile . . . . pence	9·08	7·80	7·51	7·21	**6·44**
20 PSO grant as a percentage of other receipts . . . . %	241·9	237·8	210·4	195·0	**165·4**
21 PTE grant as a percentage of other receipt . . . . %	49·7	41·7	37·1	35·5	**30·9**
22 Receipts per train mile . . . . £	3·19	3·14	3·10	3·01	**2·92**
23 Receipts per passenger mile . . . . pence	7·00	7·30	7·20	7·07	**6·78**
24 Passenger miles per loaded train mile (average train load) . . . . passengers	48	45	45	45	**45**
25 Total operating expenses per train mile . . . . £	10·31	10·30	9·63	9·10	**8·66**
26 Percentages of trains arriving within 5 minutes of booked time . . . . %	91	89	91	90	**90**
27 Percentage of trains cancelled . . . . %	n/a	n/a	0·5	0·9	**1·2**
FREIGHT BUSINESS					
Total Freight Business					
28 Operating surplus/(loss) as a percentage of receipts . . . %	(3·9)	(2·5)	3·2	5·9	**10·6**
29 Total operating expenses per train mile . . . . index	100	100	95	90	**84**
Bulk Freight					
30 Receipts per train mile . . . . index	n/a	n/a	100	89	**86**
31 Net tonnes per mainline locomotive . . . . index	n/a	n/a	100	103	**112**
32 Receipts per wagon £000	n/a	n/a	12·6	14·0	**14·7**
Railfreight Distribution					
33 Receipts per train mile . . . . index	n/a	n/a	100	100	**91**
34 Net tonnes per mainline locomotive . . . . index	n/a	n/a	100	122	**133**
35 Receipts per wagon £000	n/a	n/a	20·5	20·0	**19·4**
PARCELS BUSINESS					
36 Receipts per parcel . . . . index	100	106	113	120	**122**
37 Operating surplus/(loss) as a percentage of receipts . . . %	12·7	2·6	(9·2)	(11·7)	**(10·0)**

PERFORMANCE INDICATORS

1984/85 — 1988/89

TOTAL RAIL BUSINESS

	1984/85*	1985/86	1986/87	1987/88	1988/89
38 Total receipts per train mile .... £	9·23	9·34	9·48	9·52	**9·47**
39 Total operating expenses per train mile .... £	13·83	13·42	12·85	12·58	**11·54**
40 Train miles per member of staff (total staff productivity) .... miles	1,726	1,774	1,812	1,967	**2,123**
41 Revenue per £1,000 gross paybill costs .... £	1,430	1,479	1,510	1,594	**1,711**
42 Train miles per train crew member (train crew productivity) .... miles	8,045	8,252	8,564	9,568	**10,485**
43 Train miles per single track mile 000	12·4	12·5	12·6	13·1	**13·5**

BRITISH RAIL MAINTENANCE LTD

44 Sales per employee £000	n/a	n/a	n/a	39·2	**49·8**

INTERCITY ON BOARD SERVICES

45 Operating margin .... %	(22·0)	(22·8)	(26·3)	(23·4)	**(31·8)**
46 Sales per £000 of direct operating staff cost .... £	2,166	2,071	2,110	2,380	**2,436**
47 Percentage of train catering services cancelled .... %	3·7	4·0	3·6	4·1	**3·6**

OPERATIONAL AND NON-OPERATIONAL PROPERTY

48 Operating margin:					
Operational .... %	76·2	76·5	80·0	80·9	**79·5**
Non-operational .... %	62·2	59·2	65·5	62·1	**71·0**
49 Management expenses as a % of property income .... %	16·0	17·0	15·6	13·7	**14·6**
50 Growth in annual rental income .... index	101·2	107·1	115·2	130·4	**167·5**
51 Net income per employee £000	94·9	99·9	121·0	133·1	**165·2**
52 Net property income per £ staff costs .... £	8·34	8·45	9·21	9·90	**12·32**

TRANSMARK

53 Operating margin .... %	(0·4)	(4·9)	(5·0)	(20·2)	**6·7**
54 Sales per employee £000	67	73	61	60	**77**

*The Rail performance indicators for 1984/85 were distorted by the effects of the coal strike. In view of these exceptional circumstances an adjusted set of indicators has been calculated showing more accurately the underlying trend of the Rail business performance.

Monetary items have been converted to 1988/89 price levels using the GDP deflator. Receipts include miscellaneous receipts but exclude grant. Indicators 1 and 2 include Capital Renewal Provision but exclude PTE grant. Indicator 3 is before PSO grant for the years 1984/85 to 1987/88. Indicators 31, 32, 34 and 35 include privately owned wagons and locomotives. Indicator 36 excludes receipts relating to newspapers and Post Office traffic. Indicator 42 is only a broad indicator of overall train crew productivity. Indicators 45 and 53 are net surplus/(loss) before interest as a percentage of gross income. Indicator 48 is operating surplus (before development land tax) as a percentage of property income. Indicator 50 is rent roll value as at 31 March indexed from 1 January 1984 (100). Indicator 51 is operating surplus (before development land tax) per employee engaged on letting activities. Indicator 52 is net property income related to costs of employees engaged on letting activities.

INTERNATIONAL PERFORMANCE INDICATORS

The latest information on international performance indicators is shown below. The eight European Railways are Austria, Belgium, France, Great Britain, Italy, Netherlands, Switzerland and West Germany.

	Year to 31 March 1988		Year to 31 March 1987	
	British Rail	Average of Eight European Railways	British Rail	Average of Eight European Railways
Train kilometres (loaded and empty) per member of staff employed	**3,127**	**2,233**	2,990	2,162
Average train loading (passenger kms, divided by passenger train kms loaded and empty)...................................	**97**	**130**	95	131
Average train loading (freight tonnes kms, divided by freight trains loaded and empty)...................................	**253**	**296**	244	296
Support from public funds as proportion of Gross Domestic Product (%)	**0·22**	**0·67**	0·21	0·67

Case 12
Regional Water Authority Annual Report and Accounts

OBJECTIVES

1. To examine the current cost accounts of a regional water authority.
2. To consider financial performance targets set by central government.

MATERIALS

Extracts from Severn Trent Water Report and Accounts 1988/89:

1. Notes to Historic Cost Financial Statements, 1(f) Tangible fixed assets and depreciation; (2) Turnover and Profits (Exhibit 12.1).
2. Extracts from Supplementary Current Cost Financial Information (Exhibit 12.2).
3. Statement of performance against government controls (Exhibit 12.3).

INTRODUCTION

The 1988/89 Report and Accounts of Severn Trent Water provide an interesting example of the use of current cost accounting in the public sector. The extracts from the annual accounts of Severn Trent Water (reproduced in Exhibit 12.1) relate to the final full year before privatization. The annual report and accounts at that time were submitted to the Secretary of State for the Environment and the Minister of Agriculture, Fisheries and Food in accordance with the Water Act 1973.

The major part of water industry revenue derives from charges for water supply and sewerage services. By the very nature of its operations a heavy investment in fixed assets is required. However, it has been argued that the reluctance of successive governments to fund adequate capital investment in the water industry had meant that many of the industry's assets would need to be replaced or upgraded to meet European Community standards (see, for instance, Hills, 1987). For the privatized water authorities, the known capital expenditure programmes which would have to be carried out during the 1990s were estimated at nearly £25 billion.

ANALYSIS

It can be seen from note 2b to the historical cost accounts that costs of employment (£95.6 million) amounted to 38.8 per cent of operating costs

(£246.2 million). It is debatable whether reductions in manpower (even if made possible through increased efficiency) will have a substantial impact on overall profits. The current cost statements indicate that infrastructure assets (which comprise over half the gross replacement cost of fixed assets) are not subject to depreciation. From note 1(f)(i) to the historic cost financial statements it can be seen that infrastructure assets include such items as mains, sewers, reservoirs and dams.

One of the main difficulties with accounting in the water industry concerns the questions of depreciation and a suitable valuation for fixed assets. The argument in favour of providing no depreciation is that most of the major assets have a virtually indefinite life, provided a suitable maintenance programme is adhered to. Such a policy may lead to income measurement problems, however. For example, if maintenance expenditures are simply charged to profit and loss account in the year in which they are incurred, then the reported profit or loss could be influenced by the timing of these expenditures, which could be arbitrary. On the other hand, if depreciation is charged it is not always possible to decide exactly which expenditure falls into the category of repairs and which falls into the category of being an improvement. Often an arbitrary judgement would need to be made.

The method of asset valuation also poses problems. If the infrastructure assets are essential to the industry's operations (and are consequently not intended to be sold), how useful is market value as a basis for valuation? Also, if it is not intended to replace the infrastructure assets why use replacement cost? It might, however, be argued that if comparisons are to be made with other enterprises (not necessarily in the water industry), some valuation of assets may be essential in order to arrive at comparable measures of return on capital employed.

For the year ended 31 March 1989 the Severn Trent Water Authority was set a financial target by central government (see Exhibit 12.3). This target was expressed as the ratio of current cost operating profit to net assets (current cost basis). The pricing policies of the privatized companies are regulated by the Director General of Water Services. Prices will not be allowed to rise by more than the 'retail index plus K' (where K is calculated largely on the basis of the industry's future capital expenditure requirements).

QUESTIONS

1. What issues are involved in the accounting treatment of infrastructure assets?
2. What ways would be open to the water industry to attempt to improve its rate of return (before privatization and after privatization)?

FURTHER READING

Hills, J. S. (1987) *Cutting Water Costs and Effluent Charges*, Energy Publications, Newmarket.

Rutherford, B. A. (1983) *Financial Reporting in the Public Sector*, Butterworths, London, pp. 212–14.

Exhibit 12.1 Severn Trent Water Report and Accounts 1988/89: extracts from Notes to Historic Cost Financial Statements

Notes to the Financial Statements

Year ended 31 March 1989

f   **Tangible fixed assets and depreciation**

Tangible fixed assets comprise:

Infrastructure assets (being mains and sewers, impounding and pumped raw water storage reservoirs, dams and sludge pipe lines); and

Other assets (including properties, overground plant and equipment).

(i)   Infrastructure assets

Infrastructure assets comprise a network of systems:

Expenditure on infrastructure assets relating to increases in capacity or enhancements of the network is treated as additions which are included at cost after deducting grants and contributions.

Expenditure on maintaining the operating capability of the network in accordance with defined standards of service is charged as an operating cost.

No depreciation is charged on infrastructure assets because the network of systems is required to be maintained in perpetuity and therefore has no finite economic life.

This represents a change in accounting policy from prior years, when certain infrastructure renewals expenditure was capitalised and depreciation was charged on infrastructure assets. Depreciation charged on these assets since 1 April 1984 being the earliest practicable date for implementation of the new policy has been written back and infrastructure renewals expenditure since that date has been restated in accordance with the new policy. Infrastructure assets at 1 April 1984 have been included at their net book value at that date with subsequent additions at cost.

(ii)   Other assets

Other assets are included at cost less accumulated depreciation. Additions are included at cost, after deducting grants and contributions.

Freehold land is not depreciated. Other assets are depreciated evenly over their estimated economic lives, which are principally as follows:-

Buildings	30-60 years
Operational structures	40-80 years
Fixed plant	20-40 years
Vehicles, mobile plant and computers	4-10 years

Notes to the Financial Statements
continued

2 Turnover and Profits

a Analysis of turnover and profits by class of business	Water Resources	Water Supply	Sewerage Services
	£m	£m	£m
Unmetered charges	—	118.5	221.3
Metered charges	—	70.0	23.8
Precepts	—	—	—
Abstraction charges	22.8	—	—
Trade effluent charges	—	—	23.9
Miscellaneous charges	—	0.7	0.2
Government grants	—	0.2	0.6
Other	2.1	9.8	4.1
Inter service (see note below)	(14.9)	(0.6)	—
Turnover	10.0	198.6	273.9
Operating costs before depreciation, infrastructure renewals expenditure and exceptional items (note 2b)	11.2	117.7	101.0
Depreciation	1.0	12.5	19.7
Infrastructure renewals expenditure	2.0	29.8	18.1
Inter-service (see note below)	—	(14.9)	(0.6)
Operating costs before exceptional items	14.2	145.1	138.2
Operating profit/(loss) before exceptional items	(4.2)	53.5	135.7
Exceptional Items	0.2	2.6	2.4
Operating profit/(loss)	(4.4)	50.9	133.3
Other income (note 5)			
Profit before interest payable			
Less interest payable			
Profit on ordinary activities			

Notes
(i) Inter-service comprises abstraction charges, and internal water charges.
(ii) Other Trading Activities relate solely to overseas activities.

b Operating costs before depreciation, infrastructure renewals expenditure and exceptional items	1989 £m	1988 £m
Manpower costs	88.7	86.0
Other costs of employment	6.9	6.7
Power	23.7	22.7
Local authority rates	27.5	24.2
Water charges	19.4	17.8
Agencies	18.3	17.0
Materials and consumables	23.1	19.7
Hired and contracted services	18.8	16.6
Charge for doubtful debts	7.0	2.0
Other	12.8	14.1
Total (note 2 (a))	246.2	226.8

Environmental Services	Other Trading Activities	Total of services other than Land Drainage and Flood Protection	Land Drainage and Flood Protection	Total	1987/88
£m	£m	£m	£m	£m	£m
8.7	—	348.5	—	348.5	317.7
—	—	93.8	—	93.8	85.9
—	—	—	15.4	15.4	14.7
—	—	22.8	—	22.8	21.4
—	—	23.9	—	23.9	21.6
1.2	—	2.1	—	2.1	2.2
—	—	0.8	—	0.8	1.3
0.1	0.8	16.9	0.1	17.0	15.0
—	—	(15.5)	—	(15.5)	(14.4)
10.0	0.8	493.3	15.5	508.8	465.4
7.6	0.5	238.0	8.2	246.2	226.8
0.8	—	34.0	2.8	36.8	30.2
—	—	49.9	—	49.9	47.3
—	—	(15.5)	—	(15.5)	(14.4)
8.4	0.5	306.4	11.0	317.4	289.9
1.6	0.3	186.9	4.5	191.4	175.5
0.1	—	5.3	0.2	5.5	(17.3)
1.5	0.3	181.6	4.3	185.9	192.8
		12.1	0.2	12.3	5.0
		193.7	4.5	198.2	197.8
		86.9	2.6	89.5	91.3
		106.8	1.9	108.7	106.5

Exhibit 12.2   Severn Trent Water Report and Accounts 1988/89: extracts from Supplementary Current Cost Financial Information

Profit and Loss Account

Year ended 31 March 1989

	Note	1989 £m	1988 £m
Operating profit on historical cost basis		185.9	192.8
Current cost operating adjustments:-			
Depreciation		(38.4)	(39.0)
Current cost operating profit		147.5	153.8
Other income		12.3	5.0
Disposal of fixed assets adjustment		(0.3)	(0.8)
Current cost profit before interest payable		159.5	158.0
Interest payable		(89.5)	(91.3)
Current cost profit on ordinary activities		70.0	66.7
Extraordinary items	6	(2.8)	3.3
Current cost profit for the year		67.2	70.0

Balance Sheet
As at 31 March 1989

	Notes	1989 £m	1988 £m
Fixed assets			
Land drainage assets	4	54.4	53.4
Tangible assets	5	5,539.5	5,161.8
		5,593.9	5,215.2
Net current liabilities		(184.5)	(107.2)
Total assets less current liabilities		5,409.4	5,108.0
Creditors, amounts falling due after more than one year		744.9	810.7
Provisions for liabilities and charges		8.5	12.5
Reserves	6	4,656.0	4,284.8
		5,409.4	5,108.0

The movements on reserves are set out in note 6.

Notes to the Current Cost Statements

Year ended 31 March 1989

1   General

a   These supplementary statements have been prepared in accordance with the notification of accounts requirements made by the Secretary of State under paragraph 38(2) of Schedule 3 to the Water Act 1973. These supplementary statements have been prepared under the current cost convention having regard to the guidance contained in the publication entitled "Accounting for the effects of changing prices: A Handbook" issued by the Accounting Standards Committee. The current cost convention is not a system of accounting for general inflation, but allows for price changes specific to the Authority's operations.

b   The main accounting policies used are the same as those used in the historical cost main accounts with the exceptions set out below.

2   Principal current cost accounting policies and methods adopted

a   Tangible fixed assets

Properties

Properties are included in the Current Cost balance sheet at value to the business which is based on depreciated replacement costs. Replacement costs have been arrived at on the following bases:–

(i)   Specialised operational properties

The gross replacement cost of properties as at 1 April 1982 is arrived at using published or locally derived construction cost formulae or unit costs, indexed for the effects of subsequent price level changes. Additions since 1 April 1982 have been included at original cost indexed for the effects of changing price levels.

(ii)   Non-specialised operational properties

The net replacement cost of non-specialised operational properties is based on estimated open market value on an existing use basis.

Infrastructure assets:–

Infrastructure assets are stated in the current cost balance sheet at their value to the business, based on their estimated replacement costs. Replacement costs are calculated using estimated unit costs where appropriate.

As in the historical cost accounts, expenditure on maintaining the operating capability of the network is charged as an operating cost. Accordingly no depreciation is charged on infrastructure assets.

This represents a change in basis from prior years when, as in the historical cost accounts, certain infrastructure renewals expenditure was capitalised and depreciation was charged on infrastructure assets. Depreciation since 1 April 1984, being the earliest practicable date for implementation of the new policy, has been written back and past infrastructure renewals expenditure since that date has been restated in accordance with the new policy. Infrastructure assets at 1 April 1984 have been included at their current cost net book value at that date indexed for the effects of subsequent price level changes. Additions since 1 April 1984 have been included at replacement cost.

Other assets

Other assets, are included at estimated replacement cost less accumulated depreciation.

Land drainage assets

Land drainage assets include assets which do not normally fall to be replaced by the Authority; they are not, therefore subject to updating for inflation.

Stores

Stores are stated at their value to the business, based upon the estimated net current replacement cost, which is calculated by applying indices to reflect increases in purchase costs.

Cost of sales adjustment

This current cost adjustment has not been applied in the year ended 31 March 1989 as it is not material.

Monetary working capital adjustment

No adjustment in respect of monetary working capital has been made to reflect the impact of price changes on the amounts required to finance monetary working capital as it is not material.

Notes to the Current Cost Statements
continued

5a Tangible Fixed Assets
Analysis by asset type

	Specialised operational properties & structures £m	Non-specialised operational properties £m	Infrastructure assets £m	Plant, machinery & vehicles £m	Other £m	Total £m
Gross replacement cost						
Balance 1 April 1988	2,098.3	147.9	3,580.3	656.7	61.7	6,544.9
Additions	23.9	6.4	81.1	27.4	19.6	158.4
Disposals	(1.9)	(2.0)	—	(4.7)	(4.9)	(13.5)
Revaluation adjustment	106.6	17.4	200.2	25.6	1.5	351.3
Balance 31 March 1989	**2,226.9**	**169.7**	**3,861.6**	**705.0**	**77.9**	**7,041.1**
Depreciation						
Balance 1 April 1988	857.6	53.0	—	444.5	28.0	1,383.1
Provision for the year	30.7	2.0	—	31.3	10.0	74.0
Disposals	(1.9)	(0.3)	—	(4.5)	(4.9)	(11.6)
Revaluation adjustment	39.5	5.4	—	8.3	2.9	56.1
Balance 31 March 1989	**925.9**	**60.1**	**—**	**479.6**	**36.0**	**1,501.6**
Net Book Value						
At 31 March 1989	1,301.0	109.6	3,861.6	225.4	41.9	5,539.5
At 31 March 1988	1,240.7	94.9	3,580.3	212.2	33.7	5,161.8

Notes to 5a and 5b:-

(i)   Infrastructure assets at 1 April 1984 have been included in cost at their net book value at that date with subsequent additions at cost.

(ii) Specialised operational properties and structures principally comprise intake works, pumping stations, treatment works and boreholes.

(iii) Non-specialised operational properties comprise offices, depots, workshops, residential properties directly connected with water and sewerage services and land held for the purpose of protecting the wholesomeness of water supplies..

(iv) Infrastructure assets comprise mains and sewers, impounding and pumped raw water storage reservoirs, dams and sludge pipelines. Amounts brought forward at 1 April 1988 reflect the prior year adjustment as explained in note 1(f) (i) to the historical cost accounts. Infrastructure assets at 1 April 1988 comprise amounts of £3,339.7m and £240.6 million previously classified as mains and sewers and operational structures respectively.

(v)   Tangible fixed assets as at 31 March 1989 include £138.5 million in respect of assets in the course of construction which are not depreciated until commissioning.

(vi) External advisers have been appointed to establish on behalf of the Authority an open market value of the Authority's surplus and potentially surplus property. The results of this exercise are not yet known with sufficient certainty to include them in this supplementary current cost information.

Exhibit 12.3 Severn Trent Water Report and Accounts 1988/89: statement of performance against government controls

Statement of performance against government controls
For the year ended 31 March 1989

The members set out below the Authority's statement of performance against Government controls for the year ended 31 March 1989.

(a) Financial target on all services excluding land drainage
The Secretary of State for the Environment exercising his power under Section 29(2) of the Water Act 1973 required this Authority under the Water Authorities (Return on Assets) Order 1987 ("the Order") to discharge its functions with a view to achieving, during 1988/89, a rate of return of not less than 2.45% on the net current cost value of its assets (other than Land Drainage assets), at mid year values, as defined in the Order. The Order allowed the Authority to take into account the lesser of 0.2 per cent of the value of its net assets or the excess/shortfall brought forward from earlier years.

The following statement shows the performance of the Authority against its target:

	£m	% of Net Assets
Current cost operating profit (See note (i) below)	127.3	2.61
Amount brought forward from earlier years to count towards financial target	9.6	0.20
Adjusted amount for target purposes	136.9	2.81
Less:-		
Financial target (specified rate of return of 2.45%)	119.4	2.45
Cumulative over achievement	17.5	0.36
Current cost net asset value at 1 April 1988 (see note ii)	4,774.0	
Current cost net asset value at 31 March 1989	4,976.6	
Mean current cost net asset value 1988/89	4,875.3	

Accordingly the Authority has met its Financial Target. The monetary amount equivalent to the over-achievement of 0.36% is £17.5m.

Notes
(i) The current cost operating profit and current cost net asset values included in the above statement are different from the figures included in the Authority's 1988/89 Annual Accounts ("the Accounts").

(ii) The accounting policy in respect of infrastructure assets was changed during the year and the results and state of affairs of the Authority for the financial year 1988/89 have been included in the Accounts in accordance with the new policy. Comparative amounts in respect of the financial year 1987/88 and accumulated reserves as at 1 April 1987 have also been restated in the Accounts.

The rate of return required to be earned by the Authority and specified under the Water Authorities (Return on Assets) Order 1987 was determined having regard to the accounting policy previously used by the Authority. In order to assess the Authority's performance against the financial target the above statement includes current cost supplementary information for 1987/88 and 1988/89 based on the accounting policy previously in use.

(b) **External financing limit (all services)**

The external financing limit is notified to the Authority by the Department of the Environment and represents the capital requirements financed externally by borrowing, finance leases and certain Government grants.

	£m
Notified limit for 1988/89: Net repayment	(16.5)
Actual external finance for 1988/89.	(16.6)

(c) **Performance aims**

Performance aims are agreed between the Department of the Environment and Water Authorities as medium term targets for efficiency improvements. A sign-post aim was agreed for 1988/89 at 1985/86 prices, on total operating costs excluding depreciation, infrastructure renewals expenditure and exceptional items.

The Authority's Performance Aim achievement against sign-post in 1988/89 was as follows:

	1988/89 £m
Performance Aim sign-post	198.5
Actual achievement	194.4

This statement of performance against Government controls was approved by the Authority on 25 July 1989.

J G Bellak
Chairman

S M Larnder
Director of Finance

Case 13
University Annual Accounts

OBJECTIVES

1. To examine a set of university accounts and explore the particular features of a university accounting system.
2. To assess the information content of university accounts.
3. To consider the problems in attempting to assess university performance through a set of annual accounts.

MATERIALS

1. University of Essex Financial Statements 1989/90, pp. 2–16, (Exhibit 13.1).
2. Extracts from University of Essex Financial Statements 1988/89:

   (a) Statement of Accounting Policies (Fixed Assets) (Exhibit 13.2).
   (b) Wivenhoe Park Conference Centre, Income and Expenditure Account (Exhibit 13.3).

3. Extracts from *Statement of Recommended Practice: Accounting in UK Universities* (Committee of Vice-Chancellors and Principals, 1989), paragraphs 4–7, 27–51 (Exhibit 13.4).

INTRODUCTION

University accounting is considered in this book of case studies by virtue of the fact that a large part of university funding is allocated by the Department of Education and Science. Consequently, any pressure to reduce public expenditure generally is likely to affect the university sector.

The main influence on university financial reporting is a statement of recommended practice (SORP), *Accounting in UK Universities*, which was issued by the Committee of Vice-Chancellors and Principals (CVCP) in 1989. This document has been approved by the Accounting Standards Committee as representing approved recommended accounting practice for universities in the UK.

In 1982 the University Grants Committee had encouraged the introduction of more uniform accounting treatment in university financial reports. Hilton (1981) reviewed financial reporting by universities and suggested there was a need for an accounting standard specific to universities, and stated that the 'overwhelming impression one gains from even a cursory study of University accounts is one of variety' (ibid., p. 23). Some of the inconsistencies to which he referred included different treatment of assets and liabilities, including different methods for valuing land and buildings, different valuation policies for securities and the fact that a majority of universities did not provide a statement of source and application of funds.

The 1989 SORP is clearly intended to answer such criticisms and universities are expected to conform to the recommended practice in preparing their accounts for 1989/90 and subsequent financial years. One of the implicit goals of the SORP is to bring greater uniformity to the preparation and presentation of university accounts. The SORP states that the objectives of published financial statements should be governed by the needs of the potential users who are listed in paragraph 5 (see Exhibit 13.4). The SORP then goes on to state that 'these user groups may have differing needs in detail but certain key elements including the general need for accountability are common to all'. Paragraph 6 of the SORP then lists seven types of information which would be consistent with the needs of the users (see Exhibit 13.4).

Part 3 of the SORP (paragraphs 27 to 51 inclusive) details the scope of the recommendations (see Exhibit 13.4). The reports and financial statements are listed in paragraph 30. Paragraphs 34 and 35 cover the statement of accounting policies; paragraphs 36 to 41 the income and expenditure account; and paragraphs 42 to 48 the statement of financial position. The remaining paragraphs deal with the statement of source and application of funds, notes to the accounts and (where applicable) consolidated financial statements.

Items of particular note in the income and expenditure account are sections (iii) to (v) in paragraph 40. These sections indicate that capital expenditure on land and buildings financed by way of a loan should be reduced in line with repayment of principal on the loan. This accounting treatment is similar to that used by local authorities (see Case 8, Local Authority Capital Accounting). Section (v) states that 'any other capital expenditure, including equipment and furniture financed from general funds should be written off in full in the period of account'. As regards the statement of financial positions, paragraphs 43 and 44 are of particular interest with respect to valuation of land and buildings, and investments.

ANALYSIS

Reductions in university funding commencing in 1981 coupled with reviews carried out by the University Grants Committee (UGC) have tended to focus attention on the financial health of universities. These exercises are being continued by the UGC's successor from 1989, the Universities Funding Council (UFC).

The use of financial statements can be divided between *stewardship* purposes and *performance evaluation* purposes. Stewardship includes ensuring that resources have been managed in the way originally intended and that the organization is able to meet its continuing obligations.

Performance evaluation, by contrast, encompasses the idea of 'how well' the organization fared using the resources at its disposal. Judgements about stewardship can normally be made by looking at an organization in isolation and deciding, on the facts, the quality of stewardship. Performance evaluation, however, is normally a relative concept and requires a benchmark. 'Good' or 'bad' performance is usually judged in the light of performance by similar organizations.

One activity specifically referred to in the 1988/89 accounts was the Wivenhoe Park Conference Centre, for which a separate income and expenditure account was provided (see Exhibit 13.3). The conference centre is presumably expected to be self-financing yet, even in this fairly well defined area of activity, there are likely to be problems in measuring performance. One of the problems to be overcome would be finding a suitable capital base to provide a ratio equivalent to 'return on capital employed'.

Assessing performance in areas of academic activity is likely to prove an even more difficult task. It may be relatively easy for universities to produce graduates at a lower unit cost and therefore argue that the universities are thereby more efficient. However, a reduction in resources could mean that the quality of degree awards has suffered. Also, it could indicate a shift from research time to teaching, in which case research will have suffered.

In the university sector there is an emphasis on pure as opposed to applied research. The benefits of pure research and indications of research output can realistically be gained only by looking at evidence such as publications in academic journals, or citations in the relevant literature. Even so, the ultimate results of pure research may not be known until many years later. Given that research performance is a major factor in how universities believe they should be judged, it is difficult to see how focusing on a single year's 'results' could provide the basis for a reliable performance indicator. It may be the case that, in the future, trend data over a number of years will become increasingly important.

QUESTIONS

1. From paragraph 6 of Exhibit 13.4, classify the seven information categories according to whether they are provided to meet *stewardship* purposes or *performance measurement* purposes.

2. From the financial statements and notes to the accounts, explain how the following items have been valued:

   (a) land;
   (b) buildings;
   (c) computer hardware;
   (d) library books.

3. What problems are likely to arise in trying to assess the performance of Wivenhoe Park Conference Centre? In answering this question, discuss the treatment in the 1988/89 income and expenditure account of the following items:

	£
(a) Premises	119,769
(b) Contribution in lieu of rent	29,500

4. Would it be appropriate to calculate surplus/net assets as a measure of performance and use this for comparisons over time and between different universities? If not, why not?
5. To what extent is the SORP likely to promote greater uniformity in reporting treatment?

FURTHER READING

Cave, M., Kogan, M. and Hanney, S. (1989) Performance measurement in higher education, *Public Money and Management*, Spring, pp. 11–16.

Gray, R. and Haslam, J. (1990) External reporting by UK universities: an exploratory study of accounting change, *Financial Accountability and Management*, Spring, pp. 51–72.

Hilton, K. (1981) Are university accounts any use?, *British Accounting Review*, Autumn, pp. 21–32.

Tomkins, C. (1987) *Achieving Economy, Efficiency and Effectiveness in the Public Sector*, Institute of Chartered Accountants of Scotland, Edinburgh, pp. 36–9.

Exhibit 13.1 University of Essex Financial Statements 1989/90, pp. 2–16

TREASURER'S REPORT

The Financial Statements for the year ended 31 July 1990 are presented in the format required by the Statement of Recommended Accounting Practice in UK Universities which was prepared by the Committee of Vice-Chancellors and Principals of the Universities of the United Kingdom (CVCP) and approved and franked by the Accounting Standards Committee in May 1989. This new regime represents a major change in both presentation and the compilation of figures in the Financial Statements and the comparative figures for 1988/89 have been restated so as to provide a consistent approach between the two years. The newly prescribed Statement of Recommended Accounting Practice will provide a uniform approach to accounts presentation by all Universities in the United Kingdom thereby providing more reliable information at a national level and facilitating meaningful comparisons between Institutions.

All sources of income and all expenditure are, under the Statement of Recommended Accounting Practice, reflected in the Income and Expenditure Account rather than being dealt with in subsidiary accounts as was past practice. Examples of this are income and expenditure on residences and catering operations and the three University endowment funds. The new treatment provides a clearer picture of the total activities of the University and is welcomed.

The Financial Statements for 1989/90 show a surplus of income over expenditure of £62,123 (as compared to a surplus of £51,502 for the previous year) after making transfers to reserves of £683,584. (£533,230 for 1988/89).

Total expenditure increased from £26,809,767 in 1988/89 to £31,296,819 in 1989/90. Expenditure in academic departments has increased by 11% over the previous year, reflecting the University's commitment to real growth in academic areas. The surplus in respect of residences and catering operations for the current year of £99,314 has enabled a transfer to reserves of £100,000 to be made. This reserve will be utilised towards the capital cost of constructing additional student accommodation on campus. A comparison of the Income and Expenditure figures between 1989/90 and 1988/89 given on the Income and Expenditure Account on page 5 shows that the proportion of total income received from Parliamentary grants has again fallen. As in past recent years this has been caused by total income being enhanced by increases in income from research grants and contracts and other general income.

The Statement of Financial Position in general terms reflects the University's current financial strength and prudent financial management over its lifetime and enables members of the University to look to the future with confidence.

Finally, I welcome Mr Jon Gorringe as the University's new Director of Finance who was appointed on 1 October 1990. He succeeds Mr Harry Ford who has retired after eleven years service and to whom the University owes a great deal for the sound financial position which it now enjoys.

R.D. Hart
Treasurer

REPORT OF THE AUDITORS TO THE COUNCIL OF THE UNIVERSITY OF ESSEX

We have audited the financial statements on pages 3 to 16 in accordance with Auditing Standards.

In our opinion the financial statements give a true and fair view of the state of affairs of the University at 31 July 1990 and of its income and expenditure and source and application of funds for the year then ended.

We are also of the opinion that monies expended during the year out of non-recurrent grants have been properly applied to the purposes for which the grants were received.

SCRUTTON BLAND
Chartered Accountants
Sir Isaac's Walk
Colchester

28 November 1990

Statement of Accounting Policies

1. **Basis of Accounting**

    The financial statements have been prepared in conformity with the Statement of Recommended Accounting Practice in UK Universities franked by the Accounting Standards Committee. The statements relate to the total activities of the University as a corporate entity and follow a standard classification. The comparative figures have been restated where appropriate.

2. **Fixed Assets**

    Land and buildings are shown at historical cost less, in the case of buildings, a provision for depreciation. Expenditure on equipment and furniture is written off in full in the period of account.

3. **Depreciation**

    Depreciation on buildings has been provided using the straight line method at a rate of 2% per annum from 1 August 1988.

4. **Investments**

    Investments are included at cost and their market value at 31 July 1990 is shown by way of note.

5. **Stocks**

    Stocks for resale and other stocks of material value are included at the lower of cost and net realisable value.

6. **Restricted Income and Associated Expenditure**

    Restricted income is defined in the Statement of Recommended Accounting Practice in UK Universities as any income which is for specific purposes designated by the grantor or donor and can only be applied to those specific purposes. In accordance with recommended practice, restricted income and associated expenditure have been dealt with under the accruals concept so that they are matched in the income and expenditure account.

7. **Repairs and Maintenance**

    An annual provision is made for long-term maintenance on the basis of specific items in a long-term maintenance plan which is reviewed periodically. The sum set aside each year is intended to cover the top priorities of the University and spread the cost over a reasonable period. It does not necessarily meet the total requirements for long-term expenditure.

8. **Fabric and Furnishings**

    An annual provision is made for the upkeep of fabric and furnishings in student accommodation and catering outlets designed to spread the cost of refurbishment over a reasonable period.

9. **Pension Costs**

    Pension costs are assessed in accordance with the advice of the actuary, based on the latest actuarial valuation of the Scheme, and are accounted for on the basis of charging the cost of providing pensions over the period during which the University benefits from the employees' services. Unless it is considered prudent to recognise deficiencies over a shorter period, variations from regular cost are spread over the expected average remaining working lifetime of Members of the Scheme after making suitable allowances for future withdrawals.

10. **Taxation**

    The University is a charity with Income Tax exempt status. Except for its trading undertakings and certain consultancy and research activities, the University is wholly liable for Value Added Tax which is included under the various relevant expenditure heads.

Income and Expenditure Account for Year Ending 31 July 1990

	Note	1990 £	1989 £
Income			
Grants from Universities Funding Council	1	13,583,501	12,204,621
Contribution to Depreciation of Buildings		346,315	342,342
Academic Fees and Support Grants	2	6,498,771	5,211,478
Endowments and Donations	3	294,465	285,119
Computer Board Grants	1	164,302	205,975
Residences and Catering Operations	7	3,630,050	3,149,330
Other General Income	4	1,563,043	1,221,712
Research Grants and Contracts	5	4,742,254	3,692,100
Other Services Rendered	6	1,219,825	1,081,822
		32,042,526	27,394,499
Expenditure			
Academic Departments	8	10,458,620	9,431,553
Academic Services	9	2,262,727	2,110,675
General Educational Expenditure	10	410,647	352,161
Maintenance of Premises	11	3,151,841	3,130,837
Administration and Central Services	12	1,964,836	1,431,333
Student and Staff Facilities and Amenities	13	822,132	682,114
Residences and Catering Operations	7	3,530,736	3,158,081
Pensions	14	1,374,725	494,977
Depreciation of Buildings		346,315	342,342
Equipment and Furniture	15	1,124,388	878,276
Miscellaneous Expenditure	16	246,987	296,920
Research Grants and Contracts	5	4,505,707	3,504,641
Other Services Rendered	6	1,097,158	995,857
		31,296,819	26,809,767
Surplus/(Deficit) for Year		745,707	584,732
Transfers from (to) Reserves	17	(683,584)	(533,230)
Surplus/(Deficit) after Transfers		62,123	51,502

Statement of Financial Position at 31 July 1990

	Note	1990 £	1989 £
Land and Buildings	18	17,243,416	17,063,537
Long Term Investments	19	2,154,513	2,092,471
Net Current Assets	20	10,025,087	9,319,679
		29,423,016	28,475,687
Less: Provisions	21	2,537,108	2,361,466
Long Term Liabilities	22	1,117,478	1,153,078
Net Assets Total		25,768,430	24,961,143
Capital	23	15,977,058	15,871,103
Restricted Funds			
Specific Endowments	24	3,092,537	2,897,375
Total Restricted Funds		3,092,537	2,897,375
General Funds			
General Endowments	24	369,573	330,729
Reserves	25	6,329,262	5,861,936
Total General Funds		6,698,835	6,192,665
Total Funds		25,768,430	24,961,143

R.D. HART, Treasurer

J.P. GORRINGE, Director of Finance

28 November 1990

Statement of Source and Application of Funds for Year Ending 31 July 1990

	1990 £	1989 £
Capital		
Government Grants	—	35,001
Reserves	239,537	125,176
Loans Repaid	43,682	82,207
Research Councils	174,259	—
Other Benefactions	1,958	—
Re-allocation from previous years	(7,166)	—
	452,270	242,384
Expenditure on Land and Buildings	(526,194)	(169,214)
	(73,924)	73,170
Restricted Funds		
Specific Endowments		
Revenue for year	324,754	426,339
Expended during year	(129,592)	(171,454)
Invested during year	(64,751)	(34,273)
	130,411	220,612
General Funds		
General Endowments		
Revenue for year	73,694	64,284
Expended during year	(34,850)	(34,486)
Investments realised during year	2,709	(2,052)
	41,553	27,746
Reserves		
Surplus before transfers	745,707	584,732
Utilised for Land and Buildings	(239,537)	(125,176)
Transferred to General Endowment	(38,844)	(29,798)
	467,326	429,758
Total Funds	565,366	751,286
Increase in Provisions	175,642	(10,583)
Reduction in Long Term Liabilities	(35,600)	(45,674)
	705,408	695,029
Movements in Working Capital		
Stocks	(130,476)	37,749
Debtors and Payments in Advance	145,011	766,775
Creditors, Accruals and Prepaid income	(1,511,480)	(551,427)
	(1,496,945)	253,097
Movements in net liquid funds		
Building Society Deposit	465,549	(1,570,388)
Bank Deposits	1,367,711	1,792,253
Bank and Cash Balances	369,093	220,067
	705,408	695,029

Notes to the Financial Statements

1. Government Grants

1990

	Received £	Included in Income £	Included in Capital £	Unpaid/ (Prepaid) £
UFC Basic Recurrent Grant	10,765,088	10,705,921	—	—
UFC Specific Grants:				
Equipment and Furniture	866,280	670,820	—	324,760
Repairs and Maintenance	314,000	64,000	—	(250,000)
Library	25,000	25,000	—	—
Engineering and Technology Programme	104,000	104,000	—	—
In-Service Teacher Education and Training (INSET)	8,000	7,321	—	(679)
Professional, Industrial and Commercial Updating (PICKUP)	46,000	13,890	—	(32,110)
Capital in Recurrent	60,000	60,000	—	—
New Academic Appointment Scheme (NAAS)	115,000	115,000	—	—
Local Authority Rates	492,150	555,161	—	(330,131)
Restructuring	1,121,118	1,262,388	—	176,439
Total Grants from the UFC	13,916,636	13,583,501	—	(111,721)
Computer Board Recurrent Grant	164,302	164,302	—	—
Computer Board Equipment Grant	—	—	—	—
	14,080,938	13,747,803	—	(111,721)

1989

	Received £	Included in Income £	Included in Capital £	Unpaid/ (Prepaid) £
UFC Basic Recurrent Grant	9,951,099	9,943,933	—	59,167
UFC Specific Grants:				
Equipment and Furniture	421,262	707,998	—	520,220
Library	25,000	25,000	—	—
Engineering and Technology Programme	103,000	103,000	—	—
In-Service Teacher Education and Training (INSET)	7,000	7,000	—	—
Professional, Industrial and Commercial Updating (PICKUP)	30,000	30,000	—	—
Management and Administrative Computing (MAC)	18,400	18,400	—	—
Capital in Recurrent	84,000	84,000	—	—
Local Authority Rates	828,371	828,371	—	(393,142)
Restructuring	634,900	456,919	—	35,169
Total Grants from the UFC	12,103,032	12,204,621	—	221,414
Computer Board Recurrent Grant	205,975	205,975	—	—
Computer Board Equipment Grant	—	—	—	—
	12,309,007	12,410,596	—	221,414

Notes to the Financial Statements (continued)	1990	1989
	£	£
2. Academic Fees and Support Grants		
From Students charged Home Fees	2,522,770	1,853,406
From Students charged Overseas and Other Fees	2,974,902	2,746,086
Part time Degree and Diploma Course Fees	271,795	113,825
Research Training Support Grants	31,885	25,465
Short Courses and other Fees	697,419	472,696
	6,498,771	5,211,478
3. Endowments and Donations		
General Endowment Income	38,694	34,486
Specific Endowment Income	151,338	171,454
Donations and Subscriptions	104,433	79,179
	294,465	285,119
4. Other General Income		
Interest on Short-Term Investments	1,356,926	1,017,163
University Health Service	10,690	5,954
Athletics Facility	64,273	59,972
Rents	32,621	31,267
Day Nursery	70,240	70,017
Miscellaneous	28,293	37,339
	1,563,043	1,221,712
5. Research Grants and Contracts — Income		
Research Councils	2,724,620	1,658,225
UK Charities	481,317	344,045
UK Central Government Bodies	531,021	501,813
UK Local Authorities and Public Bodies	110,464	126,733
UK Industry and Commerce	605,649	796,359
Overseas Bodies	289,183	264,925
	4,742,254	3,692,100
Research Grants and Contracts — Expenditure		
Research Councils	2,679,070	1,644,007
UK Charities	481,317	344,045
UK Central Government Bodies	424,089	415,934
UK Local Authorities and Public Bodies	96,364	110,259
UK Industry and Commerce	555,462	740,849
Overseas Bodies	269,405	249,547
	4,505,707	3,504,641
6. Other Services Rendered — Income		
Other Services Rendered	401,828	333,813
Wivenhoe Park Conference Centre	817,997	748,009
	1,219,825	1,081,822
Other Services Rendered — Expenditure		
Other Services Rendered	391,818	335,813
Wivenhoe Park Conference Centre	705,340	660,044
	1,097,158	995,857

Notes to the Financial Statements (continued)	1990	1989
	£	£

7. Residences and Catering Operations
Income
1) Residences
  University owned properties

Termly Lodgings and Rents	1,381,824	1,316,182
Vacation, Conference and other lettings	217,563	144,636
Other	1,522	73,275

  University administered properties

Termly Lodgings and Rents	591,555	399,490
Other	11,010	6,810
	2,203,474	1,940,393

2) Catering Services

Income	973,486	825,732

3) Retail Services

Income	453,090	383,205
	3,630,050	3,149,330

Expenditure
1) Residences

Premises	1,793,645	1,499,431
Salaries, Wages and Administration	238,239	263,241
Loan Charges	86,519	127,682
Other Expenditure	9,700	12,154
	2,128,103	1,902,508

2) Catering Services

Cost of Sales	362,368	323,892
Salaries, Wages and Administration	344,287	318,869
Premises	159,359	193,940
Other Expenditure	84,492	36,493
	950,506	873,194

3) Retail Services

Cost of Sales	373,043	304,954
Salaries, Wages and Administration	63,341	51,785
Premises	13,543	25,215
Other Expenditure	2,200	425
	452,127	382,379

Total Expenditure	3,530,736	3,158,081
Operating Surplus/(Deficit) for the year	99,314	(8,751)

8. Academic Departments
Salary Costs

Academic Staff	7,516,758	6,911,845
Academic Related Staff	173,526	77,401
Technical Staff	710,405	767,931
Secretarial and Clerical Staff	426,906	366,835
Total Salaries	8,827,595	8,124,012
Departmental expenses	680,635	607,861
Short Courses and Other Academic Expenditure	950,390	699,680
	10,458,620	9,431,553

Notes to the Financial Statements (continued)	1990	1989
	£	£
9. Academic Services		
Library	1,115,366	995,742
Computing Service	616,701	695,473
Educational Technology	81,534	80,200
Data Archive	94,811	55,057
Radiation Protection	(1,233)	2,631
Continuing Education	57,145	38,408
Industrial Liaison	45,156	31,251
Admissions and Schools of Study	251,421	211,913
Other Expenditure	1,826	—
	2,262,727	2,110,675
10. General Educational Expenditure		
Examinations	54,387	29,935
Universities Central Council on Admissions	17,370	16,578
Subscriptions and Donations	11,345	40,390
Arts	132,145	110,066
Overseas Recruitment	116,249	98,312
Fellowships and Prizes	35,330	12,813
Other Educational Expenditure	43,821	44,067
	410,647	352,161
11. Maintenance of Premises		
Rates	555,178	828,371
Insurance	89,060	87,452
Heat, Light, Power and Water	456,069	410,934
Cleaning	353,348	397,954
Security	313,297	299,466
Maintenance of Buildings and Grounds	763,619	634,276
Provision for Long-Term Maintenance	601,750	290,740
Telephones	19,520	181,644
	3,151,841	3,130,837
12. Administration and Central Services		
Salaries	1,221,286	1,031,216
Other Expenses	743,550	400,117
	1,964,836	1,431,333
13. Student and Staff Facilities and Amenities		
Student Union Subvention	239,500	217,000
Health Service	45,053	38,430
Dean of Students	111,409	111,761
Careers Advisory Service	92,868	83,387
Physical Recreation	163,384	141,610
Day Nursery	85,890	85,267
Other Expenses	84,028	4,659
	822,132	682,114

Notes to the Financial Statements (continued)	1990	1989
	£	£

14. Pensions

Pensions Increase	—	9,221
Premature Retirement Compensation Scheme	1,374,725	485,756
	1,374,725	494,977

15. Equipment and Furniture

Equipment	1,065,845	818,751
Furniture	58,543	59,525
	1,124,388	878,276

16. Miscellaneous Expenditure

Hospitality	11,161	42,426
Consultants Fees	29,228	55,651
Provision for Bad Debts	21,400	105,000
Miscellaneous Expenditure	185,198	93,843
	246,987	296,920

17. Transfer from(to) Reserves

General Reserve	—	(83,468)
Early Retirement	144,888	8,079
Residences	(142,109)	(114,130)
Wivenhoe Park Conference Centre	(7,857)	(17,964)
Furniture and Equipment Fund	66,089	62,103
Capital ex Recurrent	(736,000)	(365,000)
Other Reserves	30,249	(22,850)
	(644,740)	(533,230)
Transfer to other Funds	(38,844)	—
	(683,584)	(533,230)

18. Land and Buildings

	Cost As at 31 July 1989 £	Added During Year £	Cost As at 31 July 1990 £	Accumulated Depreciation £	Net Book Value As at 31 July 1990 £
Freehold Properties					
Land	281,615	—	281,615	—	281,615
Buildings	17,124,264	526,194	17,650,458	(688,657)	16,961,801
	17,405,879	526,194	17,932,073	(688,657)	17,243,416

Notes to the Financial Statements (continued)	1990	1989
	£	£

19. Long Term Investments

General Funds
Foundation, Research and Development Fund — Home loans to staff

	7,040	9,749

Restricted Funds
Research Endowment Fund —
Quoted Equities, fixed interest debentures
and Government stocks at cost
(Market value £2,840,191)

	1,901,952	1,832,533

Trust Fund — Quoted Equities and
Government stock at Market Value 17
April 1964 with additions at cost —
(Market value £440,861)

	245,521	250,189
	2,154,513	2,092,471

20. Net Current Assets

1) Current Assets

	1990	1989
Stocks	435,100	565,576
Debtors and Prepayments	4,319,470	4,174,459
Building Society Deposits	4,647,161	4,181,612
Bank Deposits	5,409,964	4,042,253
Bank and Cash Balances	695,023	325,930
	15,506,718	13,289,830

2) Current Liabilities

	1990	1989
Prepaid Income	2,900,273	2,207,446
Creditors and Accruals	2,581,358	1,762,705
	5,481,631	3,970,151
Net Current Assets	10,025,087	9,319,679

21. Provisions

	As at 31 July 1989	Provided during Year	Expenditure during Year	As at 31 July 1990
	£	£	£	£
Long Term Maintenance				
-General	838,249	540,700	270,528	1,108,421
-Catering and Other Services	925,697	614,361	703,576	836,482
Replacement of Vehicles and Equipment	597,520	362,050	367,365	592,205
	2,361,466	1,517,111	1,341,469	2,537,108

22. Long Term Liabilities

Loans outstanding

	1990	1989
Repayable between 1 and 5 years	227,512	217,752
Repayable after 5 years	889,966	935,326
	1,117,478	1,153,078

Notes to the Financial Statements (continued)

	£
23. Capital	
At 31 July 1989	16,213,445
UFC Grants — Re-allocation from previous years	(7,166)
Additions during year	
Research Council	174,259
Reserves	239,537
Other Benefactions	1,958
Loan Repayments	43,682
	16,665,715
Less: Accumulated Contribution to Income and Expenditure Account in respect of Depreciation	688,657
At 31 July 1990	15,977,058

24. Endowment Funds

	Specific Endowments			General Endowments
	Research Endowment Fund	Trust Fund	Total Specific Endowments	Foundation Research & Development Fund
	£	£	£	£
Balance of fund at 31 July 1989	2,598,521	298,854	2,897,375	330,729
Movement in year				
Income				
Interest	86,017	4,611	90,628	38,694
Dividends	151,466	26,339	177,805	—
Net Profit on Sale of Investments	51,646	4,675	56,321	—
Contribution from Wivenhoe Park Conference Centre				35,000
	289,129	35,625	324,754	73,694
Expenditure				
Departmental Expenditure	97,743		97,743	
Consultants Fees	16,366		16,366	
Prizes, Lectures and Studentships		15,483	15,483	
Contribution to: Short Courses				2,100
Day Nursery				15,250
Wivenhoe Park Conference Centre Maintenance				17,500
	114,109	15,483	129,592	34,850
Net Movement in Year	175,020	20,142	195,162	38,844
Balance of fund at 31 July 1990	2,773,541	318,996	3,092,537	369,573

Notes to the Financial Statements (continued)

25. Reserves

	As at 31 July 1989 £	Transfers to (from) reserves during Year £	Expenditure on Land and Buildings during Year £	As at 31 July 1990 £
Specific Reserves				
Early Retirement	972,817	(144,888)		827,929
Residences	79,211	142,109	(50,000)	171,320
Wivenhoe Park Conference Centre	75,580	7,857		83,437
Furniture and Equipment Fund	330,543	(66,089)		264,454
Capital Ex Recurrent	786,224	736,000	(189,537)	1,332,687
Pension Schemes	1,674,208	—		1,674,208
Other Specific Reserves	595,738	(30,249)		565,489
	4,514,321	644,740	(239,537)	4,919,524
General Reserves				
Accumulated Surplus at 31 July 1989	1,347,615			1,347,615
Add: Surplus for year after transfers		62,123		62,123
	1,347,615	62,123		1,409,738
Total Reserves	5,861,936	706,863	(239,537)	6,329,262

26. Capital Commitments

Outstanding Capital Commitments in respect of contracts entered into for building work are estimated to be £4,200,000 at 31 July 1990. This relates to new student residential accommodation and a new building to accommodate the Inter Disciplinary Research Centre.

27. Analysis of Fund Balances between the Net Assets

	Land and Buildings £	Long Term Investments £	Net Current Assets £	Provisions & Long Term Liabilities £	Total Funds £
Capital	16,086,839		(109,781)		15,977,058
Restricted Funds		2,147,473	945,064		3,092,537
General Endowments		7,040	362,533		369,573
Reserves			8,866,370	(2,537,108)	6,329,262
Financing term loans	1,156,577		(39,099)	(1,117,478)	
Net Assets Total	17,243,416	2,154,513	10,025,087	(3,654,586)	25,768,430

Notes to the Financial Statements (continued)

28. Pension Costs

The University contributes to four pension schemes. These are set up under separate trust funds and the assets of the schemes are therefore held separately from those of the University.

The four schemes are as follows:

Name	Type of Scheme
Universities Superannuation Scheme (USS)	Defined Benefit
Essex County Scheme	Defined Benefit
University of Essex Pension & Life Assurance Scheme	Defined Benefit
Federated Superannuation Scheme for Universities (FSSU)	Defined Contribution

a) Universities Superannuation Scheme

The latest actuarial valuation of the Scheme was at 31 March 1987. The assumptions which have the most significant effect on the results of the valuation are those relating to the rate of return on investments and the rates of increase in salary and pensions. It was assumed that the investment return would be 8½% per annum, that salary scale increases would be 6½% per annum and that pensions would increase by 5% per annum.

At the date of the last actuarial valuation, which was carried out using the aggregate method, the market value of the assets of the Scheme was £3,783 million and the actuarial value of the assets was sufficient to cover 81% of the benefits which had accrued to Members after allowing for expected future increase in earnings. The level of contributions paid by the employing Institutions takes into account this actuarial deficiency. The present rates of contribution which have operated since 1 April 1983 are: USS — Member 6% of salary less £100. University 18.55% of salary less £100. USDPS — Members 0.35% of salary less £100. University nil.

b) Essex County Scheme

Present rates of contribution are 0.25% by the University and 5% or 6% by members of staff. An actuarial valuation is carried out every five years. The last such valuation as at March 1989 showed an actuarial surplus.

c) University of Essex Pension and Life Assurance Scheme

Present rates of contribution are 12% by the University and 5% by members of staff. An actuarial valuation is carried out every three years. The last such valuation as at April 1990 showed an actuarial surplus.

The pension costs of the four schemes charged in the University's accounts in 1989/90 were £1,633,302.

Exhibit 13.2 Extract from University of Essex Financial Statements 1988/89: Statement of Accounting Policies, Fixed Assets

Fixed Assets

(a) Land and buildings are included at their cost to the University.
(b) The initial cost of provision of furniture and equipment is capitalized, and replacements are either financed from the Furniture and Equipment Fund or charged to Revenue.
(c) No monetary value has been attributed to assets donated to the University other than those comprising cash and securities.
(d) No depreciation is provided in respect of fixed assets.
(e) Claims by contractors in respect of capital expenditure on buildings are not brought into the financial statements until they have been agreed and paid.

Exhibit 13.3 Extract from University of Essex Financial Statements 1988/89: Wivenhoe Park Conference Centre, Income and Expenditure Account

Wivenhoe Park Conference Centre				
Income and Expenditure Account for the year ended 31 July 1989				
	1988-89		**1987-88**	
	£	£	£	£
Income		748,009		598,400
Less Expenditure				
Purchases/Consumables	147,441		112,237	
Salaries, Wages and Administration	273,069		239,478	
Premises	119,769		227,155	
Contribution in lieu of rent	29,500		25,300	
Loan Charges	118,967		55,931	
Other	20,509		3,025	
		709,255		663,126
Surplus/(Deficit) for year		38,754		(64,726)
Uncommitted balance brought forward				
in respect of previous years surpluses		58,012		85,606
Contribution to General Account		(30,000)		(15,000)
Transfers (to) from Specific Funds		8,814		52,132
Balance carried forward to				
Balance Sheet (note 4)		75,580		58,012

Exhibit 13.4 Extracts from *Statement of Recommended Practice: Accounting in UK Universities* (Committee of Vice-Chancellors and Principals, 1989)

STATUS

4.   Universities have charitable status but they form a separate identifiable group with special characteristics and are not therefore included within the scope of SORP 2 ACCOUNTING BY CHARITIES. So far as it is relevant to university activities standard accounting practice as set out in Statements of Standard Accounting Practice and Statements of Recommended Practice issued by the Accounting Standards Committee is applicable to universities' financial statements.

OBJECTIVES OF UNIVERSITIES' FINANCIAL STATEMENTS

5.   The objectives of published financial statements should be governed by the needs of potential users. The main groups of users of universities' accounts are considered to be :-

   i)   The governing bodies of the institutions themselves.

   ii)   The Government including the UGC, Department of Education and Science, other government departments and Parliament.

   iii)   The employees.

   iv)   The students.

   v)   The alumni.

   vi)   Other universities, other institutions of higher education, schools and industry.

   vii)   The loan/creditor group.

   viii)   Donors and benefactors.

   ix)   The public.

6.   These user groups may have differing needs in detail but certain key elements including the general need for accountability are common to all. The main objectives of the financial statements are therefore considered to be the provision of the following information to users of the accounts :-

   i)   The general financial activity of the university in sufficient detail for an understanding of its affairs.

   ii)   The income from all sources within the period of the accounts.

   iii)   The expenditure on teaching and research and other activities and how it has been funded from the income.

   iv)   The assets and liabilities of the university classified in suitable form.

v) The significance and implications for the financial position of the university of any self-financing, commercial or quasi-commercial activities which are incidental to the main purposes of teaching and general research.

vi) Any known or probable major developments which might significantly affect the financial position of the university.

vii) How the university is performing financially including the adequacy of its working capital, its practical solvency or insolvency, and its investment performance.

7. These main objectives while not comprehensive should influence the scope and broad presentation of the published statements and they imply a need for comparability between the published statements of different universities. The accounting practice recommended in this statement has been determined in the light of these objectives.

PART 3 - RECOMMENDED PRACTICE

THE SCOPE OF THE RECOMMENDATIONS

27.   These recommendations are intended to be applicable to all universities in the United Kingdom. They need not be applied to immaterial items. Any departure   from the recommendations should be disclosed in the statement of accounting policies.

REPORTS AND FINANCIAL STATEMENTS

28.   These should account for income from all sources and show how it has been expended on the various purposes of the university in a manner which ensures reasonable consistency between institutions and assists in the process of performance measurement. They should also explain the overall financial position of the university in relation to its assets and liabilities, including its practical solvency and its investment performance.

29.   The financial statements, and subject to paragraph 51, the consolidated financial statements, should be prepared in such a manner and in sufficient detail so as to give a true and fair view of the income and expenditure for the year and a true and fair view of the financial position as at the end of the year.

30.   The reports and financial statements should comprise the following:-

     A.   A Treasurer's report or equivalent.

     B.   A statement of accounting policies.

     C.   An income and expenditure account.

     D.   A statement of financial position.

     E.   A statement of source and application of funds.

     F.   Notes to the accounts.

     G.   Consolidated financial statements.

     H.   An Auditors' report.

THE SCOPE AND PRESENTATION OF THE REPORTS AND FINANCIAL STATEMENTS

31.   University financial statements should be prepared in accordance with the fundamental accounting concepts referred to in paragraph 34.

32.   Corresponding amounts for the preceding financial year should be shown in the accounts and where appropriate in the notes to the accounts.

A. *The Treasurer's report*

33.   This report in narrative form should be designed to assist in the interpretation of the main features of the financial statements such as practical solvency, investment performance, and any other factors which are likely to have a material bearing on the university's financial position.

B. *The statement of accounting policies*

34. If accounts are prepared on the basis of assumptions which differ in material respects from any of the following generally accepted fundamental concepts the facts should be explained as set out in SSAP 2:-

   i)   The 'going concern' concept.
   ii)   The 'accruals' concept.
   iii)   The 'consistency' concept.
   iv)   The 'prudence' concept.

35. The accounting policies followed for dealing with items which are judged material or critical should be disclosed. The explanations should be clear, fair, and as brief as possible.

C. *The income and expenditure account*

36. The income and expenditure account should relate to the total activities of the university as a corporate entity and should follow a standard classification in accordance with the specimen layout given in appendix 1.1. The notes to the accounts should provide supplementary information on specific activities such as residences and catering operations.

37. Restricted income and associated expenditure should be dealt with under the accruals concept. The entries in the income and expenditure account will be matched but this does not necessarily mean that restricted income and associated expenditure should be equal. For example, in the case of research grants and contracts the income will include overheads recovered and will therefore be greater than direct expenditure. In the case of specific endowments the appropriate (i.e. matching) income should be shown under the heading 'Endowments, Donations and Subventions' together with income from general endowments, donations and subventions and an analysis should be given in the notes to the accounts. Expenditure financed from specific endowment income should be included under the appropriate expenditure headings. For example, chairs and lectureships should be included under 'Academic Departments' while scholarships, bursaries and prizes should be included under 'General Educational Expenditure'.

38. Subject to the need to match restricted income and associated expenditure (for example, in respect of specific endowments) as set out in paragraph 37 above, all income from investments and capital appreciation/depreciation on realisation or revaluation of investments should be treated as follows:-

   i)   Income from both short-term and long-term investments should be brought into the income and expenditure account.

   ii)   Appreciation/depreciation on realisation of short-term investments should be brought into the income and expenditure account.

   iii)   Where the accounting policy is to show investments at market value then the appreciation/depreciation on revaluation of short-term investments should also be brought into the income and expenditure account.

   iv)   Appreciation/depreciation on realisation or revaluation of long-term investments should only be brought into the income and expenditure account if the investments relate to reserves otherwise they should be added to or subtracted from the funds concerned.

v) Any investment income or appreciation/depreciation retained in separate funds and not included in the income and expenditure account should be identified in the notes to the accounts - see appendix 1.6.

39. The recommended treatment for repairs and maintenance is as follows:-

i) Expenditure on routine corrective maintenance should be charged in the income and expenditure account.

ii) Long-term maintenance should be provided for on the basis of specific items in a long-term maintenance plan. The income and expenditure account should bear an annual charge applied on a consistent basis which should be set so as to spread the total costs of long-term maintenance in accordance with the criteria disclosed in the statement of accounting policies. This charge should be separately disclosed. Actual expenditure on long-term maintenance should be made directly from the provision and should not be shown in the income and expenditure account.

iii) If a provision requires to be made for other repairs and maintenance it should be treated in the same way as the provision for long-term maintenance.

40. The recommended treatment for capital income and expenditure is as follows:-

i) Capital income and expenditure should be reflected in the income and expenditure account on a consistent basis which does not distort the surplus/deficit position of the university.

ii) Restricted income (including research grants and contracts and equipment and furniture grant) and associated expenditure should be matched in accordance with paragraph 37 of this statement and credited or written off in the period of account.

iii) Expenditure on land and buildings should be capitalised and where the asset concerned has a finite useful life it should be depreciated. Where the asset concerned has an indefinite useful life (for example, freehold land) it should not be depreciated. An amount, equivalent to the depreciation charge, should be released from capital to the income side of the account under the heading 'Contribution to depreciation of buildings' so that the surplus or deficit position of the university will not be affected by depreciation.

iv) If expenditure on land and buildings is financed by way of loan it should be capitalised and depreciated in accordance with sub-paragraph iii) above. Capital should then be increased as the loan is repaid.

v) Any other capital expenditure, including equipment and furniture expenditure financed from general funds should be written off in full in the period of account.

vi) If a minor building grant, a major building grant or a physical restructuring grant is made by the UGC, or other body, or if a benefaction is received towards the cost of a new building, it should not appear in the income and expenditure account but should be included in capital as a source of finance available only for expenditure on land and buildings.

vii)   The proceeds from disposal of land, equipment, furniture and buildings should be included in the income and expenditure account and, if material, disclosed separately from other income and expenditure. However, in the case of land and buildings only those proceeds that do not require to be surrendered to the consolidated fund under UGC rules should be included.

viii)   If expenditure on land and buildings is to be financed from general income (including the disposal proceeds referred to in sub-paragraph vii) above) then a transfer to reserve should be made in accordance with paragraph 41 of this statement.

41.   Transfers from and to reserves should be shown in the income and expenditure account after the surplus or deficit for the period has been struck. Any expenditure from reserves other than expenditure on land and buildings should be brought into the income and expenditure account under the appropriate expenditure heading and an equivalent adjustment made in the transfers section of the income and expenditure account.

D. *The statement of financial position*

42.   The statement of financial position should relate to the university as a corporate entity and should follow a standard classification which distinguishes between land and buildings, long-term investments, long-term loans, net current assets, long-term liabilities, capital, restricted funds and general funds. A specimen layout is given in appendix 1.2.

43.   The recommended treatment of land and buildings in the statement of financial position is as follows:-

i)   Land and buildings should be included at cost (or valuation) less amounts written off by way of depreciation with the exceptions stated in sub- paragraph (ii).

ii)   Land and buildings which are inalienable (in other words which the university is prohibited from disposing of) or for which neither a cost nor a market value is reasonably ascertainable need not be included in the statement of financial position but details of such assets should be given in the notes to the accounts.

iii)   Subject to sub-paragraph (ii) above benefits-in-kind involving the acquisition of land or buildings should be valued and included in the statement of financial position.

44.   Listed investments should be shown at cost or market value. If they are shown at cost, the market value should be disclosed in the notes to the accounts. If listed investments are shown at market value, then non-listed investments such as heritable property investments may be included at open market value but no firm recommendation is made on this as it is recognised that there are practical difficulties. The practice adopted should therefore be explained in the statement of accounting policies.

45.   A distinction should be made between long-term investments and short-term investments with the latter being included under the heading 'Net current assets'. This is of importance in demonstrating the practical solvency of the university.

46.   Long-term loans should appear under a separate heading as it would be misleading to include these under the heading 'Net current assets'.

47. Long-term liabilities should be deducted from assets less current liabilities to bring out the net assets total in the statement of financial position.

48. Stocks for resale and other stocks of material value should be included in the statement of financial position at the lower of cost and net realisable value. It is recognised that departmental stocks may have restrictions on realisation or may have a very limited net realisable value.

E. *The statement of source and application of funds*

49. The source and application of funds statement should cover the activities and funds which are reflected in the income and expenditure account and statement of financial position of the university. It should distinguish between capital, restricted and general funds. A specimen layout is given in appendix 1.3.

F. *The notes to the accounts*

50. The notes to the accounts should include the following information:-

i) Basic analyses of income and expenditure, and statement of financial position items: the analyses should be sufficiently detailed to enable the user to gain a proper appreciation of the spread and character of the income, expenditure, assets and liabilities of the university.

ii) Details of the distribution of assets held for the various funds of the university. A specimen layout is given in appendix 1.4.

iii) Details of the purposes of funds, reserves and provisions and of movements on them.

iv) Details of government grants received and the way in which they are reflected in the income and expenditure account and the statement of financial position. A specimen layout is given in appendix 1.5.

v) Details of the total amount and subsequent distribution of all investment income and appreciation/depreciation on realisation or revaluation of investments. A specimen layout is given in appendix 1.6.

vi) If listed investments are shown in the statement of financial position at cost the market value should be disclosed.

vii) A brief summary of the land and buildings held by the university: whether they are freehold or long or short leasehold; any restrictions as to their realisation; the broad purposes for which they are used; and whether they are included in the statement of financial position.

viii) A brief summary of all capital transactions of material value including an analysis of expenditure incurred and the sources of finance.

ix) Details of any benefits-in-kind which are of material value including land, buildings and equipment.

x) Details of any exceptional and extraordinary items.

xi) Post accounting reference date events.

xii)   Contingencies.

xiii)   Pension arrangements.

xiv)   Details of university companies excluded from consolidation because their activities or assets and liabilities are not of material value. Sufficient details should be given to enable the university's position to be understood.

xv)   Future commitments in respect of capital expenditure.

xvi)   Details of loans.

G. *The consolidated financial statements*

51.   Consolidated financial statements should conform to standard accounting practice so far as the context allows. Where the activities or assets and liabilities of university companies are not of material value a consolidated financial statement need not be presented. Where a university company is excluded from consolidation because its activities are dissimilar or for other reasons of standard accounting practice then separate financial statements for that university company should be presented.

Case 14
Regional Transport Authority and Executive Annual Report and Accounts

OBJECTIVES

1. To explain the financial relationship between a regional transport authority and executive.
2. To consider how performance is reported through the annual report and accounts.

MATERIALS

1. Extracts from Greater Manchester Passenger Transport Authority Accounts 1987/88, pp. 7–11 (Exhibit 14.1).
2. Extracts from Greater Manchester Passenger Transport Executive Accounts 1987/88, pp. 7, 9, 11 and notes 5, 7, 14 to accounts (Exhibit 14.2).
3. Extracts from Greater Manchester Passenger Transport Authority and Executive Annual Report 1987/88, including statistics for bus mileage, bus passenger journeys, bus passenger mileage and bus revenue (Exhibit 14.3).

INTRODUCTION

The reorganization of local government carried out in the mid-1980s has had profound effects on the operations of former local government organizations. On the 31 March 1986 the Greater London Council and the six metropolitan authorities were abolished. The Greater Manchester Council was one of these metropolitan authorities and its functions have now been passed to the separate metropolitan districts and joint boards. These changes were brought about as a result of the Local Government Act 1985. The Greater Manchester Passenger Transport Authority (GMPTA) has taken over the transport responsibilities of the Greater Manchester Council and is a policy-making body composed of thirty councillors appointed from the districts. The revenue of the authority derives from the rates (up to 31 March 1990), thereafter from the poll tax or community charge. In addition, revenue is provided via grants from central government.

The GMPTA is responsible for setting policy, which broadly means ensuring that the public transport needs of Greater Manchester are met. This policy is then implemented by the Greater Manchester Passenger

Transport Executive (GMPTE), whose responsibilities are set out in Exhibit 14.3. The Executive has full responsibility for the rail network, but only a limited function with regard to bus services. Thus the Executive administers concessionary travel, and funds socially necessary bus services through competitive tender. The Executive also maintains the infrastructure of bus and rail stations.

ANALYSIS

A major factor affecting the provision of transport services has been the deregulation of bus services with effect from 26 October 1986. As a result of the 1985 Transport Act and subsequent deregulation, the Authority is unable to determine fare levels for bus operations, which are now carried out on a commercial basis by private operators and by Greater Manchester Buses Ltd (GMBL). GMBL was created in 1986, taking over the buses formerly owned by Greater Manchester Council. Although GMPTA is the sole shareholder in GMBL, GMBL is required to operate on a commercial basis. The only area where GMPTA can determine fare levels on the bus system is in respect of subsidized services which the GMPTA deems necessary to meet the needs of the public and which are unlikely to be provided by the commercial operators.

The close relationship between the Authority and Executive can be seen from their accounts. Note 2 to the consolidated balance sheet of GMPTA (Exhibit 14.1) indicates total loans to GMPTE amounting to £39.534 million. In the accounts of GMPTE (see note 14(a) in Exhibit 14.2) the figure of £39.534 million appears as loans due to GMPTA. During 1987/88 GMPTE received grants from GMPTA amounting to £69.742 million. It should be noted that GMPTE is not allowed to incur a deficit, but where this is impracticable the deficit should be made good in the following year.

The annual report of the Authority and Executive (see extracts in Exhibit 14.3) provides an explanation of factors affecting service provision during the year. Also provided is more detailed information on bus mileage and revenues over the period 1975 to 1988. The Authority and Executive appear to believe that there is a strong link between the level of unemployment and the number of passenger journeys. This relationship is likely to be fairly complex. An increase in unemployment could increase the demand for public transport if it reduces car ownership. In such cases, Goodwin *et al.* (1983, p. 188) put forward the view that it can be up to two years between the unemployment occurring and its effect on public transport. On the other hand, an increase in unemployment would reduce the demand for public transport immediately where public transport is used to travel to and from the place of work. Comparable information for the rail network is not reproduced here due to space constraints, although it can be noted that over the period 1986 to 1988 there have been increases in rail mileage, rail passenger mileage and rail revenue in real terms.

QUESTIONS

1. Outline the major effects of bus deregulation in October 1986 in Greater Manchester.
2. Discuss the problems facing the Authority and Executive in trying to implement a co-ordinated transport policy for Greater Manchester.
3. Which information do you regard as important in assessing the level of bus service provision in Greater Manchester?
4. What additional information would be useful in assessing the quality of bus service provision?

FURTHER READING

Goodwin, P. B. *et al.* (1983) *Subsidised Public Transport and the Demand for Travel*, Gower, Aldershot.

Exhibit 14.1 Extracts from Greater Manchester Passenger Transport Authority Accounts 1987/88

SUMMARY OF REVENUE EXPENDITURE

1986-1987		1987-88	
Actual		Original Budget	Actual
£000	**SUPPORT TO PUBLIC TRANSPORT**	*£000*	*£000*
68,400	Revenue Grant to the Executive	68,441	69,742
	Capital Grants Financing		
174	– Principal	197	222
4,988	– Interest	6,678	5,912
73,562		75,316	75,876
	PUBLIC TRANSPORT CO-ORDINATION		
474	Authority Administration	537	607
792	Working Capital Financing	2,972	–
1,266		3,509	607
74,828	Total Expenditure	78,825	76,483
	INCOME		
227	Interest on Balances	–	400
74,601	Net Revenue Expenditure	78,825	76,083
	FINANCED BY:		
28,895	Rate Support Grant – Block Grant	31,559	31,472
64,873	Proceeds of Precept	42,066	42,247
(19,167)	Transfer (to) from Balances	5,200	2,364
74,601		78,825	76,083

CONSOLIDATED BALANCE SHEET AS AT 31st MARCH, 1988

1987 £000	CAPITAL EMPLOYED	Notes	£000	£000
	Fixed Assets:			
27,500	Long Term Investments	1	27,500	
20,000	Long Term Debtors	2	38,443	
47,500				65,943
	Current Assets:			
11,887	Short Term Debtors	3,7	4,037	
9,688	Cash at Bank	3	743	
21,575				4,780
	Other Balances:			
53,533	Deferred Charges	4		71,424
122,608				142,147
	REPRESENTED BY			
	Long Term Liabilities:			
27,000	Loans Outstanding		49,000	
48,775	Ex-GMC Debt		48,582	
75,775				97,582
	Current Liabilities:			
166	Creditors	3		261
	Other Balances:			
19,167	General Fund	6		16,804
	Acquisition of Bus Company			
27,500	– Holding Account	1		27,500
122,608				142,147

NOTES TO THE BALANCE SHEET

1. LONG TERM INVESTMENT

The Authority is sole shareholder of Greater Manchester Buses Ltd. The value shown represents the opening balance of Issued Share Capital within the books of Greater Manchester Buses Ltd.

The Company was vested in the Authority on 26th October, 1986, being transferred from the Executive. The question of consideration for the shares remains outstanding; a holding account therefore reflects this position.

2. LONG TERM DEBTORS

£39.534m was loaned to the Executive to finance the transfer of working capital and redundancies. The Executive is repaying that part of the loan (£26.0m) funded by Authority borrowing over a 10 year period. No provision has been made for the Executive to repay the balance (£13.534m) taken from the Authority General Fund.

3. CURRENT ASSETS AND LIABILITIES

Analysis between Capital and Revenue at 31st March, 1988

	Capital	Revenue	Total
	£	£	£
Debtors	–	4,036,965	4,036,965
Creditors	–	260,803	260,803
Cash	1,249,676	(506,624)	743,052

The cash at hand is temporarily invested with Manchester City Council.

4. STATEMENT OF DEFERRED CHARGES

	£
Charges at 1st April, 1987	53,532,733
Expenditure during year	18,112,872
Repaid during the year	(221,876)
Charges at 31st March, 1988	71,423,729

5. UNAPPLIED CAPITAL BALANCES

	£
a) Capital Grants	
Balance at 1st April 1987	Nil
Received during the year:	
-ERDF	Nil
-Section 56	Nil
Applied to Finance Capital Grants	Nil
Applied to repay Debts	Nil
Balance at 31st March, 1988	Nil

	£
b) Capital Receipts	
Balance held by the Authority at 1st April, 1987	Nil
Received during the year	Nil
Balance at 31st March, 1988	Nil

While the Authority has no capital receipts, receipts held by the Executive from the sale of Executive assets may be used to supplement the Authority's capital allocation by the prescribed proportion (30%).

6. GENERAL FUND BALANCE

	£
Balance at 1st April, 1987	19,167,397
Revenue Deficit	(2,363,859)
Balance at 31st March, 1988	16,803,538

7. ANALYSIS OF DEBTORS AT 31st MARCH, 1988

	£
Government Grants	227,061
Working Capital Financing	3,390,014
Others	419,890
	4,036,965

CONSOLIDATED STATEMENT OF REVENUE AND CAPITAL MOVEMENTS 1st April 1987 – 31st March 1988

EXPENDITURE	£000	£000	£000
Revenue:			
Employment costs	–		
Other operating costs	70,359		
Interest and lease payments	6,124	76,483	
Capital:			
Acquisition of fixed assets	7,408		
Long-term investments	–		
Deferred charges	17,891	25,299	
Total revenue and capital expenditure			101,782
Working capital to Executive from revenue balances			11,034
Total expenditure			112,816

INCOME			
Revenue:			
Government Grants	31,472		
Charges for goods and services	–		
Net rents (after rebates)	–		
Net rates (precept)	42,247		
Other income	400	74,119	
Capital:			
Sale of assets	–		
Capital grants	–		
Other income	–	–	
Total revenue and capital income			74,119
SHORTFALL			38,697

Financed by:			
Net change in long term borrowing		21,807	
Net change in short term indebtedness and changes in		–	
Changes in other current assets/liabilities being increase or decrease in:			
Stocks and work in progress		–	
Debtors		7,850	
Creditors		95	
Cash in hand and at bank		8,945	38,697

Exhibit 14.2 Extracts from Greater Manchester Passenger Transport Executive Accounts 1987/88

OPERATING INCOME and EXPENDITURE
for the year ended 31st March, 1988

SUMMARY OF ACTIVITIES

	1988		1987 (5 months)	
EXECUTIVE OFF BUS SALES SCHEME:	£000	£000	£000	£000
Revenue receipts	19,531		8,827	
Less: Operating expenditure	19,531	–	8,827	
CONCESSIONARY TRAVEL:		25,012		8,929
SUBSIDISED BUS SERVICE:		9,587		3,034
SPECIAL NEEDS TRANSPORT:		622		180
CO-ORDINATED RAIL ACTIVITIES:				
Revenue receipts	15,574		5,956	
Less: Operating expenditure	31,148	15,574	12,290	6,334
PTE STATUTORY DUTIES:				
Administration	7,082		2,281	
Pension increase costs	6,155	13,237	2,832	5,113
Total expenditure		64,032		23,590
Less: Allocation of grants from the Authority		69,742		24,287
Operating surplus transferred to Revenue Account		5,710		697

CONSOLIDATED BALANCE SHEET as at 31st March 1988

	Notes	1988 £000	1987 £000
FIXED ASSETS:			
Tangible fixed assets	7	50,623	35,002
Capital projects	8	157	113
Investments and long-term debtor	9	2,484	2,489
Investments in associated companies	10(a)	4,199	11,105
		57,463	48,709
CURRENT ASSETS:			
Surplus assets	11	1,672	2,655
Debtors		7,226	9,679
Short-term loans and deposits		28,400	9,002
Amount due from associated companies		260	–
Cash at bank and in hand		294	183
		37,852	21,519
CREDITORS: amounts falling due within one year			
Creditors and accrued charges		19,012	22,566
Short-term borrowing		4,500	1,750
Loan capital	14(c)	4,472	16,177
Lease finance	15	53	305
Amount due to associated companies		38	7,284
Bank overdrafts		2,020	561
		30,095	48,643
NET CURRENT ASSETS/(LIABILITIES):		7,757	(27,124)
Total assets less current liabilities		65,220	21,585
Transport Act provisions	20	(7,331)	(7,947)
		57,889	13,638
FINANCED AS FOLLOWS:			
Deferred capital grants	5	46,356	30,294
LOAN CAPITAL:			
Greater Manchester Passenger Transport Authority	14(a)	36,609	20,000
Other	14(b)	26,492	18,039
LEASE FINANCE:	15	194	246
		109,651	68,579
RESERVES:			
Undistributable reserves	12	2,601	3,060
Other	13	13,581	9,943
		16,182	13,003
DEREGULATION RESERVE:	21	(67,944)	(67,944)
		(51,762)	(54,941)
		57,889	13,638

D.A. GRAHAM C.B.E.   C.J. MULLIGAN
Director General   *Director of Finance*

NOTES ON ACCOUNTS

1. BASIS OF PREPARATION

The accounts have been prepared under the historical cost convention, modified by the revaluation of certain fixed assets.

As required by the provisions of the Transport Act 1985, the Executive transferred its bus operation to a new company on the 25th October, 1986. That company, Greater Manchester Buses Limited (GMBL), acquired certain assets from the Executive, principally properties, passenger vehicles and stocks, together with other net current and long-term liabilities.

The consideration for the transfer of assets to GMBL was the issue of shares in that company. The Transport Act 1985 provided that the beneficial ownership of GMBL should pass to the Passenger Transport Authority, for which no consideration was received.

Provision was made in the accounts for the period ended 25 October, 1986 for all expected costs arising from the implementation of the Act, including the loss arising on the transfer of the shares in GMBL.

2.(a) SURPLUS FOR THE PERIOD

In arriving at the surplus for the period the following items have been charged:-

	1988	1987 (5 months)
DEPRECIATION:	£000	£000
Owned assets	1,204	571
Leased assets	44	–
LEASING INTEREST:	20	–
AUDITORS REMUNERATION:	40	28

2.(b) EXECUTIVE MEMBERS AND SENIOR EMPLOYEES

The number of members and senior employees of the Executive who received remuneration falling within the ranges below in the period, were:

	1988	1987 (5 months)
£20,001 to £25,000	8	1
£25,001 to £30,000	2	–
£35,001 to £40,000	1	–
£45,001 to £50,000	1	–

3. VEHICLE LEASING PARTNERSHIPS - PROFITS

	1988	1987 (5 months)
Partnership profits arising from the group's	£000	£000
50% investments in Transport Leasing Company and		
Metropolitan Leasing Company	20	252

5. DEFERRED
CAPITAL GRANTS

These amounts relate to grants on expenditure on public transport facilities.
The basis of release to revenue account is as described in the statement of accounting policies.

Movements during the period were as follows:

	1988	1987 *(5 months)*
	£000	£000
Opening balance	30,294	30,704
Grants receivable	17,014	–
	47,308	30,704
Less: released to revenue account	952	410
Closing balance	46,356	30,294

7. TANGIBLE FIXED ASSETS

	Total	LAND AND BUILDINGS		Rail	Plant and
		Freehold	Long Leasehold	Improvements	equipment
	£000	£000	£000	£000	£000
COST or VALUATION:					
At 31st March, 1987	42,418	5,169	16,573	16,358	4,318
Additions at cost	17,293	6,115	2,500	8,468	210
Disposals	(1,307)	(2)	–	–	(1,305)
At 31st March, 1988 analysed below	58,404	11,282	19,073	24,826	3,223
COST:	57,909	10,932	18,928	24,826	3,223
Valuation: 1971	474	329	145	–	–
Valuation: 1976	21	21	–	–	–
	58,404	11,282	19,073	24,826	3,223
DEPRECIATION:					
At 31st March, 1987	7,416	844	2,820	1,407	2,345
Charge for the period	1,248	134	427	409	278
On disposals	(883)	–	–	–	(883)
At 31st March, 1988	7,781	978	3,247	1,816	1,740
Net book value at 31st March, 1988	50,623	10,304	15,826	23,010	1,483
Net book value at 31st March, 1987	*35,002*	*4,325*	*13,753*	*14,951*	*1,973*

Rail improvements represent expenditure incurred by the Executive in the improvement of the railway system and associated facilities.

The net book value of plant and equipment above of £1,483,000 includes an amount of £250,000 in respect of assets held under finance leases.

14. LOAN CAPITAL

(a) GREATER MANCHESTER PASSENGER TRANSPORT AUTHORITY:

	1988	1987
	£000	£000
Opening Balance	20,000	20,000
Borrowed	19,534	–
	39,534	20,000
Less: Amounts falling due within one year (included in creditors)	2,925	–
	36,609	20,000

Loan repayment arrangements are as follows:
- £23,075,000 will be repaid over nine years at interest rates varying between 9.09% and 10.12%.
- Arrangements for the repayment of the balance amounting to £13,534,000 have not been specified.

(b) OTHER:

	1988	1987
	£000	£000
Opening Balance	34,216	30,768
Borrowed	10,000	5,500
Repaid	(16,177)	(2,052)
	28,039	34,216
Less: Amounts falling due within one year (included in creditors)	1,547	16,177
	26,492	18,039
Instalments are payable as follows:		
• Within 5 years	18,182	9,196
• After 5 years	8,310	8,843
	26,492	18,039
Analysed as follows: Interest Rate Range %		
Local Authority loans 7.375 – 10.5%	492	539
PWLB loans 8.625 – 10.625%	20,000	10,000
Loans from banks and other financial institutions 9.8759% – 13.75%	6,000	7,500
	26,492	18,039

(c) ANALYSIS OF AMOUNTS FALLING DUE WITHIN ONE YEAR:

	1988	1987
Greater Manchester Passenger Transport Authority	2,925	–
Other loan capital	1,547	16,177
	4,472	16,177

Exhibit 14.3 Extracts from Greater Manchester Passenger Transport Authority and Executive Annual Report 1987/88, including statistics for bus mileage, bus passenger journeys, bus passenger mileage and bus revenue

FARES

Budgetary planning continued to reflect the Authority's recognition of the key importance of concessionary fares to children and the elderly in particular, and the hardship which would be caused by any major increase. The structure of the scheme was preserved, and concessionary fares continued to be held at the rate of 12p a journey.

This has meant that some 40 per cent of the travelling public in Greater Manchester have been protected from fares increases.

Patronage

The chart shows the patronage levels (in millions) for the quarters Feb-April 1987 to Feb-April 1988.

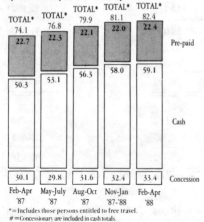

* = Includes those persons entitled to free travel.
\# = Concessionary are included in cash totals.

The maximum fare scale applied on subsidised services was increased by 9.9 per cent on 31st May, 1987 in line with fare increases implemented by the majority of operators. The rail fares increase was held down to 5 per cent.

The operators Off-Bus Sales Panel decided to bring prices of off-bus tickets into line with cash fares, and in July 1987 adjustments were made to the prices of Saver Tickets, Clipper Cards (except Concessionary ClipperCard) and 16-19 Bus Passes.

A further increase to the 16-19 Bus Pass in October 1987 brought the price to £4.75.

Changes to the range of off-bus tickets were also made on 12th July, 1987, with the introduction of the Every Bus Saver, a period ticket valid for use on any operator's buses within the Greater Manchester area.

Teentravel ClipperCards were withdrawn on the same date, with alternative facilities being provided by the 16-19 Bus Pass and the use of Off-Peak ClipperCards at any time of the day.

Although sales of off-bus tickets were declining at the beginning of the year, there are now signs that sales are stabilising.

In keeping with the Authority's committment to encouraging the development of through-ticketing arrangements, discussions were held with the operators' Off Bus Sales Panel, although these did not lead to the adoption of any new initiatives. The Executive also began consideration of the merits of electronic ticketing equipment, in terms of facilitating improved administration of the concessionary fares scheme and of widening the scope for through-ticketing facilities.

BUS NETWORK

Throughout the year, the deregulated bus network was characterised by a considerable degree of uncertainty and on-going change, as operators adjusted their services in the light of experience. Also notable was the rapid growth of minibus services, particularly in the south of the conurbation, which operated on high frequencies and in many areas previously unserved by bus. The level of competition increased, with operators providing broadly similar commercial services, resulting in overall frequency increases. Total service mileage increased within Greater Manchester by 15 per cent over the pre-deregulation level.

The Authority continued to move forward with the introduction of further improvements to the subsidised network - although it had to maintain a policy of caution in the use of its resources in order:

(i) to be able to replace withdrawn commercial services, and

(ii) not to undermine the viability of the commercial services.

The level of subsidised mileage increased as the Executive put into action a programme of network enhancements in Spring 1987. These comprised of some new services, further frequency increases and restoration of transport links broken by deregulation.

Annualised vehicle mileage

The chart shows the annualised vehicle mileage (in millions) for both the commercial and subsidised networks from April 1987 to March 1988.

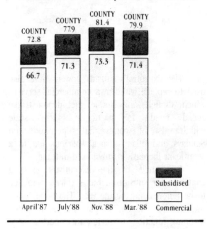

BUS STATIONS AND INFRASTRUCTURE

The provision of high quality bus facilities in major town centres throughout Greater Manchester continued with the completion on the 23rd August, 1987 of Bolton Interchange. This is now the third major bus/rail interchange in the county, following the opening of Altrincham in 1976 and Bury in 1980.

On the 29th November, 1987 a new bus station was opened at Wigan which has enabled the borough council to carry out further proposals for pedestrianisation. This has highlighted the importance of a continuing dialogue with local councils on issues of public transport, highways and traffic and town planning. In Bolton, Radcliffe and Wigan new bus routes were agreed as a result of major new shopping and road developments.

The planning of new or replacement bus stations continued. Progress was made at Tameside towards implementation of the Council's plans to relocate the bus station at Ashton-under-Lyne to improve shopping facilities in the town. Discussions with user-representatives were initiated in response to the need to maximise the safety of passengers using the new station. Work is expected to start in 1989.

Other schemes discussed were the relocation of Stalybridge Bus Station, Altrincham Interchange's role in the enlargement of shopping facilities in the town and links from the bus station to an extension of the shopping centre in Rochdale town centre.

New or reconstructed bus turnabouts were completed at Ramsbottom, Bury and Waterhead and Oldham, to reduce the impact on traffic movement of buses waiting on the highway. Contributions were also made to a number of highway authorities to encourage them to implement schemes where there was a significant benefit for buses. In one particular case, new traffic lights were installed at a junction in Offerton, Stockport, to assist visibility and reduce accidents and delays to buses.

The Executive's subsidy powers were also used to replace withdrawn commercial services which, though unprofitable, met demonstrable social need. In particular, large scale withdrawals of commercial operations on Sundays and other off-peak periods led to a significant increase in subsidised mileage.

Over half of the Executive's existing contracts for subsidised bus services were due to be renewed during the year. The opportunity was therefore taken, as part of the on-going planning function, to review their performance and the contribution they made in meeting social needs in the context of the changing pattern of commercial service provision.

A number of subsidised evening and Sunday services were converted to minibuses. Many of the contract renewals saw a change in operator including some additional new operators.

The increase in the use of minibuses on new routes has given greater penetration of areas unsuited to the use of conventional vehicles and created public interest in the possiblity of improving services. To meet this demand the Executive, after consultation, developed a programme of subsidised minibus network enhancements.

One of the areas the Authority has been keen to safeguard was its ability to fund Bank Holiday services. Therefore, further funds in the budget were earmarked for this purpose.

All the subsidised bus services were put out to competetive tender in accordance with the 1985 Transport Act.

BUS MILEAGE 1975 to 1988

The chart shows the total vehicle mileage for the 12 months up to 31st March each year.

NOTE: The mileage for 1975-86 includes all operators. The mileage for 1986-88 includes subsidised services and estimates based on vehicle registrations for commercial services.

* = 40.6 million miles for 7 months up to 25/10/86.
** = Annualised at 1st March 1988.

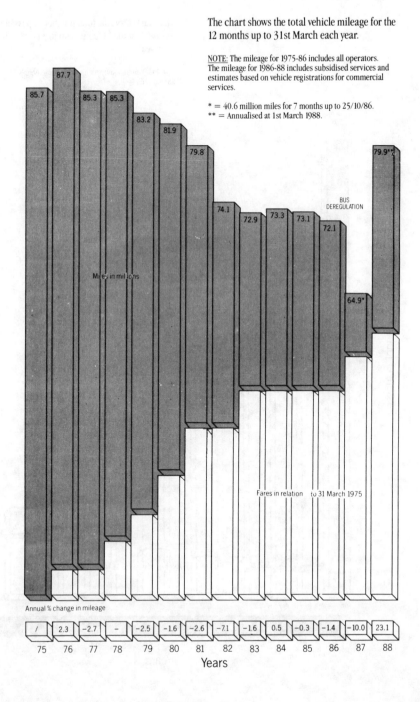

Miles in millions

Annual % change in mileage

| / | 2.3 | −2.7 | − | −2.5 | −1.6 | −2.6 | −7.1 | −1.6 | 0.5 | −0.3 | −1.4 | −10.0 | 23.1 |

| 75 | 76 | 77 | 78 | 79 | 80 | 81 | 82 | 83 | 84 | 85 | 86 | 87 | 88 |

Years

BUS PASSENGER JOURNEYS 1975 to 1988

The chart shows the total number of passenger journeys for the 12 months up to 31st March each year.

* = 192.0 million journeys up to 25/10/86 equals 337 million annualised.

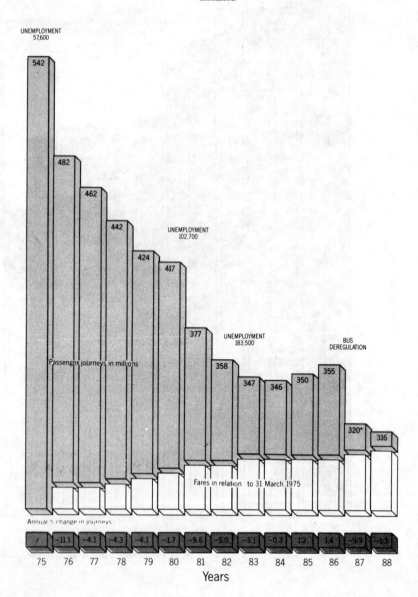

UNEMPLOYMENT
57,600

UNEMPLOYMENT
102,700

UNEMPLOYMENT
183,500

BUS
DEREGULATION

Passenger journeys in millions

542
482
462
442
424
417
377
358
347
346
350
355
320*
316

Passenger journeys in millions

Fares in relation to 31 March 1975

Annual % change in journeys

| / | −11.1 | −4.1 | −4.3 | −4.1 | −1.7 | −9.6 | −5.0 | −3.1 | −0.3 | 1.2 | 1.4 | −9.9 | −1.3 |

| 75 | 76 | 77 | 78 | 79 | 80 | 81 | 82 | 83 | 84 | 85 | 86 | 87 | 88 |

Years

BUS PASSENGER MILEAGE 1975 to 1988

The chart shows the total number of passenger miles for the 12 months up to 31st March each year.

* = 497 million passenger miles up to 25/10/86 equals 872 million annualised.

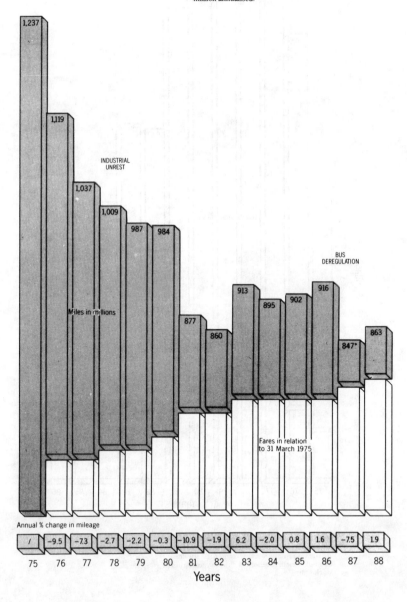

Miles in millions

INDUSTRIAL UNREST

BUS DEREGULATION

Miles in millions

Fares in relation to 31 March 1975

Annual % change in mileage

| / | −9.5 | −7.3 | −2.7 | −2.2 | −0.3 | −10.9 | −1.9 | 6.2 | −2.0 | 0.8 | 1.6 | −7.5 | 1.9 |

| 75 | 76 | 77 | 78 | 79 | 80 | 81 | 82 | 83 | 84 | 85 | 86 | 87 | 88 |

1,237 · 1,119 · 1,037 · 1,009 · 987 · 984 · 877 · 860 · 913 · 895 · 902 · 916 · 847* · 863

Years

BUS REVENUE 1975 to 1986 (at 1988 prices)

The chart shows the total revenue taken for the 12 months up to 31st March each year.

NOTE: All 1988 prices are based on the Retail Price Index.

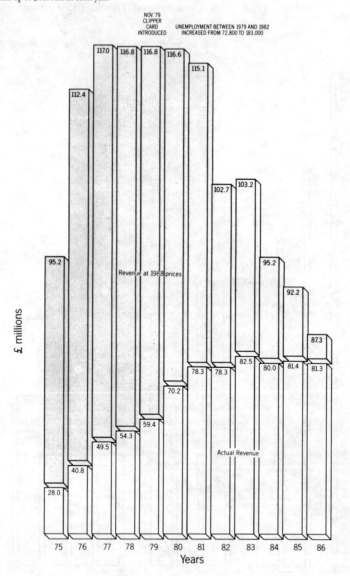

NOV.'79 CLIPPER CARD INTRODUCED

UNEMPLOYMENT BETWEEN 1979 AND 1982 INCREASED FROM 72,800 TO 183,000

£ millions

Revenue at 1988 prices

Actual Revenue

117.0 116.8 116.8 116.6 115.1
112.4
103.2
102.7
95.2   95.2
92.2
87.3
82.5   80.0   81.4   81.3
78.3   78.3
70.2
59.4
54.3
49.5
40.8
28.0

Years
75 76 77 78 79 80 81 82 83 84 85 86

NOTE: Following deregulation on 26 October 1986, the Executive has no control over the setting of standard bus fares and is not in a position to release commercially sensitive information. For these reasons the chart only goes up to 31st March 1986.